Vygotsky and Pedagogy

The theories of Vygotsky are central to any serious discussion of children's learning processes. Vygotsky argued that children do not develop in isolation, rather that learning takes place when the child is interacting with the social environment. It is the responsibility of the teacher to establish an interactive instructional situation in the classroom, where the child is an active learner and the teacher uses their knowledge to guide learning.

This book explores the growing interest in Vygotsky and the pedagogic implications of the body of work that is developing under the influence of his theories. It provides an overview of the ways in which the original writing has been extended and identifies areas for future development. The author considers how these developments are creating new and important possibilities for the practices of teaching and learning in school and beyond, and illustrates how Vygotskian theory can be applied in the classroom.

The book is intended for students and academics in education and the social sciences. It will be of interest to all those who wish to develop an analysis of pedagogic practice within and beyond the field of education.

Harry Daniels is Deputy Head of School and Professor of Special Education and Educational Psychology at the School of Education, University of Birmingham. He is Co-Director of the Centre for Sociocultural and Activity Theory Research. His previous publications include *An Introduction to Vygotsky* and *Charting the Agenda: educational activity after Vygotsky*, both published by Routledge.

Vygotsky and Pedagogy

Harry Daniels

RoutledgeFalmer
Taylor & Francis Group

NEW YORK AND LONDON

First published 2001
by RoutledgeFalmer
11 New Fetter Lane, London EC4P 4EE

Simultaneously published in the USA and Canada
by RoutledgeFalmer
29 West 35th Street, New York, NY 10001

Reprinted 2002, 2003, 2004

RoutledgeFalmer is an imprint of the Taylor & Francis Group

Typeset in Bembo by Keystroke, Jacaranda Lodge, Wolverhampton
Printed and bound in Great Britain by The Cromwell Press, Trowbridge, Wiltshire

British Library Cataloguing in Publication Data
A catalogue record for this book is available from the British Library

Library of Congress Cataloging in Publication Data
Daniels, Harry.
    Vygotsky and pedagogy / Harry Daniels.
        p. cm.
    Includes bibliographical references and index.
    1. EducationÑSocial aspects.   2. Educational psychology.   3. Vygotsky, L. S.
(Lev Semenovich), 1896Ò1934ÑContributions in education. I. Title.

    LC189 .D34 2001
    306.43Ñdc21   2001031763

ISBN 0Ö415Ö23767-X (pbk)
ISBN 0Ö415Ö23766Ö1 (hbk)

To Basil Bernstein 1924–2000
An inspirational tutor and thinker

Contents

Figures and tables

Figures

Tables

Acknowledgements

My thanks are due to the Economic and Social Research Council for funding the projects on Gender and Teacher Support and the Department for Education and Employment and the Nuffield Foundation for funding the projects on Emotional and Behavioural Difficulty discussed in Chapter 5. Friends and colleagues who either led or contributed to this work include: Ted Cole; Angela Creese; Valerie Hey; Diana Leonard; Brahm Norwich; Marjorie Smith; and John Visser. I am grateful for the thought-provoking and enjoyable times that gave rise to the publications on which I have drawn. Any shortcomings, however, are entirely my own responsibility.

The School of Education at the University of Birmingham provided me with the much-needed time for undertaking the literature review on which I have drawn in the course of writing of this book.

The Centre for Sociocultural and Activity Theory Research, which I co-direct with Anne Edwards, was founded in 2000 with Jan Derry, Mike Sharples and the late Sally Tweddle. I cherish the intellectual excitement and sense of adventure that the Centre affords. I have been privileged to work with so many people who are generous with their time and who bring such a wealth of ideas to conversation. The book would not have been written without all this support. I am deeply indebted and most grateful.

Chapter 1

Pedagogy and mediation

Introduction

The current emphasis on educational standards has given rise to a number of ways and means of scrutinising the outcomes of educational processes. In this book I wish to revisit the topic of pedagogy as it may be seen through a particular set of positions within social theory. My argument is that unless we understand the ways in which possibilities for learning are enacted within institutions we will be frustrated in our attempts to really raise standards. Through a review of a branch of social theory I will consider how social, cultural, historical and institutional factors may be seen to impact on processes of teaching and learning. My suggestion is that the term pedagogy should be construed as referring to forms of social practice which shape and form the cognitive, affective and moral development of individuals. If pedagogic practices are understood as those which influence the formation of identity as well as learning outcome as defined in, say, test scores, then a form of social theory is required that will allow us to model and investigate the factors which may be exercising some effect. The book thus seeks to understand the processes of education through models which allow for a broad range of influences and outcomes.

There is a growing interest in what has become known as 'sociocultural theory' and its near relative 'activity theory'. Both traditions are historically linked to the work of L.S.Vygotsky and both attempt to provide an account of learning and development as mediated processes. In sociocultural theory the emphasis is on semiotic mediation with a particular emphasis on speech. In activity theory it is activity itself which takes the centre stage in the analysis. Both approaches attempt to theorise and provide methodological tools for investigating the processes by which social, cultural and historical factors shape human functioning. Neither account resorts to determinism in that they both acknowledge that in the course of their own development human beings also actively shape the very forces that are active in shaping them. This mediational model which entails the mutual influence of individual and supra-individual factors lies at the heart of many attempts to develop our understanding of the possibilities for interventions in processes of human learning and development.

For many educators it provides important tools for the development of an understanding of pedagogy. Importantly, this body of theoretical work opens up, or rather insists upon, a pedagogic imagination that reflects on the processes of teaching and learning as much more than face-to-face interaction or the simple transmission of prescribed knowledge and skill. This book will discuss the theoretical developments that are taking place in this field and illustrate some of the implications through specific examples of pedagogic practice that draw from the theory.

The aim of this book is, then, to explore the pedagogic implications of the body of theoretical work that is developing under the influence of the writing of L.S.Vygotsky. His work has been translated and retranslated from the original Russian. It has given rise to a wide range of interpretations and extensions. These developments in social theory are creating new and important possibilities for practices of teaching and learning in schools and beyond. They provide us with theoretical constructs, insights and understandings which we can use to develop our own thinking about the practices of education.

Many of the ideas which inform the writing of this book were originally forged at a time of rapid and intense social upheaval – the Russian Revolution. They were developed by someone who was charged with developing a state system for the education of 'pedagogically neglected' children (Yaroshevsky, 1989, p. 96).This group included the homeless, of which there were a very large number, and those with special needs. In July 1924 the 28-year-old Lev Vygotsky was appointed to work in the People's Commissariat for Public Education. He argued that the culture of education as it had existed was itself in need of profound transformation and that this was possible in the new social circum- stances that obtained in Russia. He embarked on the creation of psychological theories which he and others used as tools for the development of new pedagogies for all learners.

We, also, are witnessing a period of very rapid social change. Transformations in the means and patterns of communication lie at the heart of fundamental changes in the labour market and social relations. These transformations have created new demands and also offer new possibilities for teaching and learning. At such a time the received wisdom or 'common sense' of education as it was practised when we were at school may no longer be appropriate.

It would seem sensible to spend some time defining the boundaries of this project. Whilst it will not comprise a comprehensive overview of all the peda- gogic initiatives that have espoused a Vygotskian root, it will attempt to illustrate the pedagogic possibilities that are being generated in the theoretical work. A basic requirement for this task is an outline of the key theoretical issues along with a discussion of the field of application. I will address these issues in Chapters 2 and 3. In this chapter I will be laying down a trace of the issues to be explored more fully later on. Thus I will open the discussion on pedagogy through questions about the breadth of its definition. The discussion concerning Vygotsky will argue that the concept of mediation is a fundamental element of his thesis. In the second half of this chapter I will introduce a number of issues which will be explored in Chapters 2 and 3 through a consideration of mediation within the Vygotskian framework.

Pedagogy

Moll (1990) argues that Vygotsky considered the capacity to teach and to benefit from instruction is a fundamental attribute of human beings.

> Vygotsky's primary contribution was in developing a general approach that brought education, as a fundamental human activity, fully into a theory of psychological development. Human pedagogy, in all its forms, is the defining characteristic of his approach, the central concept in his system.
>
> (Moll, 1990, p. 15)

He along with many others (e.g. Wertsch, 1985a) suggest that whilst Vygotsky declared an interest in more broadly defined sociocultural development he spent a major part of his time focusing on a somewhat constrained operational definition of the 'social' in his investigations of individual development. As my concern in this book is to discuss the pedagogic implications of the work that has developed under Vygotsky's influence I must take some time to reflect on how it is to be defined. Specifically, I wish to address the implicit definition of the 'social' implied by the term pedagogy itself. Moll (1990) cites Premack as an introduction to his assertion that pedagogy is central to the development of 'uniquely human psychological processes'.

> The presence of pedagogy in human affairs introduces a cognitive gap that is not found in other animals. If the adult does not take the child in tow, making him the object of pedagogy, the child will never become an adult (in competence).
>
> (Premack, 1984, p. 33)

If 'pedagogy' is *so* important in the development of human psychological functioning it is essential that a valid model of its range and possibilities is available to theoreticians, empirical researchers and practitioners. To truncate or delimit the scope of the term would be to ignore possible sources of formative influence on research and the design of formal schooling.

Best (1988) traces the changes in the use of the term pedagogy from her perspective as Director of the French Institut National de Recherche Pedagogique. Her discussion starts with the late nineteenth-century definition attributed to Henri Marion:

> Pedagogy is . . . both the science and the art of education. But as we must choose one or the other – the (French) language being usually reluctant to

allow the same word to denote both an art and its corresponding science – I would simply define pedagogy as the science of education. Why a science rather than an art? Because . . . the substance of pedagogy lies much less in the processes that it brings into play than in the theoretical reasoning through which it discovers, evaluates and co-ordinates these processes.

(Quoted in Best, 1988, p. 154)

Crucially she raises the question as to whether 'pedagogy' conflicts with 'knowledge'. In asking whether there is 'knowledge to be conveyed' on the one hand and on the other 'methods of conveying this information' she announces one of the fundamental concerns of this book. She suggests an early trajectory for common usage of the term from the practical consequences of psychology to the doctrine of non-directive teaching (which she attributes to Carl Rogers), within which pedagogy was seen as 'nothing more than intuition'. Didactics – the study of the relationship between pupils, teachers and the various branches of knowledge grouped into educational subjects – was introduced into French teacher training as a reaction to the diminution of the term pedagogy. In this way she argues that general pedagogy became the philosophy, sociology and social psychology of education, and specialised pedagogy became didactics. Jarning (1997) suggests that ambiguities between its part conceptualisation and organisation as a professional field of knowledge on the one hand and as a 'pure' discipline based knowledge field on the other, give rise to possibilities for confusion even within the Scandinavian context where the term is in common use.

Given all this Gallic and Nordic confusion it is hardly surprising that in England, where the very word 'pedagogy' sits unhappily in the mouth – (hard or soft 'g'?), Brian Simon (1985) should ask 'Why no pedagogy in England?' Simon, as Davies (1994) suggests, portrays an explicit relation between the social setting and educational practice:

Pedagogy involves a vision (theory, set of beliefs) about society, human nature, knowledge and production, in relation to educational ends, with terms and rules inserted as to the practical and mundane means of their realisation.

(Davies, 1994, p. 26)

More recently, Watkins and Mortimore (1999) reviewed three phases of research literature on pedagogy each of which adopts a particular focus. These are:

- a focus on different types of teachers;
- a focus on the contexts of teaching;
- a focus on teaching and learning.

In a statement on current views of pedagogy they propose a complex model which 'specifies relations between its elements: the teacher, the classroom or other context, content, the view of learning and learning about learning. Such a model draws attention to the creation of learning communities in which knowledge is actively co-constructed, and in which the focus of learning is sometimes learning itself', Watkins and Mortimore (1999) p. 8. Implicitly they acknowledge the force of the statement by Davies on 'vision (theory, set of beliefs) about society, human nature, knowledge and production, in relation to educational ends' in that they discuss the ways in which different views on pedagogy are created and contested by different social groups such as teachers and policy makers. However, they conclude their discussion with the definition 'any conscious activity by one person designed to enhance learning in an another', thus reverting to an account constrained to the individual level of analysis.

It may be argued that the very definition of the term pedagogy mirrors some of the issues that have arisen when researchers have approached the study of education. For example, cognitive psychologists have, in the past, studied thinking outside the natural ecology of the classroom. Anthropologists have studied many aspects of education but only recently have they looked at learning itself. They, just as the interest groups that Watkins and Mortimore discuss, have placed their own priorities/visions/values on the very definition of the field of study.

In his early writing, Vygotsky provides an emergent sociological position on pedagogy which attests to his own 'priorities/visions/values':

> Pedagogics is never and was never politically indifferent, since, willingly or unwillingly, through its own work on the psyche, it has always adopted a particular social pattern, political line, in accordance with the dominant social class that has guided its interests.
>
> (Vygotsky, 1997b, p. 348)

Vygotsky was suggesting a process of social formation in the development of educational ideas. He distances himself from naturalistic or common-sense pedagogic positions. For him pedagogies arise and are shaped in particular social circumstances. Popkewitz (1998) analyses the situations which shaped and fashioned the ideas of both Vygotsky and Dewey. He suggests that they both worked at times of intense modernisation which involved industrialisation, urbanisation and rationalisation. His argument is that their psychologies both embodied evidence of modernity. He further suggests that:

- there was a general affinity between the Russian concern with creating a new unity of community and Dewey's belief that disintegrated individuals can achieve unity only as the dominant energies of community life are incorporated to form their mind (ibid, p. 537);
- they were pragmatic theorists in the sense that they saw all teaching and learning as conditional and contingent . . . for Vygotsky teaching and learning (and upbringing) were collaborative activities in which there were no uniform methods (ibid, p. 538).

On the basis of these assertions Popkewitz develops a very broadly based definition of pedagogy.

> Pedagogy is a practice of the social administration of the social individual. Since at least the 19th century pedagogical discourses about teaching, children, and learning in schools connected the scope and aspirations of public powers with the personal and subjective capabilities of individuals. This administration of the child embodies certain norms about their capabilities from which the child can become self governing and self reliant.
>
> (Popkewitz, 1998, p. 536)

Thus, Popkewitz alerts us to the need to provide an account of pedagogic practice in which large-scale or macro factors are integrated with micro levels of analysis. This is implicit in the general definition offered by Bernstein:

> Pedagogy is a sustained process whereby somebody(s) acquires new forms or develops existing forms of conduct, knowledge, practice and criteria, from somebody(s) or something deemed to be an appropriate provider and evaluator. Appropriate either from the point of view of the acquirer or by some other body(s) or both.
>
> (Bernstein, 1999a, p. 259)

This definition emphasises that conduct, knowledge, practice and criteria may all be developed. This sets it apart from definitions that attend only to matters of skills and knowledge. It suggests that a complete analysis of processes of development and learning within pedagogic practice must consider cognitive and affective matters. It also suggests that pedagogic provision may be thought of in terms of material things as well as persons. In this book I will explore the implications of this definition in that I will consider pedagogic analysis which maintains a focus on the context within which pedagogic practice takes place.

I will attempt to develop an account of pedagogic practice which is informed by a vision/set of beliefs and theories which are developing in the wake of the Vygotsky's contribution to our understanding of human functioning. Following Bernstein (1996) I will take pedagogic practice as a fundamental social context through which cultural reproduction–production takes place. The theories that inform the social construction of pedagogic discourse and its various practices often remain tacit or ascribed to common sense. The creation of the possibilities for consciousness within particular knowledge systems is not always taken into account when analyses of teaching and learning are undertaken. In one sense it would seem that whilst there are sociological accounts of practices of teaching and learning, these are rarely connected with psychological understandings of learning and development. The purpose of this book is to provide a clear articulation of an important aspect of social theory which attempts to make such connections between social and psychological perspectives. It will then seek to trace its implications for practice.

Vygotsky

In this section I will discuss the central concept in the Vygotskian thesis – that of mediation. By necessity I will devote time to some of the core issues that are raised in reading this aspect of the Vygotskian text. In Chapter 2 I will then move to a discussion of those parts of the Vygotskian framework which revolve around the concept of mediation and are of direct relevance to the development of pedagogic practice. In Chapter 3 I will outline some of the current developments in social theory which in some way trace their existence to Vygotsky's writing. In Chapter 4 I will examine a range of pedagogic interventions that espouse a sociocultural, activity theory or general Vygotskian root.

The development of Psychology as a discipline has passed through several stages. Each part of this history provides an important legacy for the next. One of the reasons that so many Western psychologists are reading the writings of a long-dead Russian may be that they are seeking to extend the insights of the so-called cognitive revolution and yet are painfully aware of the shortcomings of so many of its products (e.g. Hirst and Manier, 1995; Sampson, 1981). The research practice of experimentation in artificial situations has provided valuable insights but incurred significant costs. Context, however defined, remained under-theorised and its effects remained under-researched.

> Flavell skillfully illustrated the role of strategies (and knowledge about strategies) in children's interior cognitive experience, and one sees in this cognitive enterprise a bold contrast to alternative theories that stress possible learning, fixed potential, and strict biological limitations. The cognitive enterprise view is, however, an essentially individualist, child-centered position, and it therefore tends to neglect a major interpersonal foundation of strategies research: strategy instruction. . . . American psychologists' experiences in the strategy-instruction laboratory were far too limited to assimilate the socio-instructional approach.
>
> (Belmont, 1989, pp. 142–3)

As an opening gambit, I will venture to suggest that Vygotsky developed a theory within which social, cultural and historical forces play a part in development. His attempts to theorise interpersonal and intrapersonal processes provide an important opening for discussions of determinism, reductionism and agency within a framework of social formation. Vygotsky discussed the way in which the psychological implications of social, cultural and historical factors could be theorised and initiated the development of appropriate methodologies for progressing the creation of appropriate forms of investigation and intervention. His free-ranging cross/multi-disciplinary contribution to twentieth-century intellectual life was supported by his own interpretation of both fellow Russian and European thinkers. He was developing a way of thinking that also found parallels with others beyond his place and time. Just as he drew on a range of disciplines so did he embed much of his own reading of European philosophical, psychological, sociological and political thought in his writing.

> In psychology the corresponding American thinkers included John Dewey, William James, and George Herbert Mead: In Germany Wilhelm Spranger, Norbert Elias, and the adherents of what they called 'cultural psychology'; and in France, it was the sociologists Emile Durkheim and Levy Bruhl who pursued the implications of a cultural-historical approach to human nature. . . . Russian psychologists were also influenced by a wide spectrum of Russian thinkers including Mikhail Bakhtin (literary and social theorist), Osip Mandelshtam (poet), Pavel Florensky (philosopher), and Sergei Eisenshtein (film maker).
>
> (Cole, 1994, p. 77)

This creative fusion and development of many perspectives and persuasions was cast adrift in the tragedy that befell the Soviet Union under Stalin. It was selectively moulded, transformed, developed and, in no small part, suppressed for many years. Although the texts themselves did achieve some small notoriety in zamisdat form, both in the Soviet Union and the West, they only really became known in the West in the 1970s.

One way of understanding Vygotsky is as a cultural psychologist. I will not engage in questions as to what is to be included or excluded in an appropriate definition of culture at this point (see Ratner, 1999, pp. 93–121 for an excellent discussion). The variation in the degree of emphasis on semiotic, activity and material components of culture is reflected in the range of contemporary interpretations of Vygotsky's work. These will be discussed in Chapters 3 and 4.

Michael Cole opens the first chapter of his book entitled *Cultural Psychology* with a discussion of Wundt's conception of a psychology composed of two parts. One part was the then (1880) new psychology of experimentation, the other, much less widely discussed, part of Wundt's contribution was concerned with 'the task of understanding how culture enters into psychological processes' Cole (1996) p. 7. If psychology is to contribute to an understanding of pedagogic practice conceived of as a fundamental social context through which cultural reproduction–production takes place then it has to fulfil demands of the task set within Wundt's second psychology. The work of the Russian school of Vygotsky, Luria and Leontiev has influenced many of the twentieth-century social theorists who sought to address this agenda. A central theme for them and for this book is that of mediation.

As a first example of the importance of the concept of mediation in the development of an understanding as to how culture enters into psychological processes I will now move to a discussion of issues raised in the 'reading' of the

Russian school of social theorists in general and Vygotsky's work in particular. In doing so I will be discussing the mediational properties of artefacts, such as texts, in the social formation of ideas.

Translation and transformation

The social theory that has developed under the influence of Vygotsky provides a rich source of potential for understanding and developing a process of social transformation such as schooling. At the outset it is important to note that I will not and, more importantly, could not adopt a fundamentalist position on Vygotsky's work. The processes of recontextualisation in time and location alone deny the possibility of such a simplistic 'reading'. I will seek to describe and analyse the major movements that have drawn on his work and then move to discuss their practical application in education.

Several writers have noted the highly selective and partial reading of Vygotsky's writing that appears in the West (see Valsiner, 1988). Many Western attempts to interpret Vygotsky have been marked more by enthusiasm for Western pedagogical preoccupations than by a concern to understand the range and depth of the arguments. This has been compounded by a marked tendency to ignore the work of more recent Russian writers. There are also logistical and linguistic reasons why over-zealous adulation would be inappropriate:

- Logistical in that, even now with the publication of the 'Collected Works', it is not at all clear that all his work is available in Russian let alone English. There are also debates and disagreements as to origins of some of the texts (see for example Veresov, 1999, p. 251).
- Linguistic in that the much discussed difficulty in translation still besets the reader of English versions despite significant advances on the very early versions.

Wertsch in the foreword to Asmolov (1998) discusses the difficulty that exists in translating Russian terms. He discusses the transformation through translation of the Russian word *lichnost* into English. The standard translation is from *lichnost* to *personality*. Wertsch's concern is with the received set of understandings associated with the term *personality* in Western psychology.

Valsiner (1998) suggests that *personality* is often thought of as a phenomenon that 'belongs inherently to the person and is not causally related to the social context'. His own sociocultural position on the meaning of *personality* is that it should be viewed as something which is created socially.

> Personality is viewed as emerging in ontogeny through social relations and their cultural organisation. In its established forms, socially emerged personality becomes relatively autonomous from the very social world within which it has emerged. Thus, personality is simultaneously socially dependent

and individually independent, with both parts of this whole being mutually interdependent.

(Valsiner, 1998, p. 1)

This definition may be read as an understanding which itself has developed under the influence of Russian writing and has also adopted a specific position within the field of interpretations that are possible. Here we have a glimpse of the possibilities afforded by the term mediation. The social/cultural/linguistic mediation of meaning serves to create a range of individual possibilities for understanding.

Another example of transformation through translation is with respect to the Russian word *obuchenie* which is often translated as *instruction*. The cultural baggage of a transmission based pedagogy is easily associated with *obuchenie* in its guise as *instruction*. Davydov's (1995) translator suggests that teaching or teaching-learning is more appropriate as the translation of *obuchenie* in that it refers to all the actions of the teacher in engendering cognitive development and growth. Sutton (1980) also notes that the word does not admit to a direct English translation. He argues that it means both teaching and learning, and refers to both sides of the two-way process, and is therefore well suited to a dialectical view of a phenomenon made up of mutually interpenetrating opposites.

> Its frequent conventional translation simply as 'learning' therefore renders much Russian work in English translation wholly meaningless, particularly the intense Soviet interest in the relationship between obuchenie and development. It should be recalled that the verb 'to develop' is transitive as well as intransitive, and that the dialectical viewpoint will therefore include a different view of the concept of 'development'. Not only do children develop, but we adults develop them. On balance, Soviet developmental psychology is a psychology of teaching and teaching difficulties, as much as ours is one of learning and learning difficulties.

(Sutton, 1980, p. 169)

Commenting on Bruner's introduction to the 1962 translation of *Thought and Language* (subsequently translated as *Thinking and Speech*) that 'Vygotsky's conception of development is at the same time a theory of education' Moll cites Cole's detailed analysis of the problems of translation:

> Taken out of their historical-cultural-linguistic context, even presumably non-problematic translation of individual terms can lead to undetected misunderstanding. This point is further illustrated by considering the mean-ing of the Russian term translated (correctly) as education, 'obrazovanie'. The etymology of English reveals that education is derived from the word, 'educe' which means to draw out or extract. How different that is from

obrazovanie, which my four volume Russian dictionary introduces with the example. 'The ocean also participated in the obrazovanie of that strip of land'. Given this context, we see a marked difference from the English which views education as a drawing out of what was in the child already, whereas the Russian emphasises a process of formation provoked by external forces. To complicate matters further, 'obrazovanie' has as its major root morpheme 'obraz' which in other contexts is the word for image, so it is akin to image making and when we look for the definition of obrazovanie we are provided with the term obuchenie. The term obuchenie . . . although often translated . . . as 'teaching' in fact can be used for both the activities of students and teachers, implicating a double sided process of teaching/learning, a mutual transformation of teacher and student. Hence, while Bruner was certainly correct that for Vygotsky there is an intimate link between education and development, when we get into the guts of the Russian, we see that he (Bruner) can be correct and (we can) still be provided with an impoverished representation of the concepts that Russian readers take for granted, e.g., that American discussion about 'learning and development' are about obuchenie and development in the USSR.

(Cole, cited in Moll, 1990, p. 24)

Thus, reading/understanding the legacy of the early Russian psychologists is in itself a problem both for and of cultural psychology. In his discussion of Asmolov's handling of *lichnost*, Wertsch uses the following quote from Bakhtin (1981) in order to try to construct a sociocultural theoretical base for the problems of translation in a very general way:

The word in language is half someone else's. It becomes 'one's own' only when the speaker populates it with his own intention, his own accent, when he appropriates the word, adapting it to his own semantic and expressive intention. Prior to this moment of appropriation, the word does not exist in a neutral and impersonal language (it is not after all out of a dictionary that a speaker gets his words!), but rather it exists in other people's mouths, in other people's context, serving other people's intentions; it's from there that anyone must take the word and make it one's own. And not all words for just anyone submit equally easily to this appropriation, to this seizure and transformation to private property; many words stubbornly resist, others remain alien, sound foreign in the mouth of the one who appropriated them and who now speaks them; they cannot be assimilated into his context and fall out of it; it is as if they put themselves in quotation marks against the will of the speaker. Language is not a neutral medium that passes freely and easily into the private property of the speaker's intentions; it is populated – over-populated – with the intentions of others.

(Bakhtin, 1981, pp. 293–4)

Wertsch encourages the reader of Asmolov's work on *lichnost* to treat its translation as *personality* as strange by mentally ascribing quotation marks to the text thus – 'personality'. In order to benefit from Asmolov's writing, Wertsch suggests that the reader must acknowledge the problematic nature of the translation. The same is true of *obuchenie*. If we accept an account of the mediation of meaning similar to that provided by Bakhtin (1981) we are faced with several levels of mediational complexity – within and between languages, cultures and, in reading Vygotsky, historical contexts. As Sutton notes:

> The problem for . . . Anglo-Saxon psychologists and educators, therefore is not solely one of linguistic translation but also, and perhaps more fundamentally, of the transition from one society to another.
>
> (Sutton, 1980, p. 33)

Taken to its extreme this statement could result in the suggestion that meaning cannot transfer across boundaries of time, space and language use. This question of the situated nature of cognition will be addressed in Chapters 2 and 3. Alternatively, a notion of fundamental meaning could be invoked and the quest for ultimate truth encapsulated within the text could drive scholarly activity. This is not the intention here. Nor is it supposed that even if the 'real Vygotsky' could be read out of the available texts would there be access to answers to what have proved to be obdurate problems in psychology. Bakhtin's suggestion that language is 'over populated with the intentions of others', reminds us that the processes of mediation are processes in which individuals operate with artefacts (words/texts) which are themselves shaped by, and have been shaped in, activities within which values are contested and meaning negotiated. In this sense cultural residues reside in and constrain the possibilities for communication. Thus the mediational process is one which neither denies individual or collective agency nor denies social, cultural, historical constraint.

In addition to the issues of selective reading and those associated with translation/translocation there are social processes which may seek to transform our 'reading' of Vygotsky. Tul'viste (1988), an Estonian, cautions against the Western 'one sided glorification of Vygotsky'. In a consideration of the prospects for the development of Vygotskian Psychology Asmolov warns of this process of glorification.

> The canonization of the basic principles of a theory entails much greater dangers than any criticism from within or without. Theories never are killed by criticism; they die in the hands of jealous disciples who are in a hurry to canonise them and then sit back in their easy chairs. Throughout the history of science in each of its stages, disciples have performed one and the same operation, that of raising principles to the rank of postulates requiring no proof.
>
> (Asmolov, 1982, p. 100)

Bearing these factors in mind, Wells (1999) argues that we should certainly read Vygotsky's texts and try to understand what he had to say; but, in appropriating his ideas and putting them to use, we should also be willing to transform those ideas so that they can be of greatest use to us in meeting the demands of our own situations (Wells, 1999, p. 334).

From a Russian perspective, Akhutina distinguishes between two kinds of scientific study:

> The findings of one kind are immediately assimilated into the body of science. The ideas of the other kind, on the other hand, only gradually gain scientific currency; each succeeding generation of scientists finds something new in them, some material that is particularly relevant for them. Vygotsky's scientific heritage certainly belongs to the latter type.
>
> (Akhutina, 1975, p. 12)

Thus, when we come to 'read' Vygotsky we are faced with a complex task. Wertsch suggests that we should try to remember the complexity or strangeness of the task and gradually work our way into *an* understanding which as Wells reminds us is appropriate in our own circumstances.

Mediation

In this section I will discuss some of the understandings of the concept of mediation. Cole (1996) places the concept at the heart of his conception of cultural psychology which owes so much to Vygotsky. He identifies the main characteristics of a general cultural psychology and develops his own version of a cultural-historical approach to the area. He suggests that:

- it emphasises mediated action in a context;
- it insists on the importance of the 'genetic method' understood broadly to include historical, ontogenetic, and microgenetic levels of analysis;
- it seeks to ground its analysis in everyday life events;
- it assumes that mind emerges in the *joint* mediated activity of people. Mind, then is in an important sense, 'co-constructed and distributed';
- it assumes that individuals are active agents in their own development but do not act in settings entirely of their own choosing;
- it rejects cause–effect, stimulus–response, explanatory science in favour of a science that emphasises the emergent nature of mind in activity and that acknowledges a central role for interpretation in its explanatory framework;
- it draws upon methodologies from the humanities as well as from the social and biological sciences. (Modified from Cole, 1996, p. 104)

This summary serves as a useful point of departure in the discussion of the Vygotskian legacy. It captures most of the major characteristics of contemporary approaches to psychology which affiliate to a post–Vygotskian position. Within this general field Cole identifies key concepts which are specific to the cultural historical psychology that in itself owes much of its origins to the Russian school comprised of Luria, Vygotsky and Leontiev.

The most important of these key concepts is that of 'mediation' which opens the way for the development of a non-deterministic account in which mediators serve as the means by which the individual acts upon and is acted upon by social, cultural and historical factors. The operational definition of those issues which are to be regarded as 'social, cultural and historical' impacts on the breadth of the conception of pedagogy. If a broad of range of factors is seen to be potentially formative at the psychological level then questions must address the pedagogy of such a process of formation. There is considerable tension and debate as to the nature of such factors. The tensions are revealed in competing definitions of 'culture' and the labelling of contemporary theoretical approaches, as for example either sociocultural or cultural–historical. These issues will be discussed in Chapter 3. There are similar debates about the means of mediation. Some approaches have tended to focus on semiotic means of mediation (Wertsch, 1991) whereas others have tended to focus more on activity itself (Engeström, 1993). These will also be discussed in Chapter 3.

In this section I wish to discuss the general concept of mediation within the Vygotskian thesis. Figure 1.1 as reproduced in Cole (1996) and many other publications represents the possibilities for subject–object relations. They are either unmediated, direct and in some sense natural or they are mediated through culturally available artefacts. In much of the literature the term 'tool' is used in place of artefact as here and in Cole (1996). Cole suggests that tool is most appropriately handled as a subcategory of artefact. I intend to discuss both the concept of tool as it appeared in the original writing and artefact as something that is embued with meaning and value through its existence within a field of human activity.

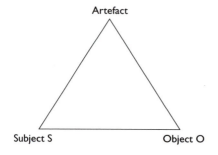

Figure 1.1 The basic triangular representation of mediation.

Reprinted by permission of the publisher from *Cultural Psychology: A Once and Future Discipline*, Michael Cole, Cambridge, MA: Harvard University Press, Copyright © 1996 by the President and Fellows of Harvard College.

Tools: material and psychological

Vygotsky described psychological tools as devices for mastering mental processes. They were seen as artificial and of social rather than organic or individual origin. He gave the following examples of psychological tools: 'language; various systems for counting; mnemonic techniques; algebraic symbol systems; works of art; writing; schemes, diagrams, maps and mechanical drawings; all sorts of conventional signs' (Vygotsky, 1960/1981, pp. 136–7).

The very idea of mediation carries with it a number of significant implications concerning pedagogic control. In that the concept denies the possibility of total determinism through external forces it is associated with an intellectual baggage which is potentially highly charged, especially in the political context in which these ideas were originally promulgated. In the extract reprinted below it is clear that Vygotsky was arguing that humans master themselves through external symbolic, cultural systems rather than being subjugated by and in them.

> Because this auxiliary stimulus possesses the specific function of reverse action, it transfers the psychological operation to higher and qualitatively new forms and permits the humans, by the aid of extrinsic stimuli, to control their behaviour from the outside.
>
> (Vygotsky, 1978, p. 40)

This emphasis on the self-construction through and with those tools which are available brings two crucial issues to the foreground. Firstly, it speaks of the individual as an active agent in development. Secondly, it affirms the importance of contextual effects in that development takes place through the use of those tools which are available at a particular time in a particular place. He distinguished between psychological and other tools and suggested that psychological tools can be used to direct the mind and behaviour. In contrast, technical tools are used to bring about changes in other objects. Rather than changing objects in the environment, psychological tools are devices for influencing the mind and behaviour of oneself or another.

Vygotsky (1978) discussed a number of examples of early psychological tools such as tying knots. He suggested that when a knot is tied in a handkerchief as a reminder it acts as an external aspect of remembering. The process of memorising is reconstructed through the transformation of an external object as a reminder of something. He contrasts the act of memorising before and after the knot is used as a psychological tool.

> In the elementary form something is remembered; in the higher form humans remember something. In the first case a temporary link is formed owing to the simultaneous occurrence of two stimuli that affect the organism; in the second case humans personally create a temporary link through an artificial combination of stimuli . . . the very essence of human

memory consists in the fact that human beings actively remember with the help of signs.

(Vygotsky, 1978, p. 51)

Thus, it was through his work on the use of knots in handkerchiefs as signs that Vygotsky revealed that 'human beings are able to control the conditions of their future remembering' (Bakhurst, 1996, p. 202). Tools and signs are the 'auxiliary means' by which interactions between subject and object are mediated (Cole and Engeström, 1993), the subject being the protagonist in activity, the object being its motivating force. Vygotsky saw tools and symbols as two aspects of the same phenomena (Cole and Engeström, 1993), a tool being technical and altering 'the process of a natural adaptation by determining the form of labour operations', a sign being psychological and altering 'the entire flow and structure of mental functions' (Vygotsky, 1981, p. 137). Lee describes it thus:

> Tools . . . and signs differ fundamentally in their organisation. A tool is externally oriented toward the goal, a mere instrument in the hands of its user who controls it. Signs, however, are inherently 'reversible' – they feed back upon or control their users.
>
> (Lee, 1985, p. 76)

Vygotsky also argues that the ways in which tools and signs are used vary as function of context and the child's own development. He refers to the 'natural history of the sign' as a way of emphasising that, in the course of development, the psychological function that may be fulfilled by signs may also develop and change. Thus, speech may have several functions (e.g. labelling and planning). In the early stages of development, Vygotsky suggests that speech may assume an important labelling function in that it enables the child to identify a particular object, to single it out and distinguish it from others. He argues that increasing sophistication in the use of language allows the child to become progressively more independent of the sensory field (Vygotsky, 1978, p. 32).

In the discussion of memory and thinking that constitutes Chapter 3 of *Mind in Society*, Vygotsky stipulates that radical transformations take place in the relationships between psychological functions as a result of such mediated psychological activity. He suggests that 'for the young child, to think means to recall; but for the adolescent, to recall means to think' (Vygotsky, 1978, p. 51). Human memory is seen as a function that is actively supported and transformed through the use of signs.

> Just as a mould gives shape to a substance, words can shape an activity into a structure. However, that structure may be changed or reshaped when children learn to use language in ways that allow them to go beyond previous experiences when planning future action . . . once children learn how to use the planning function of their language effectively, their

psychological field changes radically. A view of the future is now an integral part of their approaches to their surroundings.

(Vygotsky, 1978, p. 28)

Thus from Vygotsky's perspective the use of psychological tools:

* introduces several new functions connected with the use of the given tool and with its control;
* abolishes and makes unnecessary several natural processes, whose work is accomplished by the tool; and alters the course and individual features (the intensity, duration, sequence, etc.) of all the mental processes that enter into the composition of the instrumental act, replacing some functions with others (i.e. it re-creates and reorganises the whole structure of behaviour just as a technical tool re-creates the whole structure of labour operations) (Vygotsky, 1981, pp. 139–40).

Tools or artefacts?

Psychological tools, just as material tools, are the products of human cultural historical activity. Pea describes what can be thought of as the sedimentation of cultural historical legacies in tools. He also draws attention to the way in which this legacy may appear 'natural' or indeed be rendered invisible. This process may leave the observer with the impression that a person acting with tools is behaving intelligently in a way that reveals their own individual/asocial capability.

> [invented tools] turned from history into nature, they are invisible, un-remarkable aspects of our experiential world . . . these tools literally carry intelligence in them, in that they represent some individual's or some community's decision that the means thus offered should be reified, made stable, as a quasi permanent form, for the use by others . . . as such tools become invisible, it becomes harder to see them as bearing intelligence; instead we see intelligence as residing in the individual mind using the tools.
>
> (Pea, 1993, p. 53)

This process may happen as much with persons as objects. Cole's (1996) proposal is that the concept of tool should be treated as a subcategory of the superordinate notion of artefact. People just as objects may act as mediating artefacts. Indeed, Kozulin (1998) argues that Vygotsky envisaged a theoretical programme which accounted for three classes of mediators: material tools, psychological tools and other human beings. The development of Vygotsky's work has revealed different degrees of emphasis on these three types or classes of mediational means.

Ivic provides a citation from Vygotsky which attests to his views on mediation through interpersonal relations:

In 1932 Vygotsky wrote:'It is through the mediation of others, through the mediation of the adult that the child undertakes activities. Absolutely everything in the behaviour of the child is merged and rooted in social relations. Thus, the child's relations with reality are from the start social relations, so that the newborn baby could be said to be in the highest degree a social being.'

(Ivic, 1989, p. 429)

This general position underpins the general genetic law of cultural development which will be discussed in Chapter 2. Here the emphasis is on mediation through the activities of and with other people in sociocultural settings. It also underpins a focus on the role of another individual as a mediator of meaning (Kozulin, 1998).

Kozulin (1986) provides an illuminating discussion of the social history of Vygotsky's psychology, the core of his argument being that the Kharkov group of psychologists led by Leontiev developed what became known as 'activity theory' as a response to immediate political circumstances. In Kozulin's view they were attempting to locate the analysis of mediation through activity in such a way that it would become acceptable to the dominant interpretation of Marx that arose in the latter part of the 1930s in the Soviet Union.

While Vygotsky (and Leontiev in earlier works) focused on the mediational role of signs and symbols, the Kharkovites devoted their entire attention to activities, thus bringing them closer to the Piagetian programme with its emphasis on the internalisation of sensory-motor schemas (this rather obvious affinity, however, was played down by the Kharkovites). As a result the notion of symbolic psychological tools, and the role of culture embodied in them, became underrepresented in Soviet psychology starting in the mid-1930s. The issue of the mediating effect of interpersonal relations was taken up only in the 1960s.

(Kozulin, 1990, p. 247)

The analysis of semiotic mediation was certainly diminished in Soviet Psychology in the period 1935–1939. The activity theorists of this period suggested that the structure of cognitive processes mirrored the structure of external activity and operations. Practical activity became the mediator of the macro rather than semiotic means. It was argued that it was practical action which should predominate in psychological analysis.

Davydov and Radzikhovskii (1985) amongst others, subsequently attempted to resolve the implicit opposition to semiotic mediation of mental functions within an activity oriented approach.

The concept of sign creates one of the interesting paths of activity. . . . The fact that studies of the sign mediated nature of mental functions have not developed further in the activity, oriented approach can be considered a weakness that can be overcome in the near future.

(Davydov and Radzikhovskii, 1985, p. 39)

There is a very specific problem here, one which continues to ricochet through post-Vygotskian work. If activity is taken as the central focus then is it to be assumed that mediation through activity does not in and of itself imply a semiotic relay? Does engagement in activity imply direct psychological engagement with the objective environment. The original Vygotskian model is distanced from the suggestion that the social context of development is simply the objective environment. As I mentioned earlier, Cole (1996) distinguishes between notions of context defined as that which surrounds and notions of context defined as that which weaves together. In doing so, he draws on the legacy of Bronfenbrenner's 1979 book on the ecology of human development which portrayed layers of context in concentric circles. This image of progressive wrapping of the individual in ever wider context is transformed by Cole into the following position: 'the combination of goals tools and setting . . . constitutes simultaneously the context of behaviours and ways in which cognition can be related to that context' (Cole, 1996, p. 137). Here we have implications of active construction of context in action. The way in which individuals or groups use artefacts in effect transforms the model of contexts that obtain at any one time in a particular setting. Bronfenbrenner's 'onion rings' may be reshaped, transformed, deleted and mutually interpenetrated. The structure of as it were 'the onion rings' remains underdeveloped in this thesis and will be considered in Chapters 4 and 5. He suggests a model in which the separation of the analysis and semiotic mediation through activity is both inappropriate and inadequate.

What most concerns me in the context of this discussion is that culture was treated very much as a package of independent variables rather than as a medium, and was not directly the object of analysis.

(Cole, 1994, p. 84)

The way in which the relationship between the individual and the social is conceptualised was and remains problematic. The reasons for this may be attributed to the historical split in concern for semiotic and activity based analysis which started at or just before Vygotsky's death. The way out of the difficulty is seen to lie in a model of dialectical relations between social and individual levels which allow for levels of explanation without direct reduction of one to another. I will return to this issue in Chapter 2; however, at this point in the outline it is probably worth remembering the way in which Vygotsky's work has been distinguished from some of the more familiar Western developments in social theory. Hood-Holzman (1985) pursued an analysis of Vygotsky as a dialectical materialist rather than a symbolic interactionist.

> For Mead, the process of communication, of interpersonal interaction, is what social activity is all about. . . . For Vygotsky, social does not mean interpersonal; social interaction is not what the child has to learn. The activities of human behaviour, at all stages of development and organization, are social products and must be seen as historical developments.
>
> (Hood–Holzman, 1985, p. 357)

She proceeds to discuss the 'misreading' of the Soviet concept of activity with the Meadian concept of action. Again the analysis proceeds from questions concerning the position of the term 'social' within historical and cultural frameworks. Newman and Holzman (1993) provide a philosophical position on what they term Vygotsky's 'tool and result' methodology which grounds the tension between dialectical materialist and pragmatic accounts in, what is essentially, a political analysis. Hood–Holzman (1985) and Newman and Holzman (1993) are questioning both the breadth of interpretation that is placed on the 'social' in the formation of mind with the additional concern for the mechanism of mediation.

Interestingly, whilst attempts to develop Vygotsky's work in Russia have *not* foregrounded semiotic mediation but *have* foregrounded the analysis of social transmission in activity settings, much of the work in the West has tended to ignore the social beyond the interactional and to celebrate the individual and mediational processes at the expense of a consideration of socio-institutional, cultural and historical factors. Ideological differences between the West and the East have given rise to differences in theoretical development and of course pedagogical application. According to Davydov (1988), the emphasis on transmission in the former Soviet system of schooling had subverted the original requirement for responsive instructional dialogues. Conversely, the emphasis on interpersonal interpretation and interaction as a setting for the facilitation of developmental processes has removed the instructional invective from many Western 'Vygotskian' pedagogies. Thus it would seem that both the processes of interpretation and implementation of Vygotskian ideas must be understood in their specific social contexts. Engeström, who has done much to bring together the three types of account of mediation into a unified model, mounts a defence of the work of Leontiev, claiming that he has suffered at the hands of many Western interpreters.

> A careful reading of Leontiev's work reveals that both mediation by signs and subject–subject relations do play an important role in his theory. Proponents of the cultural–historical school repeatedly point out that communication is an inherent aspect of all object-related activities. Leontiev's account of the emergence of speech and language emphasises the original unity of labour actions and social intercourse. . . . So, there is a curious discrepancy between the ways Leontiev is read by critics and those sympathetic to his ideas.
>
> (Engeström, 1990, p. 7)

The ideal and the material

The notion of artefact raises a central concern in the philosophy underpinning many sociocultural psychologies – the relation between the ideal and the material. Bakhurst (1995) has done much to clarify the contribution of the Russian philosopher Ilyenkov to our understanding of the framework within which so much of the Russian perspective on mediation may be read. A starting point from which to untangle some of the ramifications of this philosophical position is with reference to the concept of 'objectification'. It is with this concept that connection can be made to the cultural historical production of the artefacts which humans use to order and construct their lives. The idea of meaning embodied or, as I have suggested above, sedimented in objects as they are put into use in social worlds is central to the conceptual apparatus of theories of culturally mediated, historically developing, practical activity.

> This notion of 'objectification' (*opredmechivanie*) is easiest to understand in the case of artefacts. What distinguishes an artefact from a brutally physical object? (e.g. what distinguishes a table from the raw material from which it is fashioned?) The answer lies in the fact that the artefact bears a certain significance which it possesses, not by virtue of its physical nature, but because it has been produced for a certain use and incorporated into a system of human ends and purposes. The object thus confronts us as an embodiment of meaning, placed and sustained in it by 'aimed-oriented' human activity.
>
> (Bakhurst, 1995, p. 160)

This model of the process is part of the conceptual apparatus which is associated with Ilyenkov's philosophy of 'ideality'. This provides an account of the way in which humans inscribe significance and value into the very physical objects of their environment. This 'ideality' results from 'the transforming, form creating, activity of social beings, their aim mediated, sensuously objective activity'. As Bakhurst notes: 'Ilyenkov's transcendental account of the origin of subject and object in activity portrays nature as a kind of shapeless raw material given form by human agency. Nature is the clay on which humanity inscribes its mark' (Bakhurst, 1995, p. 173).

Bakhurst applies the same logic to the object of his discussion. He seeks an understanding of the concept of objectification in the history of the philosophical culture of Russia. He suggests that Russian thinking has developed in a culture which embodies a powerful anti-Cartesian element. He contrasts this kind of intellectual environment with that which obtains in many settings in the West where so much effort has been expended in conceptualising the mind as a 'self-contained private realm, set over against the objective, "external" world of material things, and populated by subjective states revealed only to the "self" presiding over them' (Bakhurst, 1995, pp. 155–6). The argument is that culture and community are not merely independent factors which discriminate between settings. They are, as it were, the mediational medium with and through which ideas are developed. This argument underpins Cole's (1996) model of culture as that which weaves together as mentioned above.

Ilyenkov emphasises the cultural-historical nature of the development of ideality at the macro and micro level of analysis. He also seeks to unify the analysis of the ideal and the material. Cole joins with Bakhurst in theorising artefacts as being both ideal (conceptual) and material.

> Artifacts exhibit a dual nature in that they are simultaneously ideal and material. Their creators and users exhibit a corresponding duality of thought, at once grounded in the material here and now, yet simultaneously capable of entertaining the far away, the long ago, and the never has-been.
>
> (Cole, 1994, p. 94)

Cole (1996) employs Wartofsky's definition of artefacts (including tools and language) as objectifications of human needs and intentions already invested with cognitive and affective content (Wartofsky, 1973, p. 204). He distinguishes between three hierarchical levels of the notion of artefacts. Primary artefacts are those such as needles, clubs, bowls, which are used directly in the making of things. Secondary artefacts are representations of primary artefacts and of modes of action using primary artefacts. They are therefore traditions or beliefs. Tertiary artefacts were referred to by Wartofsky as imagined worlds. He sees works of art as examples of these tertiary artefacts or imagined worlds. He proceeds to outline how these three levels of artefact function in processes of cultural mediation.

Discourse and schema

A number of tensions will be explored throughout this book: the ideal and material; formative effects inside the mind and outside the body; internalisation and appropriation; transmission based and acquisition based pedagogies and so on. Some may be resolved, some will not – indeed should not be resolved. As Lemke (1997) reminds us, the intellectual culture which still runs deep through much contemporary thinking is that of cleavages where, perhaps, dynamic tensions should remain.

> We blame the early Moderns of Rene Descartes' 17th-century Europe for cleaving Mind from Body and Society from Nature. From them we inherited a chain – cognition in the mind, mind 'in' a material brain, brain in a mindless body, body in a natural environment separate from society, society made up of persons not bodies, persons defined by cultures, cultures created by minds – a chain that binds us still and runs us 'round and 'round in ever smaller circles.
>
> (Lemke, 1997)

In Chapter 2 I will discuss Vygotsky's dialectical alternative to dualism in more detail. At this point I wish to pursue one particular dualism. To some extent a discussion of the concept of mediation must make either direct or indirect reference to the major issues in the development of Vygotskian theory. It is central to all other facets of the thesis. A theory of mediation through artefacts infers that in the course of human activity meaning is sedimented, accumulated or deposited in things. These meanings are remembered both collectively and individually. The artefact is thus both material and ideal. How is the relationship, this intertwining to be conceptualised? In the early 1980s I re-read the schema and script theory which had been developed by writers such as Rumelhart (1978), Schank and Abelson (1977), and Nelson (1981). At the time I was struggling with a PhD in which I wished to theorise a connection between a Vygotskian account of the social formation of mind, some notion of mental representation and also a sociology which allowed for empirical study of the psychological consequences of activity within different forms of socio-institutional structures. It is reasonable to say that I failed. At the time I had not read Bakhurst (1995), Wartofsky (1973), Holland and Cole (1995) and Cole (1996).

At the time I felt that an appropriate theory of mental representation was required to account for the transfer of understanding across locations and through time. I find Nelson's (1981) remark that without shared scripts every social act would need to be negotiated afresh, a simple yet effective challenge! However, more recently, Cole (1991) has suggested that 'a script is part of a social process with distributions of authority and responsibility; it may or may not be an intrapersonal, mental structure, but it is certainly an interpersonal one' (Cole, 1991, p. 201). This hint of a question concerning the existence of mental representations is taken much further by Shotter.

Shotter (1993 a, b) argued against a mechanical and systematic character to Vygotsky's account of internalisation. His position was that rather than functioning in terms of already well-formed mental representations 'inner lives' exhibit the characteristics of communication in the interpersonal world. Drawing on Bakhtin's writings, he suggested that mental activities are only 'given form' at the time of their expression. His argument was for a cognitive psychology without mental representations. I will return to this matter of mental representation within a post-Vygotskian model in Chapter 2 where I will discuss the internalisation–appropriation debate. The tension concerning the specificity and duration of mental representations is played out within that debate.

I also felt that those aspects of Vygotsky's work with which I was familiar at the time were almost silent on socio-institutional factors. I will return to this issue in Chapters 4 and 5. I was convinced that Vygotsky had developed the point of departure for the re-thinking of the outer world at work in the inner world. Interestingly, Prawat (1999) has approached the issue from another point of view and come to a similar conclusion. He starts with an analysis of the differences between modernist and postmodernist views of cognition. He critiques the dualist epistemology of modernism and the failure of postmodernist approaches to adequately theorise the connection between local and societal level language practice. Prawat (1999) argues that Vygotsky offers a mediational account of meaning-making which is also social, embodied and transactional. This position is elaborated by Kozulin (1998) who discusses three possible generators of consciousness:

- the historical nature of human experience: 'human beings make a wide use of non-biological heredity transmitting knowledge, experiences and symbolic tools from generation to generation';
- the social environment and experiences of others: through drawing out the similarities between Mead and Vygotsky he emphasises that 'an individual becomes aware of him- or herself only in and through interactions with others';
- the existence of mental images and schemas prior to actual action: 'human experience is always present in two different planes – the plane of actual occurrences and the plane of their internal cognitive schematizations' (Kozulin, 1998, p. 10).

Where Prawat speaks in terms of social, embodied and transactional, Kozulin speaks of history, interaction and internal cognitive schematisations. There are tensions between the two positions: Kozulin's emphasis on history which is not made explicit in Prawat's use of the term 'social'; Prawat's use of trans-action has a more dialectical turn than 'interaction' within Kozulin's work; and schematisations is much more specific than embodied. Whilst differences of emphasis are clear, there remains an agreement about the existence of multiple levels of representational activity which occurs in between and within persons. The relationship between Wartofsky's tertiary artefacts or imagined worlds and the schemas and scripts of cognitive psychology has been made possible through the understanding of artefact as simultaneously material and ideal which is available in Ilyenkov's work.

Holland and Cole (1995) use discourse and schema theory to elaborate the concept of cultural artefact. Discourse theory is used to initiate a discussion of how representations/artefacts that operate in the social world may be regarded as cultural products and exhibit historical legacies. Speech genres and stories both reveal these qualities. Schema theory is used to explore the possibilities for mental representations which are socially formed and are modifiable.

Anderson (1980) summarised work on schema theory and suggested that humans appear to have a powerful ability to build schemas from correlations detected in stimulus events. Whilst he recognised the inadequacy inherent in the stereotypical nature of schema abstraction and that schemas might best be described as 'quick and dirty' methods of thinking, he indicates their value in some circumstances.

> Some schemas serve to help us recognize objects, make judgements, comprehend stories and otherwise act in the world. Schemas are important knowledge structures that enable us to deal effectively with the information processing demands of a large and complex world. They serve to extract and categorize clusters of experiences in that world!
>
> (Anderson, 1980, p. 158)

In his use of the metaphor of cultural context as that 'which weaves together' rather than 'that which surrounds' Cole (1996) draws on Rumelhart *et al.* (1986), who argue that external mediators help to simplify complex tasks in such a way that they can be managed through and by various forms of mental representation. For example, words acting as labels help to sort a complex stimulus field. The approach is therefore based on the belief that by studying individuals' developing ability to acquire knowledge from or produce discourse, one is investigating fundamental characteristics of how individuals acquire, represent and construct extended knowledge structures. Whilst these theories may well be sufficient for treating internal and external structures as independent entities, a theory is required which posits their dynamic mutual influence.

Schemas may be thought of as selection mechanisms and be used to explain the differences between the way in which experts behave and the behaviour of novices. In that experts notice features and meaningful patterns of information that are not noticed by novices it may be inferred that they are using socially acquired, expert schemas through participation in particular forms of practice (Glaser, 1999). To my mind, this may accord with Greeno's (1991) notion of 'learning the landscape'. Greeno proposes that experts are good at learning their way around a knowledge landscape knowing what's available in it and how to use what is available in order to be both productive and fulfilled. There is, of course, a tension between the production and development of general schema and their application in specific circumstances.

> Most of the reasoning we do apparently does not involve the general purpose reasoning skills. Rather it seems that most of our reasoning ability is tied to particular schemata related to particular bodies of knowledge.
>
> (Rumelhart, 1978, p. 39)

D'Andrade (1990) extends these ideas into the formulation of the notion of cultural schema which include social interaction, discourse and word meaning. Importantly, Cole (1996) emphasises that no script, or generalised event schema, fully specifies behaviour. He argues that every schema leaves out an enormous amount and is a great simplification of the potential visual, acoustic, sensory and propositional information that could be experienced (D'Andrade, 1990, p. 98). He discusses how Bruner and Nelson have developed the notion of scripts comprising both mental representations and patterns of talk and action. This position invokes notions of culturally shaped cognitive representations operating within social interchange in specific settings.

> What we learn and what we know, and what our culture knows for us in the form of the structure of artefacts and social organisations are these hunks of mediating structure. Thinking consists of bringing these structures into co-ordination with each other such that they can shape (and be shaped by) each other. The thinker in this world is a very special medium that can provide co-ordination among many structured media, some internal, some external, some embodied in artefacts, some in ideas, and some in social relationships.
>
> (Hutchins, 1986, p. 57)

Wertsch (1998) and Bruner (1990) both analyse narrative and historical texts as cultural tools. Wertsch (1998) emphasises that tools or artefacts such as 'conventional' stories or popular histories may not always 'fit' well with a particular personal narrative. As ever with a Vygotskian account there is no necessary recourse to determinism. Wertsch suggests that individuals may resist the way in which such texts 'shape their actions, but they are often highly constrained in the forms that such resistance can take' (Wertsch, 1998, p. 108). This emphasis on the individual who is active in shaping a response to being shaped by engagement with cultural artefacts is central to the Vygotskian argument. The relative emphasis on agency (whether individual or collective – Wertsch, 1998) and the affordances (Gibson, 1979) that social, cultural and historical factors offer forms the stage on which the development of new and improved forms of thought is enacted.

As is now well known, Vygotsky was involved in a variety of intellectual pursuits. These ranged from medicine and law to literary theory. Kozulin reminds his readers that Vygotsky was a member of the Russian intelligentsia for whom literature assumed a particular significance.

> A particular feature of the Russian intelligentsia was the importance they attached to literature, which they saw not only as the ultimate embodiment of culture but as the most concentrated form of life itself. Literary characters were routinely judged by the Russian intelligentsia as real social and psychological types, while political and historical debates were commonly conducted in the form of literature and about literature.
>
> (Kozulin, 1990, pp. 22–3)

He has subsequently expanded on this position in an essay on literature as a psychological tool in which he discusses the notion of human psychological life as 'authoring' alongside a consideration of the role of internalised literary modalities as mediators of human experience (Kozulin, 1998, p. 130). I will return to the implications of this position in theoretical terms in Chapter 2 when I discuss the implications of Bakhtin's work, and in Chapter 3 when I consider some of the pedagogic implications. It is clear that aspects of this part of his thinking are still being developed today, most notably by Bruner.

What is unique about us as a species is that we not only adapt to the natural and social worlds through appropriate actions, but we also create theories and stories to help us *understand* and even *explain* the world and our actions in it.

(Bruner, 1997, p. 63)

As with many aspects of his work, an analysis of his writing over time reveals some fundamental shifts in Vygotsky's thinking on these matters.

The belief that imaginative literature (or art in general) is merely a manner of signalling, like birdsong or rat squeak, to be explained by its biological and social functions, versus the belief that it is also a thing in itself, to be not only explained but also understood as beautiful truths accumulating in a cultural process, which creates the human mind even as it is created by it. Vygotsky began with the second belief, was drawn against his aesthetic inclination toward the first, tried to fuse them, but did not succeed.

(Joravsky, 1987, p. 192)

Recent advances in neurophysiology suggest that representation at the neurological level is an activity which is in many ways isomorphic to forms of social representation.

Images are not stored as facsimile pictures of things or events or words or sentences. The brain does not file Polaroid pictures of people, objects, land-scapes; nor does it store audio tapes of music or speech; it does not store films of scenes in our lives; nor does it hold the type of cue cards and TelePromTer transparencies that help politicians earn their daily bread. In brief, there seem to be no permanently held pictures of anything, even miniaturised, no microfiches or microfilms, no hard copies. . . . Mental images are momentary constructions, attempts at replication of patterns that were once experienced, in which the probability of exact replication is low but the probability of substantial replication can be higher or lower, depending on the circumstances in which the images were learned and are being recalled.

(Damasio, 1994, pp. 100–1)

This contribution from the natural sciences allows for the development of a theoretical account of representation and mediation in which several levels of representation operate at the same time. Forms of representation which are both sociocultural and historical such as stories may transact/interact with representations which are embodied but not immutable. Bruner provides a characteristically engaging illustration of the social appearance of such a process.

When we enter human life, it is as if we walk on stage into a play whose enactment is in progress – a play whose somewhat open plot determines what parts we may play and toward what denouements we may be heading. Others on stage already have a sense of what the play is about, enough of a sense to make negotiation with a newcomer possible.

(Bruner, 1990, p. 34)

The concept of mediation has developed far beyond the original notion of psychological tools. Contributions from disciplines as seemingly diverse as Philosophy, Cognitive Psychology and Neurophysiology have given rise to the possibility of reconsidering the original Vygotskian position. This concept on which so much of the thesis depends has gained explicit and implicit support from a wide range of contributions. A model of dynamic interplay between discourses and other artefacts, mental representations and patterns of neurological activity in the formation of human thought has started to evolve. Discussions of the constraints and control over those discourses and other artefacts which are available socially in particular cultural contexts and which have specific historical origins and commitments give rise to sociological considerations of production and distribution. Biological constraints and limitations are also to be understood in a robust model of the way in which social, cultural and historical factors exercise a formative effect on human development. Crucially the emphasis on the human use of tools, signs/artefacts for self-creation removes the Vygotskian model from the domain of crude social determinism. The attempt to develop an account of the way in which active learning has a formative effect has clear implications for pedagogy.

His (Vygotsky's) views on pedagogy and learning are more consistent with recent discoveries that children learn in a variety of ways rather than by a single path of development. For several decades, theories of learning and development proceeded on separate tracks, with little overlap.

(Emihovich and Souza Lima, 1995, p. 377)

This connection between learning and development will be discussed in Chapter 2. Part of the position that I have argued in this chapter asserts that the 'social' within Vygotsky's account of the social formation of mind should be defined very broadly. It has cultural and historical elements and should take account of the way in which particular activities are regulated. Given this assertion concerning the nature of the 'social' then it is hardly surprising that I should have argued for a broad definition of pedagogy – it is after all the means through which education arranges social influences. As I will make clear in subsequent chapters I believe that the formative effects of schooling are attributable to far more than the mechanical unfolding of a curriculum script. I will also seek to emphasise that just as the model of mediation within Vygotsky's account of development suggests that single pathways are not to be expected, so the action of teachers should not be expected to conform to rigid pre-scriptions. The following quote from the writings of Davydov provides what I feel is a fitting close to this initial chapter.

It is worth noting specially that Vygotsky did not recognise the presence of some separate reality containing only the teacher and child. He singled out and studied the dynamic social surroundings that connect the teacher and child (that is, the other adults and children with whom a given child actually lives and interacts). The teacher's work is particularly complex because, in the first place, the teacher must be well oriented to the regularities of the child's personal activity, that is, know the child's psychology; in the second place, the teacher must know the particular social dynamics of the child's social setting; and in the third place, the teacher must know about the possibilities of his or her own pedagogical activity to use these sensibly and thus raise to a new level the activity, consciousness, and personality of his or her charges. This is why the work of a genuine teacher can never be stereotyped or routine; the teacher's work always carries a profoundly creative character.

(Davydov, 1995, p. 17)

Chapter 2

Vygotskian theory and education

In this chapter I will attempt to present an overview of Vygotsky's theoretical contribution to the field. The discussion concerning mediation that is to be found in Chapter 1 lays the foundation for this overview. Scribner captured the essence of this foundation in the following way:

> Vygotsky's special genius was in grasping the significance of the social in things as well as people. The world in which we live is humanised, full of material and symbolic objects (signs, knowledge systems) that are culturally constructed, historical in origin and social in content. Since all human actions, including acts of thought, involve the mediation of such objects ('tools and signs') they are, on this score alone, social in essence. This is the case whether acts are initiated by single agents or a collective and whether they are performed individually or with others.
>
> (Scribner, 1990, p. 92)

This will not be an attempt to discuss the entire collection of writings as in the case of Kozulin (1990), Yaroshevsky (1989) and Van der Veer and Valsiner (1991). As the 'field' here is pedagogy the discussion will be constrained to the issues raised by Vygotsky which have a direct bearing on educational matters. Chapter 3 will consist of a discussion of current developments which derive some inspiration from this body of work.

The task I have set myself is not as straightforward as it may appear. The original body of writing itself cannot be considered to be coherent and unified. As Minick (1987) shows the stages and phases of Vygotsky's work were marked by some profound shifts in orientation, albeit with a common frame of reference. The exact nature of these stages and phases is the matter of some dispute (see Veresov, 1999); however, the general point that significant changes occurred is undeniable.

The last two years of Vygotsky's life were marked by the increasing emphasis in his writing on the analysis of the development of psychological systems in connection with the development of social behaviour. Minick (1987) traced the progression of Vygotsky's thinking through three phases and argued that in contrast to his earlier work, his writing in the period 1933–4 insisted that the analysis of the development of word meaning should begin with the analysis of the function of the word in communication. Here was the connection between the analysis of social and psychological systems albeit with little direct reference to the material circumstances within which communication was enacted. The analysis proceeds from that of specific forms of social practice through an analysis of the function of the word in mediating specific types of social interaction and communication, to an understanding of the development of the word.

Both Wertsch (1985a) and Kozulin (1990) discuss the significance of Vygotsky's writings in terms of methodology. Their view is that Vygotsky's study of the general theoretical and metatheoretical issues that underlie any investigation of psychological phenomena constitutes his major contribution to social theory (Wertsch, 1985a). This contribution remains remarkable particularly as it was made so far in advance of its time. His time was one of major change and a concern to develop ways of understanding the human condition which did not revert to the reductionism and dualism of the past. Consequently it is of great importance to distinguish between the general framework and the practical implementation of his ideas and also to allow for changes in the methodological basis of his writing.

There are at least three translations of the text originally referred to as *Thought and Language* and now known as *Thinking and Speech* which differ substantially in the way in which the theory is presented and within which specific approaches to translation may give rise to fundamentally different interpretations (Vygotsky, 1962, 1986, 1987). Minick (Vygotsky, 1987) has made a major contribution to our understanding of Vygotsky's writing through his translation of a complete version of *Thinking and Speech*, although, as Kozulin (1990) points out, this widely cited text does not represent a coherent view of Vygotsky's ideas. The book, published in 1934, is not entirely representative of the final stages of Vygotsky's work. Indeed some of the writing incorporated into this volume is drawn from the mid-1920s phase of his studies. It is, therefore, not an easy book to read. As Minick (1985) has shown, the stages of development of the work reflect shifts in priority and conceptual development. A compilation of Vygotsky's writing such as this requires a reading which is sensitive to the developments which are represented by the various chapters of the book. The transitions between chapters five, six and seven remain the subject of much speculation. For example, Wertsch (2000) discusses the change in the view of meaning that is to be seen in the comparison of chapter seven with chapters five and six.

Basic to Vygotsky's methodology or metatheory is the insistence that psychological theory must involve the elucidation of the 'explanatory principle', the object of study (or analytic unit) and the dynamics of the relations between these two. Minick's (1985) analysis of three phases of Vygotsky's work enables a reader to gain a perspective on the development of Vygotsky's methodological writings. The first transition was from a focus on an analytic unit called the instrumental act in 1925/30, to an analytic unit of the psychological system in

1930. This was followed in 1933/4 by a refinement of the explanatory principle which became the differentiation and development of systems of interaction and action in which the individual participates (Minick, 1987). This final phase has remained obscure until very recently. It is evidenced in papers and lectures written in the last two years of his life. These sources are often difficult to obtain and remain elusive as his work was often left in the form of sketches rather than fully fledged arguments (Vygotsky, 1983). This final phase of Vygotsky's work suggests the need to move towards a broad analysis of behaviour and consciousness which articulates and clarifies the social cultural and historical basis of development.

There is a sense in which one can feel Vygotsky 'talking his way in' to a thesis that was never finished. This image of an obviously hugely talented thinker grappling with disciplines such as Psychology, in which he was, like Piaget, to a large part untrained, carries with it a sense of excitement and verve.

The paradox of learning

The concepts developed by Vygotsky sometimes appear as a web of tightly related notions. Breaking into this web of understanding is not easy. The network of cross-references requires a prior understanding before entry into the network! In one sense the issue referred to as the paradox of development by Fodor (1983) or the learning paradox as discussed by Bereiter (1985) applies. Cole (1996) discusses the same issue with reference to children's reading:

> Assuming that children do not enter school able to expand their ability to comprehend their experience by reading alphabetic text, how can we arrange for them to develop this new system of mediated action? In attempting to answer this question we are simultaneously tackling the crucial question of how it is possible to acquire a more powerful cognitive structure unless, in some sense, it is already present to begin with.
>
> (Cole, 1996, p. 274)

The same issue is raised by Smith (1996) who regards the learning paradox as a severe challenge to all forms of constructivism.

> If hypothesis-testing is the only way in which a new predicate (concept, structure) could be acquired, then all novel acquisition is impossible. According to Fodor, there is a minimal condition that a theory of novel learning must meet, namely the extensional equivalent of the novel concept and an available concept: something is an instance of (novel) concept if and only if it is an instance of (available) concept. This condition states that the learning of a novel concept is possible only if some connection is made with a concept equivalence in that the available and novel concepts should be subsumed in all-and-only the same individual instances. The implication

is that nativism must be accepted by default as there is currently no better alternative than hypothesis-testing.

(Smith, 1996, p. 115)

I will use Cole's (1996) resolution of the paradox to resolve my own difficulty in finding a point of departure. He invokes Vygotsky's (1978) 'general genetic law of genetic development':

> Every function in the child's cultural development appears twice: first, on the social level, and later, on the individual level; first between people (interpsychological), and then inside the child (intrapsychological). This applies equally to voluntary attention, to logical memory, and to the formation of concepts. All the higher functions originate as actual relations between human individuals.

(Vygotsky, 1978, p. 57)

Cole uses Figure 2.1 to illustrate the to-be-co-ordinated systems of mediation that exist when a novice begins to learn to read from an expert.

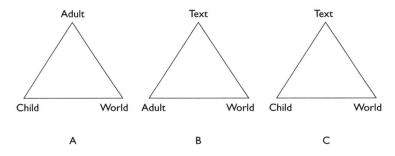

Figure 2.1 The to-be-co-ordinated systems of mediation that exist when a novice begins to learn to read from an expert.

Reprinted by permission of the publisher from *Cultural Psychology: A Once and Future Discipline*, Michael Cole, Cambridge, MA: Harvard University Press, Copyright © 1996 by the President and Fellows of Harvard College.

A and B represent resources for the instructional strategy. A represents the experience that children have of the world mediated by adults. Adults have experience of the world mediated by text B. C becomes the goal of instruction. Figure 2.2 shows how Cole argues that the given and the to-be-developed systems are juxtaposed in an approach to reading where the text based and the prior-world-knowledge based systems are co-ordinated.

The adult creates a means by which the child can participate in the activity of reading before they can actually read alone. A social activity of reading is created with the object of transferring control of the activity from the adult to

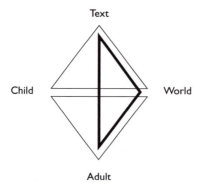

Text

Child

World

Adult

Figure 2.2 Existing and to-be-formed systems of mediation that have to be co-ordinated.

the child. This approach models the statement – 'every function in the child's cultural development appears twice: first, on the social level, and later, on the individual level'. The adult creates a social setting in which reading takes place as a collaborative act. The setting is designed to facilitate the gradual development of individual unsupported reading.

Smith (1996) and Bereiter (1997) remain sceptical about the extent to which such approaches do genuinely resolve the learning paradox. They both suggest that approaches which situate cognition do not provide an adequate account of knowledge within Popper's third world,[1] the 'world wholly created by the human intellect, that enables us, for better or worse, to escape the situational embeddedness of cognition' (Bereiter, 1997, p. 284). Smith (1996) infers 'social platonism' and Bereiter (1997) returns to education as the escape route from a radically situated account of cognition. His criticism of situated constructivist approaches is that, whilst they contribute to an understanding of the kind of knowledge that is implicit in practice by treating all knowledge as situated, it renders the world of knowledge objects invisible (Bereiter, 1997, p. 299). Bereiter argues that to overcome situatedness one has to 'create symbolic representations of situations and carry out operations on those symbols' (p. 288). This position is countered by Engeström and Cole (1997) who argue that the manipulation of symbolic representations is itself situated.

This debate raises important issues with respect to the ways in which a 'function . . . appears later, on the individual level'. That is, it questions the mechanism by which that which was social becomes individual and the extent to which that which is individual understanding can transfer from one social setting to another. This debate is ongoing. The paradox gives rise to questions about the creation of new knowledge at ontological and cultural–historical levels of analysis. It will not be resolved here. I raise it because it remains one of the central dilemmas in the development of cultural psychology, sociocultural and activity theory. Cole (1996) cites Milan Kundera's remark:

We leave childhood without knowing what youth is, we marry without knowing what it is to be married, and even when we enter old age, we don't know what it is we are heading for; the old are innocent children of their old age. In that sense, man's world is a planet of inexperience.

(Kundera, 1988, pp. 132–3)

Vygotsky makes a related point in his discussion of the processes involved in learning in the recently published edition of *Educational Psychology*:

Just as you cannot learn how to swim by standing at the seashore . . . to learn how to swim you have to, out of necessity, plunge right into the water even though you still don't know how to swim, so the only way to learn something, say, how to acquire knowledge, is by doing so, in other words, by acquiring knowledge.

(Vygotsky, 1997b, p. 324)

This reference to the extent to which we go forward through time without scripts which are sufficient for making sense of new situations and circumstances provides an appropriately grounded reminder of certain tensions within developmental theory.

I will return to this matter when I discuss the concept of 'internalisation' within Vygotsky's work. I will also discuss the details of Cole's modification of reciprocal teaching (Palinscar and Brown, 1984) in Chapter 4. The purpose of entering the discussion of the learning paradox at this point is two-fold. Firstly, it provides a way of entering the discussion of Vygotsky's work, and secondly, the learning paradox is seen as a significant challenge to many theories of learning and requires discussion even if resolution is not easily achieved (see Cox (1997) for a defence of a Vygotskian resolution of the problems of the learning paradox).

In this discussion I have introduced the general genetic law of cultural development which is defined in terms of 'social' and 'individual' and 'development'. I have also used the concept 'mediation'. I hope that, in this context, the use of these terms is relatively unproblematic. They are familiar, everyday terms. I have drawn on, what I hope is, a common cultural legacy to create a space in which an initial communication about Vygotsky's ideas can take place. What I wanted to try to do was draw on the familiar in order to enter the network of concepts. I will now move to render problematic that which we have taken as common or everyday.

Dialectical method

The general genetic law of cultural development introduces the notion of some form of relationship between something which is defined as 'social' and something which is defined as 'individual'. My use of the term 'mediation' suggests that this is not necessarily a direct relationship from the social to the individual. However, there is an important conceptual move to be made between the dualism I infer above and the dialectical relationship which Cole implies below:

> The dual process of shaping and being shaped through culture implies that humans inhabit 'intentional' (constituted) worlds within which the traditional dichotomies of subject and object, person and environment, and so on cannot be analytically separated and temporally ordered into independent and dependent variables.
>
> (Cole, 1996, p. 103)

Before embarking on my proposed discussion of Vygotsky's original contribution to our understanding of pedagogic matters I wish to make a methodological point. Having made this point I will illustrate its significance through a discussion of the Piaget–Vygotsky debate.

A dialectical world view

Sameroff (1980) provided an important contribution to the debates on psychology and systems theory with the introduction of a concept of 'dialectics' within which development was seen as driven by internal contradictions. Earlier, Riegel (1976) and Wozniak (1975) had criticised traditional psychology with its emphasis on balance and equilibrium. It was Riegel who produced a manifesto for Dialectical Psychology which emphasised contradictions and their synchronisations in short- and long-term development both in the individual and in society (Riegel, 1976, p. 689). Surprisingly this work is rarely cited in discussions of Vygotsky's work. The details of their approach differ whilst the key emphasis on dialectical processes remains very similar. As Van der Veer and Valsiner (1991) remind us, Vygotsky most definitely adopted a dialectical world view. This was the case for his theories as well as his approach to method and criticism.

> A present day psychologist is most likely to adopt a non-dialectical 'either-or' perspective when determining the 'class membership' of one or other approach in psychology. Hence the frequent non-dialectical contrasts between 'Piagetian' and 'Vygotskian' approaches, or the widespread separation of psychologists into 'social' versus 'cognitive' categories which seem to occupy our minds in their meta-psychological activities . . . in direct contrast, for Vygotsky any two opposing directions of thought serve as opposites united with one another in the continuous whole – the discourse on ideas. This discourse is expected to lead us to a more adequate understanding of the human psyche, that is, to transcend the present state of theoretical knowledge, rather than force the existing variety of ideas into a strict classification of tendencies in the socially constructed scientific discipline of psychology.
>
> (Van der Veer and Valsiner, 1991, pp. 392–3)

Piaget and Vygotsky

Discussions of the relative merits of Piaget and Vygotsky often seek refuge in dimensions of difference which are on the one hand cast in terms of causation (biological versus social) or locational/contextual (Swiss versus Russian). Bidell (1992) is one of a small group of writers who move beyond such analyses in his consideration of the issues which serve to distinguish between Piaget's stage theory and Vygotsky's socio-historical theory.

In an attempt to draw on the strengths of both writers he suggests that the differences are to be found in the extent to which the social dimension of development is refined and also how relations between the social and the personal are conceptualised. His suggestion is that much is to be gained by making an initial distinction between Piaget's stage theory of development and Piaget's constructivist theory of knowledge:

> Piaget's stage theory of development tacitly reflects the ideology of individualism. The stage theory is based on an interactionist metaphor in which the relation between the person and the social world is conceived as an individual standing apart from and interacting with a social environment. Piaget's constructivist theory of knowledge in contrast, rejects the Cartesian tradition of reductionism (in both nativist and empiricist versions), affirming a relational and even dialectical view of development.
>
> (Bidell, 1992, p. 307)

Bidell's is an important contribution in that it moves the Vygotsky versus Piaget debate beyond the somewhat sterile opposition that has been re-iterated many times over the last fifteen years. Bidell argues that the internal inconsistency within the Piagetian thesis opens the door on powerful theoretical developments. These developments would allow for the practical integration of Piaget's constructivism and Vygotsky's dialectical method. He suggests that:

> Piaget's constructivism implicitly supports a contextualist approach to knowledge development and stands in contradiction to the individualism and interactionism of his stage theory . . . Vygotsky presents a dialectical conception of the relations between personal and social that differs diametrically from reductionist views . . . dimensions of reality such as the social and the personal are not separate and self-contained but have a shared existence as differing tendencies united within real developing systems . . . replaces the reductionist metaphor of separation and interaction with the dialectical metaphor of participation.
>
> (Bidell, 1992, p. 307)

Smith's (1996) positioning of Vygotsky within the possibilities afforded by the various strains of constructivism contrasts with Bidell's and yet both remind us that the labelling of Piaget as a writer who posits asocial individual development is incorrect. Recourse to the recently translated *Sociological Studies* serves to reinforce this contention.

> Human knowledge is essentially collective and social life constitutes an essential factor in the creation and growth of knowledge, both prescientific and scientific.
>
> (Piaget, 1995, p. 30)

> The isolated individual would never be capable of complete conservation or reversibility, and it is the exigencies of reciprocity which allow this double conquest, through the intermediary of a common language and a common scale of definitions. But at the same time, reciprocity is only possible between subjects capable of equilibrated thought, i.e. of the conservation and reversibility imposed by exchange. In short, however the question is approached, individual functions and collective functions require each other in the explanation of the conditions necessary for logical equilibrium.
>
> (Piaget, 1995, p. 94)

> In conclusion, we believe that social life is a necessary condition for the development of logic. Thus, we believe that social life transforms the very nature of the individual, making him pass from an autistic state to one involving personality. In speaking of co-operation, therefore, we understand a process that creates new realities and not a mere exchange between fully developed individuals.
>
> (Piaget, 1995, p. 210)

These statements drawn from Piaget's writing affirm the poverty of an analysis which asserts the need for an 'either-or' position on the Piaget–Vygotsky debate. Moscovici (1996) goes as far as to question which of the two writers was most influenced by Marx. He dismisses superficial analysis which posits each writer within a particular ideological camp and suggests that it is the interplay between their respective personal intellectual developments which is instructive. The tensions between their respective positions should be taken as productive start points for development of new ideas. Whatever Vygotsky's politics were it is clear that he would have suffered under Stalinism. His affiliation to aspects of Marx's writing was within a framework that would not have found favour within the determining philosophy and practice of a command control state. Moscow in the 1920s was a place where political ideas did not conform to the stereotype that subsequent periods have bequeathed us. 'I cannot stress enough the liberationist quality of Vygotsky's Marxism. But it was not that unusual in his day' (Bruner, 1997, p. 70).

Bruner (1997) in his address to the 1996 joint meeting of the 'Growing Mind Conference' in honour of Jean Piaget's birth, and the 'Vygotsky–Piaget Conference' of the 2nd Congress of Socio-Cultural Research, honouring both

Lev Vygotsky's and Piaget's centennial, suggests that there may be a case for regarding the contradictions between them as having reached a stage of incommensurability by the end of their respective careers. Drawing on an analogy from Psychology itself – that depth perception requires disparity – he welcomes the difference as a source of development for the field. If this is a reasonable depiction of the way in which forms of understanding may interact then how can we think about the process at the level of ontology? In the next section of this chapter I will introduce the debates that are taking place concerning the process by which the 'interpersonal becomes the intrapersonal'.

Cultural development: the tension between internalisation and participation

Within the swathe of approaches that claim a Vygotskian root the term 'individual development' raises a number of questions. Vygotsky spoke of social, cultural and historical influences on individual development. One possible extension of this starting point is to suggest that all thinking is inextricably bound up with context and that to speak of the individual development is inappropriate. The argument becomes one which insists that all that we think of as cognition is situated in specific social, cultural and historical circumstances. Such speculations on the nature of cognition must try to provide and account for sources of continuity in everyday life. Matusov (1998) defines two possibilities for models, both of which lay emphasis on the sociocultural nature of human activity and development. He terms these possibilities the internalisation model and the participation model.

> The internalization model of cultural development, emphasizing transformation of social functions into individual skills, leads to a chain of mutually related dualisms between oppositional abstractions such as the social and the individual, the external and the internal, and the environment and the organism. Attempts to bridge these dualistic gaps seem problematic because these dual abstractions mutually constitute each other and are, thus, inseparable from the beginning. . . . The participation model considers individual cultural development as a validated process of transformation of individual participation in sociocultural activity. Transformation of participation involves assuming changed responsibility for the activity, redefining membership in a community of practice, and changing the sociocultural practice itself.
>
> (Matusov, 1998, p. 326)

Matusov argues that participation and internalisation models of development are not just two slightly different points in a general argument but two different world views. In an important paper he adheres to the dialogic conception of method which is close to that which Vygotsky himself adopted.

> I appreciate the internalisation world view as a dialogic partner that stimulates and even shapes the development of the participation model.
>
> (Matusov, 1998, p. 327)

He employs the device of discussing the two models as thesis and antithesis in accordance with his avowed commitment to a dialectical method. Table 2.1 attempts to capture the essence of the dualities and tensions he is seeking to construct in his analysis.

Table 2.1 Internalisation and participation models

	Internalisation thesis	*Participation antithesis*
Social and psychological planes	• Separate • The social precedes the psychological in ontogenesis	• Mutually constitutive and inseparable • Transformation of participation
Joint and solo activities	• Separate • Solo being psychologically and developmentally more advanced	• Mutually constitute each other • Solo activities occur in the context of sociocultural activity rather as context free mental functions
Transfer and continuity	• Transfer of skills and functions from one activity to another • Skills and functions exist outside activities	• Skills and functions embedded in activities • Meaning is distributed across time, space and participants – it is interpreted and re-negotiated
Course of development	• Objectively defined by human sociocultural nature • Original thesis (Vygotsky) suggested universal teleology Current interpretations more relativistic with immediate societal influence	• Child creatively shapes process of development and contributes to defining direction • Community activity level of definition
Study of development	• Comparison of skills and functions before, after and during intervention (e.g. teaching)	• Study of processes of change of and in participation • Individual test construed as joint activity with tester in test activity context

Developed from Matusov (1998, pp. 229–30).

Matusov clearly positions himself within the frame of the participation model. Along with Rogoff (1990, 1992, 1994), Lave (1988, 1993) and Lave with Wenger (1991) he announces a radical alternative to a version of the internalisation model. My purpose here is not so much to 'decide' which of these positions is 'correct'; rather I am concerned to identify the possible theoretical positions that may come to influence pedagogic practice. These theoretical debates may be seen as sites for the generation of tools which may inform pedagogic innovation.

There are of course many 'dialects' of the internalisation model. Lawrence and Valsiner (1993) argue that the conceptual roots of internalisation need to be clarified. They suggest that the analysis of internalisation as constructive transformation makes it possible to understand the uniqueness of personal subjective worlds and their social (intersubjective) developmental roots. Matusov (1998) has a somewhat different perspective on the conceptual roots of internalisation and participation models. Whilst Lawrence and Valsiner (1993) discuss the origins of the models in terms of specific psychological theories, Matusov (1998) invokes a more avowedly sociocultural analysis.

> Vygotsky shaped and gave the major impetus for the internalization model of development. He ethnocentrically considered Western societies as the historically most progressive and advanced (Rogoff, 1990; Wertsch, 1985). His life project [using Sartre's term] seemed to be how to facilitate people's connection with the network of Western sociocultural practices of mass production, formal schooling, vast institutional bureaucracy, and alienated labor. That is why, in my view, Vygotsky mainly focused on studying children, people with disabilities, and people from 'primitive' cultures. In contrast, his contemporary Russian theoretician Bakhtin, whose scholarship was deeply literary, had a very different life project. Bakhtin seemed to be concerned with how people constitute each other in their diversity, agency, and dialogue. According to Bakhtin, people need each other not so much to successfully accomplish some goal in their cooperative efforts but because of their 'transgradience' (it literally means 'the outsideness'), which allows them to be participants of never-ending dialogue. Bakhtin's project was much closer to the participation worldview than Vygotsky's.
>
> (Matusov, 1998, pp. 237–8)

More recently Valsiner (1997) has argued that much of the theoretical debate about internalisation and appropriation has been 'lost in the middle of unclarified general assumptions'. He attempts to bring some clarity to the debate through his identification of two core oppositions that he identifies in the field. Firstly he suggests that there is an opposition between internalisation models which posit a separation between the inner and outer personal worlds and appropriation models which posit no boundary or separation. He distinguishes dualisms from dualities, arguing that the denial of dualism (inner, outer) in appropriation models leads to a denial of the dualities which are the constituent elements in dialectical or dialogical theory. Secondly, Valsiner suggests that the opposition of active versus passive role is central to the debate. He argues that both internalisation and appropriation models can be viewed in terms of active or passive roles for the individual. The question of individual agency is therefore a crucial distinguishing feature in the discussion of models of cultural development. This debate is played out in pedagogic theory in terms of an acquisition-transmission dimension. Transmission based pedagogies assume passivity where acquisition based pedagogies assume activity on the part of the learner.

Winegar (1997) discusses internalisation as person–environment negotiation. He focuses on the key issue of continuity. If a radical appropriation model is pursued how is continuity of self across time and space to be discussed? Winegar seeks to distinguish between models of internalisation which provide a within person account and those which discuss a process which takes place within the person–environment relationship. Ratner (1999) also takes issue with the within person version:

> Divorcing personal interactions from social activities and conditions, the individualistic approach to cultural psychology acts as a deculturizing agent just as psychoanalysis, behaviourism, phenomenology, and other traditional psychological approaches do. The individualistic approach to cultural psychology not only undermines a cultural analysis of psychological phenomena. Exaggerating individual agency, autonomy, and diversity also denigrates the reality of culture altogether. Shared, organized culture becomes devalued.
>
> (Ratner, 1999, p. 19)

Ratner suggests that Valsiner (Lightfoot and Valsiner, 1992) represents the individualistic approach. My own reading of this work is that it could conform to Winegar's (1997) description of person–environment negotiation:

> Belief systems that exist within a collective culture do not have an effect in the sense of being copied directly (or appropriated) by individuals. Instead, they constitute resources from which active persons construct their own (personal) belief structures.
>
> (Lightfoot and Valsiner, 1992, p. 395)

The critical issue is with respect to whether the resources that a collective culture embodies are regarded as fixed offerings from which the individual selects or they constitute the starting points for negotiation.

Clearly there are many positions that have developed within the internalisation-participation debate. One obvious question for the pedagogue is whether all these positions are supposed to apply to all aspects of knowledge/skill/functioning or do some apply more to one than another? These theories clearly hold very different implications for pedagogy in the widest sense (school organisation, division of labour, rule structures, etc.) as well as the narrow sense (curriculum structure, face-to-face interactional practices, control over sequence and pace, etc.). They may also apply differentially across the knowledge domains of schooling.

Wells (1999) provides a good example of participation model in action:

> Dancing is a cultural activity that is far older than any individual participant and, although new forms emerge and are, in turn, replaced by still newer, the basic patterns tend to persist from one generation to the next. In learning to dance, therefore, the newcomer is joining an ongoing community of practice. To begin with, as the novice takes the first faltering steps, he or she is carried along by the rhythm of the music and guided by the movements of the other dancers (and even in some, characteristically Western, genres, quite forcibly 'led' by his or her partner). Before long, however, the novice begins to get a feel for the dance and is soon able to participate on equal terms, both creating new variations that are taken up by others and adapting easily to those that they introduce. In explaining this learning process, talk of internalisation seems unnecessary; no knowledge passes to the novice from the more expert participants, as they move together with increasing synchrony. Rather, within the framework provided by the structure of the activity as a whole, of which the entraining movements of the other participants are just one part, the novice gradually constructs the organising cognitive structures for him or herself and brings his or her actions into conformity with the culture-given pattern. In the words with which W.B. Yeats concludes his poem, Among School Children: 'How can we know the dancer from the dance?'
>
> (Wells, 1999, pp. 322–3)

As someone who has been a singular failure at learning to dance (or ski for that matter) through participation I wonder whether the recourse to global application of particular theories is appropriate. In a discussion of a range of definitions of internalisation that had been announced in a collection of chapters, Tudge (1997) provides a clear reminder of the multilevel analysis which is embedded in Vygotsky's work:

> Development is a function of factors that relate to the immediate activity in which one or more people are involved (the microgenetic level of analysis), age and developmental characteristics of the studied person or people as they are developing over the life span (the ontogenetic level), the culturewide symbols, values and beliefs, technologies, and institutions (factors relating to the cultural-historical level of analysis), as well as the development of the species (the phylogenetic level). There is hierarchial organization, but also interconnections at each and every level. Because of

the interconnections, understanding development requires analysis that captures all levels, although the phylogenetic level, being virtually unchanging for all except those studying development over archaeological time, is rarely considered. This means, in effect, studying aspects of developing individuals, relations between those individuals and their immediately surrounding world (both people and objectives), and the broader cultural-historical context. Analysis at only one level is insufficient to make sense of development.

(Tudge, 1997, pp. 120–1)

Externalisation

It is of interest that so much effort has been expended attempting to clarify the movement from the social to the individual and yet relatively little attention has been paid to the reverse direction. Bruner's (1997) reminder about Vygotsky's liberationist version of Marxism serves to reinforce the view that his was a psychology which posited the active role of the person in their own cognitive and emotional creation. Whether the emphasis was directly on creativity itself or through the use of expressions such as 'mastering themselves from the outside' in his early work Vygotsky discussed externalisation at some length. Engeström (1999) reports that there has been a reawakening of interest in the topic in Russia. He links this development to political shifts that have taken place:

> In a Russian collection on the concept of activity edited by Lektorsky this emphasis was suddenly almost turned around. Nearly all authors emphasised that the most important aspect of human activity is its creativity and its ability to exceed or transcend given constraints and instructions. Perhaps this conclusion reflected the impact of perestroika in philosophy and psychology.
>
> (Engeström, 1999, p. 231)

Engeström has developed a model of transformation which he calls the expansive cycle in which internalisation and externalisation develop complementary roles. Engeström and Miettinen (1999) provide a discussion of the internalisation-externalisation process at every level of activity. They relate internalisation to the reproduction of culture and externalisation to the creation of artefacts that may be used to transform culture. These processes will be discussed in Chapter 3. The rediscovered emphasis on externalisation is important because it brings a perspective to concept formation which affirms the notion of active agency in learning and development.

> Like Ilyenkov after him, Vygotsky recognises that as much as culture creates individuals, culture itself remains a human creation.
>
> (Bakhurst and Sypnowich, 1995, p. 11)

Leontiev's work on internalisation and externalisation also revealed that the internal and the external were not identical. He saw externalisation as the process that 'produces artefacts . . . that enter into and channel subsequent streams of activity' (Prior, 1997, p. 278). Ways of thinking and feeling may be influenced and shaped by the availability of cultural artefacts which may themselves be the products of mediated activity. In his discussion of Leontiev's work Glassman (1996) characterised this process as 'expansion' originating in the 'development of symbols in a joint community'. Leontiev also argues that there are two layers of thinking and consciousness, one of which is 'objective reality in consciousness' and the second being 'consciousness of consciousness', or reflection (Zinchenko, 1985, p. 114). This points to the need to develop pedagogies which are informed by, what may be crudely termed, some form of metacognitive perspective. Leontiev was thus directing attention to the production of cultural artefacts some of which may act to inform self-reflection. The statement concerning the 'development of symbols in a joint community' suggests that collaborative activity assumes a particular pedagogic significance. The production of cultural artefacts through collaborative activity may lead to enhanced self-reflection and metacognitive development. This theoretical position extends the argument of the 'general genetic law of cultural development'. The latter argues the case for the primacy of interpersonal exchange in development. The former takes this idea somewhat further by suggesting that specific forms of activity lead to the production of artefacts which may subsequently promote specific forms of intrapersonal development. Collaborative activity is seen as the site of production of tools for promoting reflection as well as other forms of development. In Chapter 4 I will discuss some of the research which has sought to identify those forms of collaborative activity which do function in this way.

Functions and concepts

In this section I will engage with some of the debates concerning the ways in which functions and concepts develop. Vygotsky (1997a) discussed the development of higher mental functions, which he contrasted with elementary mental functions. He also discussed the relationship between spontaneous or everyday concepts and scientific concepts. In her discussion of this aspect of his work, Nelson (1995) stressed that there were two moves: from the natural to the socio-historical; and from spontaneous to scientific. However, both the spontaneous and the scientific are located in the socio-historical. In that Vygotsky provides an account within which so much emphasis is placed on social, cultural and historical forces it would be easy to ignore biology in an overview of his work. This would be a grave error.

Biology in development

Moll, I. (1994) argues that an adequate account of Vygotsky's theory must ground the social construction of cognition in a fundamental recognition of natural and biological possibility. He argues that natural constraints in cognitive development are not given enough attention in contemporary discussions of his work. Tudge and Winterhoff (1993) also explore this theme in the context of a critical review of Vygotsky's views on biological influences.

> The child's system of activity is determined at each specific stage both by the child's degree of organic development and by his or her degree of organic development and by his or her degree of mastery in the use of tools.
>
> (Vygotsky, 1997b, p. 21)

It is inescapable that Vygotsky did account for biological factors and individual differences. In his work on 'defectology' he insists that individual differences in patterns of communication give rise to differences in patterns of social mediation and hence development.

> A bodily defect is, first of all, a social and not an organic abnormality of behaviour. A bodily defect in a person causes a certain attitude towards that person among the people around him. It is this attitude, and not the defect in itself, that affects the character of psychological relations to a child with impaired sense organs.
>
> (Yaroshevsky, 1989, p. 107)

However, it is in the manner of social engagement that differences may arise and form their own dynamic.

> Whatever the anticipated outcome, always and in all circumstances, development, complicated by a defect, represents a creative (physical and psychological) process: the creation and re-creation of a child's personality based upon the restructuring of all the adaptive functions and upon the formation of new processes – overarching, substituting, equalising – generated by the handicap, and creating new, roundabout paths for development.
>
> (Knox and Stevens, 1993, p. 17)

Similarly, Vygotsky was concerned that social responses to people with disabilities should not create problems of their own. Given that he argues that cultural tools and practices have a formative effect on development, then barriers to participation are a cause for concern. Barriers may be both social and biological. Specific forms of impairment may give rise to difficulty in participation in a society where most participants do not experience similar difficulties. The solution could be to seek alternative forms of participation either through transforming social practices in such a way as not to marginalise those with the impairment, or through specific interventions such as supplementary forms of communication such as braille. In the past, and to a slightly lesser extent now, many people with disabilities remove themselves or are removed from certain aspects of society. Gallaudet University is an example of a setting where deaf people are educated with other deaf people. This setting is usually regarded as positive. There are many examples of social responses to people with disabilities where satisfactory communities are not the outcome. Vygotsky's suggestion is that transformations in patterns of participation carry with them implications for cognitive development. Exclusion carries cognitive consequences.

Ratner (1998) argues that higher psychological functions actually stimulate neuronal growth in particular directions and that they create their own biological mediations. He draws on Donald (1991) in his assertion that they do not depend upon specialised biological mechanisms which pre-determine them. This accords with Vygotsky's position that:

> There is every reason to assume that the historical development of behaviour from primitive forms to the most complex and highest did not occur as a result of the appearance of new parts of the brain or the growth of parts already existing.
>
> (Vygotsky, 1998, p. 35)

Recent advances in neuroscience (Damasio, 1999) and cognitive psychology (Clark, 1996, 1998) open the way for rethinking mind/biology/social setting transactions. Damasio is concerned with the role of feelings in the ways that humans make sense of the information that the social world provides to the sense organs. He presents a dynamic view of the construction of the 'auto-biographical self' which is the product of continual revision and change. Clark reconsiders the role of language as a tool which he argues acts as an adjunct of the brain in problem solving – 'a tool that alters the nature of the computational tasks involved in various kinds of problem solving' (Clark, 1996, p. 193).

Similarly, Dennett (1991) argues that advanced cognitive skills should be viewed as not so much the manifestation of the innate hardware of the brain but more as the ways in which the biological material is programmed and reprogrammed through the input that arises from specific cultures and use of language. He discusses the 'myriad microsettings in the plasticity of the brain' (Dennett, 1991, p. 219).

Moves to develop a dynamic account of plasticity at the level of neurological function echo the assertion that Tomasello (1999) makes with respect to the role of genetic material in human cognitive evolution. His argument is that the dichotomies, such as 'nature–nurture', which have linguistically structured so much of the debate are outmoded. They are not sufficiently powerful tools for the consideration of the issues. Tomasello, Dennett, Clark and Damasio in their differing ways suggest a forthcoming development within which are new conceptions of the place of biology in the development of thinking. The early stages of this development suggest a high degree of compatibility with a sociogenetic account of development.

Elementary and higher functions

Ratner (1998) argued that a central principle within the framework of Vygotsky's developmental psychology is the transition from 'lower' processes to 'higher' functions. The 'lower' psychobiological processes include reflexes, and spontaneous, rudimentary conscious processes. The 'higher' conscious psychological functions include developed, voluntary, mental functions, categorical perception, voluntary attention, and voluntary movements. He understood the development of higher functions in terms of mediated social, collaborative activity. Language is the most crucial of these 'mediational means'. He argued that with its onset in childhood, thought becomes linguistic and speech rational. During the second phase of his writing he argued that speech acts to develop the interrelation of all the higher mental functions (Minick, 1985). He maintained a dialectical concept of the relation between speech and thinking which incorporated biological and cultural influences.

> All higher mental functions are mediated processes. A central and basic aspect of their structure is the use of the sign as a means of directing and mastering mental processes . . . [higher mental functions] are an aspect of the child's cultural development and have their source in collaboration and instruction . . . initially these [higher mental] functions arise as forms of co-operative activity. Only later are they transformed by the child into the sphere of his own mental activity.
>
> (Vygotsky, 1987, pp. 126, 213, 259)

> Considering the history of the development of higher mental functions that comprise the basic nucleus in the structure of personality, we find that the relation between higher mental functions was at one time a concrete relation between people; collective social forms of behaviour in the process of development become a method of individual adaptations and forms of behaviour and thinking of the personality . . . Put more simply, higher mental functions arise from collective forms of behaviour.
>
> (Vygotsky, 1998, p. 168)

Vygotsky's (1981) suggestion is that mastery of a psychological tool and, through it, mastery of a natural mental function, is involved in the development of a lower function to a higher stage. In its higher form it is restructured and its field of application widened. Davydov (1988) disagreed with Vygotsky's division of functions into higher and lower or elementary forms. He argued that all mental processes arise and are maintained through complex mediational processes albeit that the onset of speech marks a particularly important phase. Van der Veer and Van Ijzendoorn (1985) also argued that what is often considered to be the problem of the sharp distinction drawn by Vygotsky between higher and lower psychological processes may be resolved through recent studies in activity theory which consider the possibility of demonstrating that 'natural' processes may be influenced by direction and instruction/training.

Bower (1974), Gibson and Walker (1984) and Baillargeon (1987) amongst many others, have conducted detailed empirical studies which suggest that very young children function in such a way that suggests a high level of cognitive sophistication. Subbotsky (1996) argued that these data do not necessarily cast doubt on the existence of qualitative differences between lower and higher mental functions. However complex they appear, the neonate functions are, according to Subbotsky, still exhibiting lower mental functions and have to go through the route of development.

Veresov's (1999) detailed analysis of Vygotsky's work makes claims for transitions in the way in which the notions of higher and lower are handled: from the writing in which higher functions were presented as inhibited reflexes to 1925 when he defined 'higher psychical functions' and 'higher forms of behaviour' as synonyms. This was the phase in which Minick (1985) notes Vygotsky was concerned with interfunctional relationships. By 1927 (approximately) Veresov argues that Vygotsky began to represent higher functions as higher psychical processes which gradually replace the natural (not elementary) processes in the development of consciousness. Whether one agrees with the details of Veresov's assertions is, perhaps, not as important as the recognition that Vygotsky's ideas were changing rapidly.

One of the great dangers with the early interpretations of this work was the suggestion that children whose elementary functions were damaged or deficient were beyond the reach of education. Children would be assessed to see if they could benefit from education. This assessment would consist of a means of scrutinising those functions deemed elementary. Those who 'failed' the assessment were removed from the educational community. The work of early years developmentalists and Russians such as Davydov gives ground for rejecting the sharp delineation between functions deemed higher and lower and the practices that were associated with the demarcation. The development of Vygotsky's own thinking on this matter was incomplete. He certainly changed his views on several occasions. He was also working at a time when the cultural artefacts of the late twentieth century were not even imagined. He had no access to tape recorders, freeze frame video recorders, etc. and was not in a position to 'see' the data on development that those who followed him have examined. A modern position such as that of Nelson (1995), mentioned above, seems more appropriate. Her depiction is of three levels of conceptual development yields: the first is constructed by individuals on the basis of direct experience with the world without the mediational effects of language; the second level of knowledge is a product of the 'language using community'; and the third level is that of a formally organised cultural system − theoretical knowledge. Thus, she proposes transitions from the natural to the socio-historical; and from spontaneous to scientific. As noted above, both the spontaneous and the scientific are located in the socio-historical.

Scientific and everyday concepts

As the, now accepted, correct translation of Vygotsky's work *Thinking and Speech* implies, he was concerned to show how the social activity of speaking was connected with the active processes of thinking. For him thinking was a culturally mediated social process of communication. Cole (1994, p. 78) uses the same quote from O.E. Mandelstam's poem 'The Swallow' as did Vygotsky at the start of chapter seven of *Thinking and Speech* to open up a discussion of the relationship.

> I forgot the word I wanted to say,
> And thought, unembodied,
> Returns to the hall of shadows.

In his discussion of concept development, Vygotsky argued that specific ways of using words was a necessary part of the process – 'the concept is not possible without the word. Thinking in concepts is not possible in the absence of verbal thinking' (Vygotsky, 1987, p. 131). Such theories about the relationships between thought processes, conceptual development and social communication, including instruction, are clearly central to any pedagogic project.

The period 1927–1934 was when Vygotsky was particularly interested in concept formation. For Vygotsky scientific concepts are characterised by a high degree of generality and their relationship to objects as mediated through other concepts. By the use of 'scientific concept' Vygotsky referred to concepts introduced by a teacher in school, and spontaneous concepts were those that were acquired by the child outside contexts in which explicit instruction was in place. Scientific concepts were described as those which form a coherent, logical hierarchical system. According to Vygotsky (1987) children can make deliberate use of scientific concepts, they are consciously aware of them and can reflect upon them.

Lave and Wenger's (1991) representation is of the scientific as 'understood' or 'cultural' and the everyday as 'active' and 'individual'; the 'mature' concept being achieved when they have merged. The complexity of mastering scientific concepts is brought home by the distinction between the 'sense' (*smyl*) and the 'meaning' (*znachenie*) of a word.

> A word's sense is the aggregate of all the psychological facts that arise in our consciousness as a result of the word. Sense is a dynamic fluid, and complex formation which has several zones that vary in their stability. Meaning is only one of these zones of sense that the word acquires in the context of speech. It is the most stable, unified and precise of these zones. In different contexts, a word's sense changes. In contrast, meaning is a comparatively fixed and stable point, one that remains constant with all the changes of the word's sense that are associated with its use in various contexts.
>
> (Vygotsky, 1987, pp. 275–6)

In chapter seven of *Thinking and Speech* Vygotsky discusses the complexities of the relationships between sense and meaning on the one hand and oral and inner speech on the other. In this rather beautiful and poetic chapter, Vygotsky provided what could be taken as the background for the preceding chapters on concept development. The ongoing dynamic between the use of social speech and relatively stable social meanings in the creation of particular forms and patterns of personal sense is construed as the motor of development. The notion of the scientific concept can be seen as a particular historical cultural form of relatively stable meaning which is brought into productive interchange with the sense of the world that is acquired in specific everyday circumstances.

The editors of the most recent translation of *Thinking and Speech* argue that when Vygotsky (1987) uses the terms 'spontaneous thinking' or 'spontaneous concepts' he is referring to the context of formation which is that of immediate, social, practical activity as against a context of instruction in a formal system of knowledge. Scientific concepts are through their very systematic nature open to the voluntary control of the child.

> The dependence of scientific concepts on spontaneous concepts and their influence on them stems from the unique relationship that exists between the scientific concept and its object . . . this relationship is characterised by the fact that it is mediated through other concepts. Consequently, in its relationship to the object, the scientific concept includes a relationship to another concept, that is it includes the most basic element of a concept system.
>
> (Vygotsky, 1987, p. 192)

Vygotsky argued that it was in communication that social understanding was made available for individual understanding. Within schooling word meanings themselves form the object of study. As Minick (1987) has argued, the difference between communication *with* words and communication *about* words marks the significant difference between communication within schooling and communication in everyday life. This difference is what Kozulin (1998) refers to as repositioning. Communication about words within schooling leads to the development of scientific concepts by the individual. In this way communication performs a mediational function between the society of schooling and the individual. The need for instruction remains paramount within the original thesis. This is associated with the institution of the school and the teacher.

> The fundamental difference between the problem which involves everyday concepts and that which involves scientific concepts is that the child solves the latter with the teacher's help . . . in a problem involving everyday concepts he must do with volition something that he does with ease spontaneously.
>
> (Vygotsky, 1987, p. 216)

Van der Veer (1998) has questioned the extent to which scientific knowledge can be articulated and through reference to Polanyi suggests that much scientific knowledge may remain tacit and only partially open to conscious manipulation. The modernist project of early twentieth-century Russia had no doubts about such vagary. I believe that it is important to understand Vygotsky's writing about 'schooled' or 'scientific' concepts as historically located. The modernisation of Russia required clear formulations of 'the good life' and agencies which would ensure that the conceptual equipment for this new world was at hand. The school was to be the state's agency for ensuring the development of advanced conceptual tools. The recognition that scientific concepts may develop outside the formal institutions of schooling would not necessarily have been considered at the time. Lima (1998) draws on ethnographic studies in which she suggests that European American traditions of schooling still represent a specific case of the separation of scientific and everyday learning experiences.

The distinction has recently been refined. In his last journal article Bernstein (1999b) distinguishes between vertical and horizontal discourse. Horizontal discourse arising out of everyday activity is usually oral, local, context dependent and specific, tacit, multilayered and contradictory across but not within contexts. Its structure reflects the way a particular culture is segmented and its activities are specialised. Horizontal discourse is thus segmentally organised. In contrast, vertical discourse has a coherent, explicit and systematically principled structure which is hierarchically organised or takes the form of a series of specialised languages with specialised criteria for the production and circulation of texts (Bernstein, 1999b, p. 159). Bernstein suggests that Bourdieu's notion of discursive forms which give rise to symbolic and practical mastery respectively and Habermas's reference to the discursive construction of life worlds of individuals and instrumental rationality both refer to parts of a complex field of parameters which in turn refer to both individual and social experience and relate to the model of horizontal and vertical discourse which he seeks to develop. He offers an initial set of contrasts and indicates that many more exist. His lament is for the lack of a language of description of these forms which can serve to generate and relate the possibilities for difference.

Table 2.2 Horizontal and vertical discourse

	Horizontal discourse	*Vertical discourse*
Evaluative	Spontaneous	Contrived
Epistemological	Subjective	Objective
Cognitive	Operations	Principles
Social	Intimacy	Distance
Contextual	Inside	Outside
Voice	Dominated	Dominant
Mode	Linear	Non-linear
Institutional	Gemeinschaft	Gessellschaft

After Bernstein (1999b, p. 158)

This paper serves as an important reminder that the theoretical derivation of 'scientific and everyday' in the original writing was somewhat provisional. For example, the association of the scientific with the school does not help to distinguish those aspects of schooling that merely act to add to everyday understanding without fostering the development of scientific concepts. The association also suggests that the development of scientific concepts must take place in the school and not outside it. Bernstein's analysis is suggestive of a more powerful means of conceptualising the forms which Vygotsky announced.

It may be as a consequence of the dualist perspective, which remains so powerful, that the emphasis on the interdependence between the development of scientific and everyday concepts is also not always appreciated. Vygotsky argued that the systematic, organised and hierarchical thinking that he associated with scientific concepts becomes gradually embedded in everyday referents and thus achieves a general sense in the contextual richness of everyday thought. Vygotsky thus presented an interconnected model of the relationship between scientific and everyday or spontaneous concepts. Similarly he argued that everyday thought is given structure and order in the context of systematic scientific thought. Vygotsky was keen to point out the relative strengths of both as they both contributed to each other.

> The formation of concepts develops simultaneously from two directions: from the direction of the general and the particular . . . the development of a scientific concept begins with the verbal definition. As part of an organised system, this verbal definition descends to concrete; it descends to phenomena which the concept represents. In contrast, the everyday concept tends to develop outside any definite system; it tends to move upwards toward abstraction and generalisation . . . the weakness of the everyday concept lies in its incapacity for abstraction, in the child's incapacity to operate on it in a voluntary manner . . . the weakness of the scientific concept lies in its verbalism, in its insufficient saturation with the concrete.
>
> (Vygotsky, 1987, pp. 163, 168, 169)

One way of understanding part of the teaching process is in terms of helping children to makes links between their everyday understanding and, what Lemke (1990) refers to as, that form of schooled knowledge which is expressed in the synoptic mode of written language. The movement between teacher and taught and between written text and talk is part of the process by which progressively more powerful conceptual tools are developed. In this way scientific concepts are developed through different levels of dialogue: in the social space between teacher and taught; and in the conceptual space between the everyday and scientific. The result is the production of webs or patterns of conceptual connection.

> The concept of 'flower' is not actually more general than the concept of 'rose'. When the child has mastered only a single concept, its relationship

to the object is different than it is after he masters a second. However, after he masters a second concept, there is a long period during which the concept of 'flower' continues to stand alongside, rather than above, the concept of 'rose'. The former does not include the latter. The narrower concept is not subordinated. Rather, the broader concept acts as a substitute for the narrower one. It stands alongside it in a single series. When the concept 'flower' is generalized, the relationship between it and the concept of 'rose' changes as well. Indeed, there is a change in its relationship with all subordinate concepts. This marks the emergence of a concept system.

(Vygotsky, 1987, p. 193)

As the previous quote makes clear, Vygotsky argued that scientific concepts are not assimilated in ready-made or pre-packaged form. He insisted that the two forms of concept are brought into forms of relationship within which they both develop. An important corollary of this model of conceptual development is the denial of the possibility of direct pedagogic transmission of concepts.

Pedagogical experience demonstrates that direct instruction in concepts is impossible. It is pedagogically fruitless. The teacher who attempts to use this approach achieves nothing but a mindless learning of words, an empty verbalism that stimulates or imitates the presence of concepts in the child. Under these conditions, the child learns not the concept but the word, and this word is taken over by the child through memory rather than thought. Such knowledge turns out to be inadequate in any meaningful application. This mode of instruction is the basic defect of the purely scholastic verbal modes of teaching which have been universally condemned. It substitutes the learning of dead and empty verbal schemes for the mastery of living knowledge.

(Vygotsky, 1987, p. 170)

If it is to be effective in the formation of scientific concepts instruction must, according to Davydov (1988), be designed to foster conscious awareness of conceptual form and structure and thereby allow for individual access and control over acquired scientific concepts. It must also foster the interaction and development of everyday concepts with scientific concepts.

Learning a foreign language raises the level of development of the child's native speech. His conscious awareness of linguistic forms, and the level of his abstraction of linguistic phenomena, increases. He develops a more conscious, voluntary capacity to use words as tools of thought and as a means of expressing ideas . . . by learning algebra, the child comes to understand arithmetic operations as particular instantiations of algebraic operations. This gives the child a freer, more abstract and generalised view of his operations with concrete quantities. Just as algebra frees the child's thought from the grasp of concrete numerical relations and raises it to the level of more abstract thought, learning a foreign language frees the child's verbal thought from the grasp of concrete linguistic forms of phenomena.

(Vygotsky, 1987, p. 180)

Van der Veer (1994) argues that conceptual thinking positively influences not only the cognitive domain but also aesthetic reactions and emotions. He argues that Vygotsky's view of conceptual development is overly rationalistic and that the notion of scientific concepts seems to imply a somewhat static view of science. Bozhovich (1977), who was one of Vygotsky's co-workers, also suggests that the cognitive skew in Vygotsky's project needs to be redressed. Wardekker (1998) adds to the suggestion that concept development should not be seen solely as a cognitive endeavour. For him the development of scientific concepts also includes a moral dimension. He argues that 'scientific (or 'scholarly') concepts as the products of reflection in a practice that includes choices about the future development of that praxis are, in that sense, of a moral nature' (Wardekker, 1998, p. 143). In Chapter 5 I will discuss some of the effects of social and moral aspects of pedagogic practice.

In this chapter I have outlined some aspects of concept development from a Vygotskian perspective. I have stressed the complex nature of the relationship between the everyday and the scientific and discussed the importance given to the pedagogue and the institutional setting. In the sections that follow I will discuss the context in which instruction takes place.

Instruction was the driving force of development for Vygotsky. I will close this section with a quotation which underlines Vygotsky's insistence on collaborative instructional practice. Co-operation and collaboration are seen as crucial within effective teaching. In Chapters 4 and 5 I will discuss ways in which this principle has been applied.

> The development of the scientific . . . concept, a phenomenon that occurs as part of the educational process, constitutes a unique form of systematic co-operation between the teacher and the child. The maturation of the child's higher mental functions occurs in this co-operative process, that is, it occurs through the adult's assistance and participation. In the domain of interest to us, this is expressed in the growth of the relativeness of causal thinking and in the development of a certain degree of voluntary control in scientific thinking. This element of voluntary control is a product of the instructional process itself. . . . In a problem involving scientific concepts, he must be able to do in collaboration with the teacher something that he has never done spontaneously . . . we know that the child can do more in collaboration that he can independently.
>
> (Vygotsky, 1987, pp. 168, 169, 216)

The zone of proximal development

Schneuwly (1994) discussed Vygotsky's theory of development in terms of the individual's reorganisation of lower psychological functions to form new higher ones whilst emphasising that psychological functions are themselves historical-cultural constructions. He viewed the concept of zone of proximal development (ZPD) as the theoretical attempt to understand the operation of contradiction between internal possibilities and external needs that constitutes the driving force of development. The concept of ZPD was created by Vygotsky as a metaphor to assist in explaining the way in which social and participatory learning takes place (John–Steiner and Mahn, 1996). The general genetic law of cultural development asserts the primacy of the social in development. I have sought to emphasise that Vygotsky was concerned to develop an account in which humans were seen as 'making themselves from the outside'. Through acting on things in the world they engage with the meanings that those things assumed within social activity. Humans both shape those meanings and are shaped by them. This process takes place within the ZPD. This well-known concept is often cited as Vygotsky's most profound contribution to educational debate. However, as Veresov (1999) argued, Vygotsky did not devote much of his extensive writing in psychology to the topic. Van der Veer and Valsiner (1991) debated whether Vygotsky claimed the ZPD as his original contribution. Whilst this issue is, to say the least, hazy, it is undoubtedly the case that whilst many of the current interpretations may not be 'wrong', some may be best described as partial.

The ZPD is certainly a concept that has shaped some aspects of educational thinking and in turn it has also been shaped and appropriated by different voices within educational debate. Valsiner (1998) sounded a warning note here. He suggested that some uses of the ZPD concept have merely served the purpose of labelling complex phenomena with another equally complex concept. The attachment of the label in and of itself may not yield clarity or understanding. I will now discuss Vygotsky's use of the term and then move to discuss more recent developments in the definition

Moll (1990) argued that a close reading of *Mind in Society* reveals the development of the ZPD concept from the method of double stimulation that emphasised the child's active engagement in finding new means to solve problems.

> Using words to create a specific plan, the child achieves a much broader range of activity, applying as tools not only those objects that lie near at hand, but searching for and preparing such stimuli as can be useful in the solution of the task, and planning future actions.
>
> (Vygotsky, 1978, p. 26)

The shift that takes place between the method of double stimulation and the ZPD is in terms of emphasis from sign mediated to socially mediated activity.

Moll suggested that Vygotsky incorporated the former into the latter. This was part of the development of the ZPD concept which may be traced through his writing. The search for a method of studying psychological change, which was arguably Vygotsky's central concern, was stated as follows:

> The search for method becomes one of the most important problems of the entire enterprise of understanding the uniquely human forms of psychological activity. In this case the method is simultaneously prerequisite and product, the tool and result of the study.
>
> (Vygotsky, 1978, p. 65)

Holzman (1995) and Newman and Holzman (1993) explored the 'tool and result' understanding of method in detail. The crucial point here is that in order to both study and promote learning one and the same methodological understanding is required.

Wells (1999) distinguished between two definitions within Vygotsky's original writing. One version in chapter six of *Mind in Society* places emphasis on dynamic assessment of children's intellectual abilities rather than more static measures such as IQ scores. Here Vygotsky defines the ZPD as:

> 'actual developmental level as determined by independent problem solving' and the higher level of 'potential development as determined through problem solving under adult guidance or in collaboration with more capable peers'.
>
> (Vygotsky, 1978, p. 86)

He elaborates on this definition in order to emphasise the difference between aided and unsupported performance.

> 'Suppose I investigate two children upon entrance into school, both of whom are twelve years old chronologically and eight years old in terms of mental development. Can I say that they are the same age mentally? Of course. What does this mean? It means that they can independently deal with tasks up to the degree of difficulty that has been standardized for the eight-year-old level. If I stop at this point, people would imagine that the subsequent course of development and of school learning of these children will be the same, because it depends on their intellect. . . . Now imagine that I do not terminate my study at this point, but only begin it. . . . Suppose I show . . . [these children] have various ways of dealing with a task . . . that the children solve the problem with my assistance. Under these circumstances it turns out that the first child can deal with problems up to a twelve-year-old's level. The second up to a nine-year-old's. Now are these children mentally the same? When it was first shown that the capability of children with equal levels of mental development to learn under a teacher's guidance varied to a high degree, it became apparent that those children

were not mentally the same and that the subsequent course of their learning would obviously be different. This difference between twelve and eight, or between nine and eight, is what we call the zone of proximal development.

(Vygotsky, 1978, pp. 85–6)

His interest was in assessing the ways in which learners make progress. The focus on process as well as product in assessment has become embedded in the range of techniques now called 'dynamic assessment' (Campione, 1996). The general practice of dynamic assessment is either explicitly or tacitly inspired by the work of Vygotsky. This contrasts sharply with practices which theorise a lag of learning behind development as in the case of Piaget or which theorise learning as development as in the case of Skinner. There are stark differences in the ways in which this idea which has, at least, some root in Vygotskian theory, becomes embedded in other psychological traditions. I will discuss some of these differences and their implications in Chapters 3 and 4.

Wells (1999) pointed out that the second version of ZPD is to be found in Vygotsky's last major work, *Thinking and Speech* (1934/1987), and is embedded in chapter six, in which he discussed 'The Development of Scientific Concepts in Childhood'. Instruction is foregrounded here rather than assessment.

We have seen that instruction and development do not coincide. They are two different processes with very complex interrelationships. Instruction is only useful when it moves ahead of development. When it does, it impels or awakens a whole series of functions that are in a stage of maturation lying in the zone of proximal development. This is the major role of instruction in development. This is what distinguishes the instruction of the child from the training of animals. This is also what distinguishes instruction of the child which is directed toward his full development from instruction in specialised, technical skills such as typing or riding a bicycle. The formal aspect of each school subject is that in which the influence of instruction on development is realised. Instruction would be completely unnecessary if it merely utilised what had already matured in the developmental process, if it were not itself a source of development.

(Vygotsky, 1987, p. 212)

Arguably, Vygotsky has not shifted his position on the nature of the ZPD in the time that lapsed between the writing of these two texts. Perhaps the differences of emphasis may be attributable to the changes in the social/political/professional circumstances in which he was working. In the earlier writing he was more concerned with assessment and indeed it was more acceptable to write about assessment. As his career developed the political pressure against assessment grew and his own interests, as Minick (1987) has shown, shifted away from relations between psychological functions and towards relations between psychological functioning and social circumstances.

In summary, Vygotsky discussed the ZPD in terms of assessment and instruction. Within both frames of reference he discussed the relationship between an individual learner and a supportive other or others even if that other was not physically present in the context in which learning was taking place. In many ways the concept of ZPD lies at the heart of Vygotsky's social account of learning. It is, therefore, often the point of departure for many of the tensions and dilemmas in the development of the theory. It raises questions about the nature of the 'social' in the pedagogic relationship alongside questions concerning the nature of the relationship itself. I will now address these issues.

The nature of the 'social' within the ZPD

Lave and Wenger (1991) argue that the operational definition of ZPD has itself undergone many differing interpretations. Many different researchers have interpreted and developed the notion of the ZPD (for example Tharp and Gallimore, 1988a; Matusov, 1998; Wells, 1999), with the result that various models have emerged which apply, extend and reconstruct Vygotsky's original conception. These differences may be seen to reveal the more general theoretical drift towards a broader more cultural and historical view of the 'social' which is theorised as being progressively more intimately a part of the 'individual'. Thus Lave and Wenger (1991) distinguish between a 'scaffolding', a 'cultural' and a 'collectivist' or 'societal' of the original formulation of the ZPD. The 'scaffolding' interpretation is one in which a distinction is made between support for the initial performance of tasks and subsequent performance without assistance: 'the distance between problem-solving abilities exhibited by a learner working alone and that learner's problem-solving abilities when assisted by or collaborating with more-experienced people'.

The term scaffolding could be taken to infer a 'one-way' process wherein the 'scaffolder' constructs the scaffold alone and presents it for use to the novice. Newman *et al.* (1989) argued that the ZPD is created through negotiation between the more advanced partner and the learner, rather than through the donation of a scaffold as some kind of prefabricated climbing frame. There is a similar emphasis on negotiation in Tharp and Gallimore (1988b) who discussed 'teaching as assisted performance', in those stages of the ZPD where assistance is required. The key question here seems to be with respect to where the 'hints', 'supports', or 'scaffold' come from. Are they produced by 'the more capable partner' or are they negotiated? Vygotsky is unclear on this matter.

> Vygotsky never specified the forms of social assistance to learners that constitute a ZPD. . . . He wrote about collaboration and direction, and about assisting children 'through demonstration, leading questions, and by introducing the initial elements of the task's solution' . . . but did not specify beyond these general prescriptions.
>
> (Moll, 1990, p. 11)

Moll (1990) suggested that the focus of change within the ZPD should be on the creation, development and communication of meaning through the collaborative use of mediational means rather than on the transfer of skills from the more to less capable partner. Thus, even within the 'scaffolding' interpretation there are fundamental differences. A rigid scaffold may appear little different from a task analysis produced by teaching which has been informed by applied behaviour analysis. A negotiated scaffold would arise in a very different form of teaching and may well be associated with collaborative activity as discussed by Moll. The application and subsequent development of the scaffolding metaphor will be discussed in Chapter 4.

The 'cultural' interpretation of the ZPD is based on Vygotsky's distinction between scientific and everyday concepts. It is argued that a mature concept is achieved when the scientific and everyday versions have merged. However, as Lave and Wenger (1991) note, no account is taken of 'the place of learning in the broader context of the structure in the social world'.

> . . . the distance between the cultural knowledge provided by the socio-historical context – usually made accessible through instruction – and the everyday experience of individuals. Hedegaard calls this the distance between understood knowledge, as provided by instruction, and active knowledge, as owned by individuals.
>
> (Lave and Wenger, 1991, p. 76)

Hedegaard discusses what she calls the 'double move approach' in the process of concept formation within the ZPD. She suggests that 'the teacher guides the learning activity both from the perspective of general concepts and from the perspective of engaging students in "situated" problems that are meaningful in relation to their developmental stage and life situations' (Hedegaard, 1998, p. 120).

In the 'collectivist', or 'societal' perspective, Engeström defined ZPD as the 'distance between the everyday actions of individuals and the historically new form of the societal activity that can be collectively generated' (Engeström, 1987, p. 174). Under such societal interpretations of the concept of the ZPD researchers tend to concentrate on processes of social transformation. This involves the study of learning beyond the context of pedagogical structuring, including the structure of the social world in the analysis, and taking into account in a central way the conflictual nature of social practice (Lave and Wenger, 1991, pp. 48–9). I will discuss this approach to activity theory in Chapter 3.

These types of definition carry with them different implications for schooling and instruction. If the 'social' in teaching and learning is constrained to a view of particular teaching technologies and procedures then the analysis of schooling is both truncated and partial. If the 'social' in schooling is considered in socio-institutional terms then the gaze of the analysis of the outcomes is altered and/or extended. This question of the scope of the definition is fundamental to one of my concerns about the ways in which pedagogy is theorised, described and investigated. In Chapter 1 I was keen to promote a socially extended definition of pedagogy. Throughout this book I will be exploring the ways in which post-Vygotskian studies can be developed to meet the requirements of an account which is capable of advancing the theory and practice of pedagogy so defined. Following Vygotsky's own insistence on the use of genetic (historical/developmental) analysis it is possible to discern a trajectory in his own writing towards a more socially connected account.

> Vygotsky seemed to be coming to recognise this issue near the end of his life. It is reflected in the difference between Chapters five and six of *Thinking and Speech* (1987). Both chapters deal with the ontogenetic transition from 'complexes' to 'genuine', or 'scientific' concepts. However, the two chapters differ markedly in what they see as relevant developmental forces. In Chapter five (based on research with Shif and written during the early 1930s), concept development is treated primarily in terms of intramental processes, that is, children's conceptual development as they move from 'unorganised heaps' to 'complexes' to 'concepts'. In Chapter six (written in 1934), there is an essential shift in the way Vygotsky approaches these issues. He clearly continued to be interested in intramental functioning, but he shifted to approaching concept development from the perspective of how it emerges in institutionally situated activity. Specifically, he was concerned with how the forms of discourse encountered in the social institution of formal schooling provide a framework for the development of conceptual thinking. He did it by the teacher–child intermental functioning found in this setting.
>
> (Wertsch *et al.*, 1993, p. 344)

It remains the case that most of Vygotsky's writing tends to focus on the more immediate interactional/interpersonal antecedents of independent or seemingly independent functioning. The first important implication of this for pedagogy is that teaching and assessment should be focused on the potential of the learner, rather than on a demonstrated level of achievement or understanding. The second is that teaching, or instruction, should create the possibilities for development, through the kind of active participation that characterises collaboration, that it should be socially negotiated and that it should entail transfer of control to the learner. Theories concerning the regulation of such practices within specific schools remained beyond the scope of Vygotsky's writing. The institutional regulation of the social practices of schooling is beyond the gaze of much of the empirical work that claims to be drawing on his work. I will return to this matter briefly in Chapter 4 and again in Chapter 5.

Valsiner (1998) has reconstructed the notion of the ZPD, as part of a zone system, which extends beyond other notions of the ZPD. In a model which emphasises canalisation and co-construction he discussed organisational devices that provide the framework for constraint on development and possible directions of nearest future development. The constraints come within the Zone of Free Movement (ZFM) and possibility is promoted within the Zone of Promoted Action (ZPA). Valsiner (1997) argued that the zones are useful tools for explaining regulation of the developmental process, through the restructuring of the zones and the relationships between them.

The ZFM is a means he uses to describe the internal and external structuring of a child's access to different aspects of his or her environment (Valsiner, 1997, 1998). Valsiner (1997) argued that as the child develops, the ZFM becomes internalised, providing a structure for personal thinking and feeling through semiotic regulation. The ZFM promotes canalisation, through the constraints or restrictions created on and through possible child–environment interactions. This argument reminds me of Waddington's (1951) developmental chreods which were proposed as models of cell development within embryology. In Figure 2.3 the ball represents cell fate. The valleys are the different fates the cell might roll into.

At the beginning of its journey, development is plastic, and a cell can become many fates. However, as development proceeds, certain decisions cannot be reversed. The surface down which the ball rolls is itself subject to change.

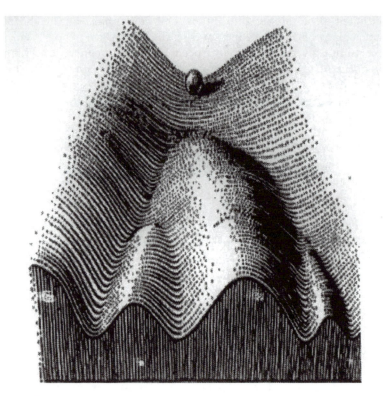

Figure 2.3 Developmental chreods.

Valsiner's ZFM could be linked with Gibson's (1979) idea of ecological affordance or Waddington's model of developmental chreods. All three speak of constraint yet not in an overdetermined manner. However, it is important to remember that in Vygotsky's original writings he most certainly did not subscribe to the extreme relativism with which he has been popularly associated.

> We said that in collaboration the child can always do more than he can independently. We must add the stipulation that he cannot do infinitely more. What collaboration contributes to the child's performance is restricted to limits which are determined by the state of his development and his intellectual potential.
>
> (Vygotsky, 1987, p. 209)

Valsiner incorporates an account of the canalisation of interest within cultural meaning systems. He also argued that the meanings and values of the caregiver will canalise and constrain the possibilities for interest and interaction. He recognised that this canalisation process may lead to conflict. This conflict remained somewhat under-theorised within his model. There is no attempt to discuss how different modalities of caregiving, upbringing or teaching with their embedded practices of regulation may give rise to different possibilities for transgression. The ZFM remains a depiction of the social without a model of regulation. The same criticism can, of course, be levelled at Vygotsky who failed to develop an approach that would allow for the empirical investigation of the consequences of different configurations of power and control either at the social interactional or the institutional level. Clearly this is a major omission when social practices such as schooling are to be considered. As I mentioned earlier, I will return to this matter in Chapters 4 and 5.

Valsiner conceptualised the ZPA as those actions of the child with a set of activities, objects or areas in the environment that are encouraged (Valsiner, 1997, 1998). Again it is envisaged that encouragement may be resisted or ignored and it is recognised that the ZPA may encourage activity outside the ZFM. Together the encouragement and constraint of the ZPA and ZFM constitute co-constructed cultural and personal meaning systems which are themselves mediated by others.

> In the context of intersubjective processes of child–other interaction, the child constructs his or her own personal sense system under the guidance of other people: parents and other adult relatives, older siblings, peers and even younger siblings.
>
> (Valsiner, 1997, p. 175)

The ZFM/ZPA system creates the field for activity within a ZPD. This extension moves some way to specifying the 'specific social nature of . . . the intellectual life of those around them'.

> Human learning presupposes a specific social nature and a process by which children grow into the intellectual life of those around them.
>
> (Vygotsky, 1978, p. 88)

My own view is that this theory has not yet developed to the point where operational definitions of different forms of social practice may be generated, their consequences hypothesised and investigated.

The specific social nature of an activity may be characterised, or indeed, realised, in the speech which is used. In a discussion of the way in which speech is theorised Cazden (1993) dismissed 'dialect' and 'register' as inadequate for the task of providing a unit of analysis which could connect mind with social interaction. She turned to Bakhtin's term 'voice':

> Voice is Bakhtin's term for the 'speaking consciousness': the person acting – that is speaking or writing in a particular time and place to known or unknown others. Voice and its utterances always express a point of view, always enact particular values. They are also social in still a third meaning: taking account of the voices being addressed, whether in speech or writing. This dialogic quality of utterances Bakhtin calls 'responsivity' or 'addressivity'.
>
> (Cazden, 1993, p. 198)

Cazden suggested that whilst Vygotsky and Bakhtin had not necessarily met or heard of each other they shared a common intellectual milieu which may well have been the significant precursor in the development of compatible ideas. Wertsch *et al.* (1993) noted complementary features of their work. Bakhtin provides a situated sociocultural account of semiotic mediation. His emphasis on dialogue and what he termed 'ventriloquism' made way for an understanding of the processes by which the voice or voices of the other or others are appropriated by individuals. As with Wittgenstein's notion of 'language game' so in Bakhtin's notion of dialogue is the insistence that meaning is developed through the interplay and mutual transformation that results from dialogic exchange between two or more influences. Social languages are associated with particular forms of social practice. Social languages can be viewed as a connection between individual functioning and socio-institutional activity which is at one time cultural and historical. They are mediating artefacts. Clearly they must be analytically connected with the activity within which they arise. However, this activity may not always be physically present. Vygotsky's attempts at providing the theoretical account of the production of cultural artefacts within specific activities were somewhat underdeveloped. He did discuss the notion of the 'internal social voice'.

Vygotsky insisted that there is no necessary recourse to physical presence in accounts of support within the ZPD. With the following quotation he announced the possibility of virtual collaboration without the physical presence of the adult/teacher.

When the school child solves a problem at home on the basis of a model that he has been shown in class, he continues to act in collaboration, though at the moment the teacher is not standing near him. From a psychological perspective, the solution of the second problem is similar to this solution of a problem at home. It is a solution accomplished with the teacher's help. This help – this aspect of collaboration – is invisibly present. It is contained in what looks from the outside like the child's independent solution of the problem.

(Vygotsky, 1987, p. 216)

If we accept the notion of support without presence as discussed by Vygotsky (1987, p. 216) and elaborated by Clark (1998) we are then faced with the fundamental question of the extent to which the mind can be considered as an individual attribute. Clark discusses the social attributes of inner speech.

When the child, confronted by a tricky challenge, is 'talked through' the problem by a more experienced agent, the child can often succeed at tasks which would otherwise prove impossible (think of learning to tie your shoelaces). Later on, when the adult is absent, the child can conduct a similar dialogue, but this time with herself. But even in this latter case, it is argued, the speech (be it vocal or 'internalized') functions so as to guide behavior, to focus attention, and to guard against common errors. In such cases, the role of language is to guide and shape our own behavior – it is a tool for structuring and controlling action and not merely a medium of information transfer between agents.

(Clark, 1998, p. 66)

Clark proceeds to question whether the use of linguistic support for thinking is ever truly an individual act or remains a form of social dimension.

I suspect that our intuitive notions of mind and cognition actually do pick out these larger extended systems and that as a result the biological brain is only one component of the intelligent system we call the mind. But I will settle for a weaker conclusion – one that merely implicates our linguistic capacities in some highly productive transformations of our overall compu- tational powers. This power of computational transformation constitutes a neglected virtue of linguistic practice. It reveals language as the ultimate upgrade: so ubiquitous it is almost invisible; so intimate, it is not clear whether it is a kind of tool or an added dimension of the user. But whatever the boundaries, we confront a complex coalition in which the basic biological brain is fantastically empowered by some of its strangest and most recent creations: words in the air, symbols on the printed page.

(Clark, 1998, p. 180)

Clearly, Vygotsky's reference to virtual support raises some important issues. If support within the ZPD may come from the 'voice' of an absent tutor then surely there is a place for several voices within a particular ZPD. If this is the case then each voice or influence may not necessarily be in agreement. This faces us with a series of decisions or interpretations.

Cheyne and Tarulli (1999) announce their intention to develop a broad cultural historical view of the ZPD by discussing issues of dialogue, others and what they refer to as 'third voice'. They compared and contrasted the positions adopted by Bakhtin and Vygotsky on dialogue and noted a crucial distinction:

> In what way would it enrich the event even if I merge with the other and instead of two there would now only be one? And what would I myself gain by the other's merging with me? If he did, he would see and know no more that what I see and know myself; he would merely repeat in himself that want of any issue of itself that characterises my own life. Let him rather remain outside of me, for in that position he can see and know what I myself do not see and do not know from my own place, and he can essentially enrich the event of my own life.
>
> (Bakhtin, 1990, p. 87)

Here we have a rejection of the notion of consensus. As Cheyne and Tarulli noted 'a dialogical mind does not itself constitute a common apperceptive mass, but rather a community of different and often conflicting voices that may not be resolved into one comprehensive self . . . it is in the struggle with difference and misunderstanding that dialogue and thought are productive and that productivity is not necessarily measured in consensus' (Cheyne and Tarulli, 1999, p. 89).

Vygotsky's explicit claims about dialogue do not seem to have extended beyond external social speech. Wertsch (1980) suggested that when Vygotsky wrote about egocentric and inner speech it may be that that more appropriate terms for what he was studying would be 'egocentric dialogue' and 'inner dialogue' (p. 151). Burkitt (1998) argued that the similarities between the two are to be found in the extent to which each is a manifestation of the situation in which the speaker utters. The analysis is firmly on the communication of meaning and how that meaning is developed rather than on the decontextualised text/utterance.

> Oral speech is regulated by the dynamics of the situation. It flows entirely from the situation in accordance with the type of situational-motivational and situational-conditioning process.
>
> (Vygotsky, 1987, p. 203)

Whether Vygotsky was really writing about speech or dialogue will remain a mystery. He certainly did not progress the analysis of the psychological implications of contradictory social voices to the same extent as did Bakhtin. One of the most important differences to be found between Vygotsky and Bakhtin is then with respect to the 'difference of the other'. For Bakhtin it is

through and in difference and misunderstanding in dialogue that the contradictions that generate development are to be found. Vygotsky often seems to be
concerned with a ZPD as a space where the learner is brought into the 'knowing'
of the other. The emphasis on multiple voices engaged in the construction of a
form meaning which is not necessarily located within the individual characterises
many current interpretations of Bakhtin's influence on a Vygotskian account.

Valsiner cautioned against too much theoretical speculation of this nature and
ponders on the social implications of an ordinary person announcing that
they were either 'seamlessly tied' to their living room or that their mind was
filled with the 'voices of others' (Valsiner, 1997, p. 237). On the other hand,
Gergen (1999) developed a radical constructionist account of the learning
processes. He was critical of both Vygotsky and Bruner, suggesting 'they remain
deeply ambivalent concerning the significance of the social as opposed to the
individual'. These two positions serve to illustrate the ongoing tensions in
the interpretation of the ZPD concept.

However, if the Bakhtinian approach is, to some extent, a reasonable model
of possible activity within the ZPD, we are faced with the prospect of the learner
actively making decisions about which actions/pathways to progress. At a
particular time a learner makes decisions with the benefit (or otherwise) of the
influence of others both present and absent. This position opens the way for a
non-determinist account in which the learner finds a way forward through what
may be contradictory influences. This does not deny the possibility of the single
voice of influence. There may be times when a learner follows a single path
through a ZPD as a diligent apprentice to an all-powerful 'master'.[2] However
this is not a necessary concomitant of the ZPD model:

- the learner's own prior understanding may come into conflict with the
  support given;
- the learner may receive influence from several conflicting sources.

This speculation on the nature of support within the ZPD raises questions
about broader social influences. Multiple and possibly conflicting discourses with
different sociocultural historical origins may be in play within the ZPD. This
view of the ZPD as the nexus of social, cultural, historical influences takes us
far beyond the image of the lone learner with the directive and determining
tutor. It provides a much expanded view of the 'social' and the possibility of a
dialectical conception of interaction within the ZPD.

Valsiner provides another important cautionary note that must enter into this
debate. He reminds us that much of the empirical work that has been undertaken
runs the risk of confusing microgenetic and ontogenetic processes.

> There exists an unwarranted (and implicit) assumption in received empirical
> practices in developmental psychology to consider the microgenetic and
> ontogenetic levels of development similar in their organisation.
>
> (Valsiner, 1997, p. 241)

If this slippage is permitted then the concept of appropriation can be used to render any form of social activity as formative in ontogenetic terms. Clearly this is not justified.

In summary, the discussion of ZPD has raised a number of questions. For example, to what extent is the 'social' other in the ZPD an individual with whom the learner interacts? The anthropologist Erickson (1996) argued that much of the application of the ZPD concept is within dyadic settings with a single expert and a single novice. He reminded his readers that such a situation may not be typical of patterns of communication in learning situations.

> Teachers and students interact in classrooms, they construct an ecology of social and cognitive relations in which influence between any and all parties is mutual, simultaneous and continuous. One aspect of this social and cognitive ecology is the multiparty character of the scene – many participants, all of them continually 'on task' albeit working on different kinds of tasks, some of which may be at cross purposes. Although teachers in group discussion may attempt to enforce a participant framework of successive dyadic teacher–student exchanges, often the conversation is more complicated than that.
>
> (Erickson, 1996, p. 33)

The reduction of the complexity of classroom life to a quasi-experimental dyad carries significant restrictions in terms of the generalisability and validity of findings. Crucially such studies do not allow for a critical examination of the effect of different forms of participant structure in learning situations. When considering different models of ZPD it thus seems reasonable to ask – to what extent should we consider social groups, institutions, communities and other cultural historical dimensions within the ZPD. It also seems important to ask whether the changes that take place as a consequence of activity in a ZPD are best considered as acts of internalisation or as incorporation of aspects of the social that may or may not remain present. Lastly and somewhat portentously – to what extent is the developing conscious mind an individual mind.

These issues ricochet through contemporary fractions of social theory. In the next chapter I will review a number of recent developments in this field and consider their assumptions and implications.

Notes

1 Popper (1972) provides a metaphoric schema of three worlds: World 1 – the material world of inanimate and animate things (including human beings); World 2 – the subjective world of individual mental life; and World 3 – the world of immaterial knowledge object.

2 I know of no gender free alternative.

Chapter 3

Current approaches to sociocultural and activity theory

In Chapters 1 and 2 I provided a restricted discussion of elements of Vygotsky's theoretical contribution. In Chapter 1 I also sketched an outline of issues that arise in the operational definition of the term 'pedagogy'. I opted for a general definition of pedagogic practice as the fundamental social context through which cultural reproduction-production takes place. I see this 'fundamental social context' as far more than pupil–teacher interaction. I also discussed Vygotsky's speculations on mediation. This discussion emphasised the mutual shaping and development of person and cultural artefacts. In Chapter 2 I drew attention to Vygotsky's emphasis on a dialectical method and the tensions that have arisen between models of internalisation and appropriation of social, cultural and historical influences in development. I also brought biology into the discussion of the elementary and higher functions and everyday and scientific concepts. My outline of debates concerning the Zone of Proximal Development, within which the social/individual dialectical machine of development operates, emphasised the dangers of reducing the complexities of formative effects to a narrow conception of the 'social'. In this chapter I will provide an outline of the current field of activity within what could be called post-Vygotskian studies. This discussion will consist of a consideration of approaches which refer to cognition as situated and/or distributed. This will be followed by an attempt to unravel some of the complexities and tensions that exist in the use of the terms 'social', 'cultural' and historical' with reference to the analysis of 'action' and 'activity'.

Initial studies of developing cognition tended to ignore the context or to provide a very partial view of the relationship between context and cognition. The early cognitivist approach tended to exclude societal and cultural factors from its notion of context. The initial theorising in ecological psychology tended to focus on the description of settings and to ignore the relations between persons acting and those settings. More recent times have witnessed a rapid growth in the number of approaches which attempt to investigate the development of cognition in context using non-deterministic, non-reductionist theories. Amongst these are cultural-historical activity theory (Cole *et al.*, 1997) sociocultural approaches (Wertsch, 1991; Wertsch *et al.*, 1995), situated learning models (Lave, 1996), distributed cognition approaches (Salomon, 1993b). They all share the view that the theory developed by L.S. Vygotsky provides a valuable tool with which to interrogate and attempt to understand the processes of social formation of mind (see Daniels, 1996).

Situated learning and distributed cognition

In the introduction to his edited book on distributed cognitions, Salomon (1993a) asserts that 'a clearer understanding of human cognition would be achieved if studies were based on the concept that cognition is distributed among individuals, that knowledge is socially constructed through collaborative efforts to achieve shared objectives in cultural surroundings and that information is processed between individuals and tools and artefacts provided by the culture' (Salomon, 1993a, p. 3). The concept of cognition as a phenomenon that extends beyond the individual, that arises in shared activity, owes a clear debt to the original Vygotskian understanding that the interpersonal precedes the intra-personal. Anthropologists have long been attracted to this concept of distributed cognition. Their approach has tended to regard cultures as repositories of accumulated cognitive resources. For anthropologists such as Hutchins, distributed cognition is a necessary characteristic of human functioning.

> All human societies face cognitive tasks that are beyond the capabilities of any individual member. Even the simplest culture contains more information than could be learned by any individual in a life-time, so that tasks of learning, remembering, and transmitting cultural knowledge are inevitably distributed. The performance of cognitive tasks that exceed individual abilities is always shaped by a social organisation of distributed cognition. Doing without a social organisation of distributed cognition is not an option.
>
> (Hutchins, 1995, p. 262)

When this approach is linked with the concept of cultural artefact, as discussed in Chapters 1 and 2, the importance of contextual resources for and in learning is raised. As I have already noted, Vygotsky was keen to emphasise that what could appear to be individual problem solving may still be thought of as a collaborative activity given that the 'voice' of the 'other' may still serve to guide individual actions. This calls into question whether the partners in acts of distributed cognition have to be present in the same location (see Salomon, 1993b, pp. 114–16 for a discussion). However, the twin notions of situated and distributed cognition are, as Salomon (1993b) argues, in many senses, inextricably linked.

> If cognitions are distributed, then by necessity they are also situated . . . since the distribution of cognitions depends on situational affordances.
>
> (Salomon, 1993b, p. 114)

The situational affordances of which Salomon speaks may of course be networks of cognition distributed across time and space. Shared learning activity does not necessarily require shared physical space and may be thought of as occurring through networks which are both proximal and distal. Clark (1998) has argued that there is a need to give 'more attention, and credit, to the many ways in which networks can learn to exploit external environmental structures so as to simplify and transform the nature of internal processing' (Clark, 1998, p. 16). In this section I will handle these two aspects of the literature together on the understanding that they refer to a central concern about the relationship between a broadly defined concept of context (people and things) and cognition.

Of the many texts which refer to situated cognition and/or situated learning, two of the most influential are Lave and Wenger's (1991) *Situated Learning: Legitimate Peripheral Participation* and Kirshner and Whitson's (1997) *Situated Cognition: Social, Semiotic, and Psychological Perspectives*. The latter provides a wideranging commentary on the field and draws on a number of disciplinary perspectives. The former has become widely regarded as a seminal text in which a particular view of learning was established.

> Learning viewed as situated activity has as its central defining characteristic a process that we call legitimate peripheral participation. By this we mean to draw attention to the point that learners inevitably participate in communities of practitioners and that the mastery of knowledge and practice requires newcomers to move toward full participation in the sociocultural practices of a community. 'Legitimate peripheral participation' provides a way to speak about activities, identities, artefacts, and communities of knowledge and practice. It concerns the process by which newcomers become part of a community of practice. A person's intentions to learn are engaged and the meaning of the learning is configured through the process of becoming a full participant in a sociocultural practice. This social process includes, indeed it subsumes, the learning of knowledgeable skills.
>
> (Lave and Wenger, 1991, p. 29)

They report observations of people engaged in problem solving in the course of their participation in ongoing everyday activities. They discuss midwives, tailors, quartermasters, butchers and non-drinking alcoholics in chapter three of Lave and Wenger (1991). As Lemke (1997, p. 38) notes, these reports are of people 'functioning in micro-ecologies, material environments endowed with cultural meanings; acting and being acted on directly or with the mediation of physical-cultural tools and cultural-material systems of words, signs, and other symbolic values. In these activities, "things" contribute to solutions every bit as much as "minds" do; information and meaning is coded into configurations of objects, material constraints, and possible environmental options, as well as in verbal routines and formulas or "mental" operations.'

Lave argues that situated learning is usually unintentional and occurs as individuals come to participate more and more in a 'community of practice'. The beliefs and behaviours which are constituted, sustained and developed in communities of practice are progressively acquired as the new entrant to a community, the beginner or newcomer, becomes more central to that community. Accordingly, Lave (1993) describes cognition as 'stretched over, not divided among – mind, body, activity and culturally organized settings (which include other actors)'. The trajectory from what Lave and Wenger (1991) call the process of 'legitimate peripheral participation' to central engagement as an 'old timer' within a community is the move from novice to expert within a particular situation. Learning is situated in that community and is, by definition, something that takes place with other members of that community.

Prior draws on Lave and Wenger (1991) and invokes their view of the process of becoming an expert not as mastering a shared core of abstract knowledge and internalising language but as operating within a community characterised by 'a set of relations among persons, activity, and world, over time and in relation with other tangential and overlapping communities of practice' (Prior, 1997, p. 98). Similarly, Lewis talks of a collective core of knowledge in a community where some people's core knowledge overlaps and one person's zone of proximal development overlaps with the core knowledge of others (Lewis, 1997).

This point is also handled by Hatano who sees active learners as bringing together multiple sources of information including their own previous informal knowledge (Hatano, 1993). Lave and Wenger's emphasis on learning as 'collaborative production' which takes place as part of a range of activities and practices constitutes the background to their assertion that legitimate peripheral participation relates to a 'way of being in the social world, not a way of coming to know about it' and thus denotes the process of moving from being a novice to an expert. Language is central to it in that 'Language is part of practice, and it is in practice that people learn' (Lave and Wenger, 1991, p. 85); and 'For newcomers . . . the purpose is not to learn *from* talk as a substitute for legitimate peripheral participation; it is to learn *to* talk as a key to legitimate peripheral participation' (Lave and Wenger, 1991, p. 109). This is, as it were, a reference to the process of talking one's way in to the expertise of a community.

Resources are also key and Lave and Wenger engage with how teachers can limit the meaning of what is learned through structuring of resources and how relations of power and control constrain newcomers' access to a community. Star, who describes learning as 'something which occurs only in the presence of a knowledgeable community', identifies as problematic the fact that 'many new users are ashamed to admit ignorance and, pretending to know already, must learn through the . . . indirect means of observation and imitation' (Star, 1998, p. 308). Participation in web-based interest groups provides a good example of such situated learning which is not defined in terms of a particular location. The 'newcomer' often simply reads what is taking place. Initial participation often takes place when the newcomer feels that the situation affords an opportunity to participate in such a way that the risk of offending or disrupting the community is minimal. Old timers are much more likely to engage in risk taking contributions. The process of learning the rules of engagement and protocols is one in which the newcomer takes a gradually more central position within the community. Importantly, the newcomer to such a community may seek to solve problems in other settings within which they may be guided by the physically and electronically absent community. The voices of the community may be carried outside the network in which they reside.

Other researchers have also developed theories of situated learning. Brown *et al.* (1989, p. 32) develop the idea of cognitive apprenticeship: 'Cognitive apprenticeship supports learning in a domain by enabling students to acquire, develop and use cognitive tools in authentic domain activity. Learning, both outside and inside school, advances through collaborative social interaction and the social construction of knowledge.' This position has been the subject of some criticism by Lave and Wenger who suggest that the approach may direct attention to a rather constrained view of the processes which concern them.

> To be able to participate in a legitimately peripheral way entails that newcomers have broad access to arenas of mature practice. . . . An apprentice's contributions to ongoing activity gain value in practice . . . a value which increases as the apprentice becomes more adept. As opportunities for understanding how well or poorly one's efforts contribute are evident in practice, legitimate participation of a peripheral kind provides an immediate ground for self evaluation. The sparsity of tests, praise, or blame typical of apprenticeship follows from the apprentice's legitimacy as a participant. Notions like those of 'intrinsic rewards' in empirical studies of apprenticeship focus quite narrowly on task knowledge and skill as the activities to be learned. Such knowledge is of course important; but a deeper sense of the value of participation to the community and the learner lies in becoming part of the community.
>
> (Lave and Wenger, 1991, pp. 110–11)

Their emphasis on identity formation with increasing participation marks out their approach from some models of apprenticeship. For them, learning is a part of social practice, and they focus on the structure of social practice rather than the structure of pedagogy, pedagogic practice and forms of knowledge in learning. This position demarcates their work from the more instructionally driven conceptions of learning and development which espouse a Vygotskian root whilst also having some parallels with accounts of situated learning and distributed cognition. For example, Hedegaard (1998) is very critical of the accounts of situated learning and cognition which have been developed by both Jean Lave and Ann Brown. She is concerned about:

> the narrowness of cognition and learning promoted by this approach because it does not differentiate between the types of learning and cognition

as Vygotsky does when he differentiates between learning and cognition in every day community life and school life.

(Hedegaard, 1998, p. 117)

Another concern is raised by Lemke (1997) who draws on the tradition of social semiotics in his attempt to go beyond the radically situated position which is one of the possible out-turns of the Lave and Wenger (1991) formulation of peripheral participation. The model of social semiotics on which he draws suggests that it is not only the context of the situation that is relevant but also the context of culture when an analysis of meaning is undertaken. He suggests that 'we interpret a text, or a situation, in part by connecting it to other texts and situations which our community, or our individual history, has made us see as relevant to the meaning of the present one' (Lemke, 1997 p. 50). This use of notions of intertextuality, of networked activities, or networks of connections provides Lemke with tools for the creation of an account of ecosocial systems which transcend immediate contexts. This allows him to discuss learning in and across activities and communities of practice. For Lemke, this is the 'way out of' what could be a conservative view of situated cognition. The prospect of too close a tie between situation and thinking could result in a model within which a change or movement from one situation to another and is cognitively very challenging. If the linkage with situation is very strong and notions of transfer are seen as inadmissible then every change of situation would make huge demands on the individual. The concept of development itself becomes problematic. Lemke explicates a situated model which avoids the pitfalls of an account which denies personal involvement in establishing continuities across domains and situations. I am not arguing that this, essentially pessimistic, dialect of situated learning is the necessary interpretation of Lave and Wenger's work. I am raising the prospect of such a position by way of a warning against what I see as an unrealistic and untenable interpretation of situated learning.

Pea examines the shaping effect of the design of activity and its goals and argues that the importance of 'cultural artefacts and representations as carriers of meaning' has been insufficiently recognised to date. He adopts and adapts Gibson's notion of affordances, which he defines as 'the perceived and actual properties of a thing, primarily those functional properties that determine just how the thing could possibly be used' (Pea, 1993, p. 51). He sees intelligence as residing in the interaction of memory and available resources with embedded intelligence, and desires, which guide the exploitation or appropriation of the resources' affordances. Pea also raises important questions about the aims of education through his distinction between effects *of* and effects *with* technology and solitary and collaborative performance with tools. He sees technological tools as expanding intelligence, not relocating it and learners as designers of tools (Pea, 1993). Like Lave and Wenger he considers the effect on action and purposes for action of the opaqueness or the visibility and invisibility, of technological tools (Lave and Wenger, 1991).

Through his work on the aircraft pilot's checklist, Bazerman shows how a text can 'organize and regulate' activity, including the 'relations and interactions among participants' (Bazerman, 1997). Salomon sees means of communication as having a reciprocal influence on interaction between individual and distributed cognitions. He considers how 'powers afforded by writing systems transform cognitive processes which, in turn, affect the kinds of literate activities one engages in, and these, in turn, lead to the development of yet more powerful means of communication' (Salomon, 1993b). Prior, who like Pea and Wertsch adopts Gibson's notion of affordances, makes a case for the weakness of defining literacy based on features of texts rather than textual practices, seeing literate activity 'as cultural forms of life saturated with textuality' (Prior, 1997, p. 280). Providing an example of the effect of textual practices on texts, Toulmin points out that the conventions for writing on parchment were changed to accommodate the practice of reading in the head rather than aloud (Toulmin, 1999). The importance of this work is that it directs attention to learner activity with objects of learning as well as the texts themselves. These questions of what people actually do in learning situations suggest that pedagogic analysis needs to focus on the social dynamics of learning.

Moll and Whitmore have proposed that the *purpose* of formal instruction is to enable children to 'consciously manipulate and voluntarily control crucial sociocultural symbolic systems' (Moll and Whitmore, 1993, p. 20). With Tapia they argue that multiple socially distributed funds of historically accumulated knowledge and networks of relationships form a mediational role along with texts, teaching practices and systems. The consequence is a view of people and their social and cultural worlds as 'embedded in each other' and their thinking as 'irreducible to individual properties, intelligences, or traits' (Moll *et al.*, 1993, p. 162). Moll and his colleagues discovered that Mexican-American households are clustered according to kinship ties and exchange relationships. These clusters of households develop rich funds of knowledge that provide information about practices and resources useful in ensuring the well-being of the households.

In the context of a discussion concerned with activity theory and human computer interaction, Nardi (1996) provides a useful summary of similarities and differences in the situated learning (she uses the descriptor 'situated action') and distributed cognition models. I will draw from this chapter in the following summary which concludes this section.

Situated action models lay emphasis on the way in which activity grows out of a situation. The focus of study becomes situated practices rather than artefacts or social relations or cultural knowledge and values. The basic unit of analysis becomes 'the activity of persons acting in setting'. Attention is given to the development and changes in activities in settings. The emphasis tends to be on particular events rather than more general enduring patterns of change.

Distributed cognition is seen by Nardi as concerned with the analysis of the cognitive system composed of individuals and the artefacts that they use. The functioning of the distributed cognitive system is the central unit of analysis.

In part it carries the legacy of cognitive science whereas situated models owe more to anthropology. Distributed cognition is more concerned with structure, internal and external representations and transformations of these representations. The search is often for stable principles which may inform designs for use across settings. It also seeks to study the patterns of co-ordination of persons and artefacts.

Nardi argues the two approaches differ in the extent to which goals shape action. For the distributed cognition theorists there is much more emphasis on conscious human or systemic goals whereas situated learning theorists argue that goals are not priors to action. They are seen as retrospective speculations following action. These differences in the way that the structuring of activity is theorised lead to differences in application. One approach, distributed cognition, lends itself more to comparative studies whereas the radically situated nature of the other renders comparison problematic at best or to some extent irrelevant.

A concomitant of the latter is that one approach tends to seek for persistent structures. On the other hand, the radical interpretation of a situated account would not posit, or rather be concerned with, structures that transfer or persisted across situations (Nardi, 1996).

In Chapter 4 I will discuss the applications of the 'communities of practice' concept to education along with other examples of pedagogic practice which seek to apply insights developed from the perspectives of situated learning and distributed cognition theorists. I will now move to a discussion of the two broad fields of theoretical work which dominate the post-Vygotskian field. One, activity theory, has much in common with distributed cognition; the other, sociocultural approach, is more closely aligned with the situated approach. They differ in the relative emphasis they place on particular forms or means of mediation.

Mediation: activity or semiotic means?

Activity theory posits psychological development and thus psychological analysis as grounded in practical cultural activities. The symbolic approach understands psychology in terms of collective symbols and concepts. The individualistic approach emphasises individual construction of psychological functions from collective symbols and artefacts.

See Table 3.1 for the strengths and weaknesses of the three approaches to cultural psychology as tabulated by Ratner (1999).

The distinctions drawn in the table provide a useful summary and point of departure for the discussion of tensions and differences which exist in these aspects of the post-Vygotskian field. I will now use a series of quotes from major researchers in this field to illustrate the differences between positions that have been taken up. This is not the place to speculate on the reasons why these individuals have developed ideas in the ways that they have. However, the basic principles of the theory would lead to a suspicion that these may, in part, be ascribed to the cultural circumstances and the communities of practice in which they are located.

Table 3.1 Strengths and weaknesses of three approaches to cultural psychology

Approach	Strengths	Weaknesses
Symbolic	• Emphasises cognitive basis of psychological processes • Elaborates social content of psychological processes • Recognises social construction and sharing of concepts	• Overlooks practical activities, artefacts and conditions • Symbols appear arbitrary • Minimises individual differences in concepts and processes • Indefinite process of social construction
Personal	• Emphasises individual agency in constructing psychological phenomena from social influences • Emphasises individual differences in psychological phenomena	• Overlooks practical activities, artefacts and conditions which affect psychology • Overlooks organised social action necessary to alter cultural and psychological phenomena
Activity	• Emphasises action rather than pure cognition • Emphasises tools • Emphasises social agency • Recognises heterogeneity of psychological processes	• Activity and tools are conceived as devoid of social content • Unclear about how activity organises psychological processes • Minimises individual agency

In Chapter 1 I discussed the importance of mediation within the framework of the Vygotskian thesis. I referred to the differences that have arisen, or been supposed, between approaches which lay emphasis on semiotic means of mediation and those which privilege an analysis of activity. I used the following quote from Engeström to suggest the complexity of the development of these supposedly distinct forms of analysis. Here Engeström is arguing that the positioning of Leont'ev, one of the progenitors of activity theory, as someone who took no account of semiotic mediation, was and is erroneous.

> A careful reading of Leont'ev's work reveals that both mediation by signs and subject–subject relations do play an important role in his theory. Proponents of the cultural–historical school repeatedly point out that communication is an inherent aspect of all object-related activities. Leont'ev's account of the emergence of speech and language emphasises the original unity of labour actions and social intercourse. . . . So, there is a curious discrepancy between the ways Leont'ev is read by critics and those sympathetic to his ideas.
>
> (Engeström, 1990, p. 7)

Here then is the suggestion that the supposed origins of differences are not responsible for the tensions that have developed. Lave (1993) discusses some of the tensions between some of the research traditions which have been developed.

> The major difficulties of phenomenological and activity theory in the eyes of the other will be plain: those who start with the view that social activity is its own context dispute claims that objective social structures exist other than in their social interactional construction in-situ. Activity theorists argue, on the other hand, that the concrete connectiveness and meaning of activity cannot be accounted for by analysis of the immediate situation.
>
> (Lave, 1993, p. 20)

The terms that are used to describe these positions are not without their problems. I have already discussed the distributed–situated tension. The field abounds with descriptors such as 'sociocultural psychology', 'cultural historical activity theory', etc. each of which has been defined with great care. However, confusions persist alongside what still appear to be genuine differences of emphasis. The emphasis on the historical plane is thought by some to have been diminished in the relocation of theories from Russian to Western academic cultures.

> We would agree that 'cultural-historical' and 'sociohistorical' are more appropriate terms when referring to the heritage we recognize from Vygotsky, Leont'ev, Luria, and many other Soviet psychologists. However, we believe that 'sociocultural' is a better term when it comes to dealing with how this heritage has been appropriated in contemporary debates in the human sciences, at least in the West.
>
> (Wertsch et al., 1995, p. 6)

However they continue to assert that:

> The goal of a sociocultural approach is to explicate the relationships between human action, on the one hand, and the cultural, institutional, and historical situations in which this action occurs on the other.
>
> (Wertsch et al., 1995, p. 11)

This position has led Wertsch (1998) to advance the case for the use of mediated action as a unit of analysis in sociocultural research because, in his view, it provides a kind of natural link between action, including mental action, and the cultural, institutional and historical context in which such action occurs. This is so because the mediational means, or cultural tools, are inherently situated, culturally, institutionally and historically.

As Cole (1996) remarks: 'So the level of activity is present in Wertsch's formulation; it is simply backgrounded when it is focused on mediated action.' Engeström (1993) points out the danger of the relative under-theorising of context: 'Individual experience is described and analysed as if consisting of relatively discrete and situated actions while the system or objectively given context of which those actions are a part is either treated as an immutable given or barely described at all' (Engeström, 1993, p. 66).

Cole tries to develop a middle line between the two traditions. 'Mediated action and its activity contexts are two moments of a single process, and whatever we want to specify as psychological processes is but a moment of their combined properties. It is possible to argue how best to parse their contribution in individual cases, in practice, but attempting such a parse "in general" results in empty abstractions, unconstrained by the circumstances' (Cole, 1996, p. 334).

It is with this caveat in mind that I will now discuss the sociocultural and activity theory approaches within the post-Vygotskian field.

Sociocultural approaches

Wertsch (1991) provides a very clear exposition of his approach to analysing how specific forms of mental functioning reflect and reproduce concrete social, cultural and historical settings. As I noted above, Werstch *et al.* (1995) decided to use the term sociocultural to refer to the future for their own work whilst recognising that the term socio-historical was an important reference to what they saw as the Vygotskian heritage.

In Werstch's (1991, 1998) hands the sociocultural emphasis on the use of cultural tools in mediated action is revealed in studies of how humans employ speech in the course of particular forms of action. The Vygotskian heritage is evidenced in the focus on the mediational function and capacity of speech. At the centre of Wertsch's work is the concept of mediated action, predicated on the idea of a basic 'irreducible' description of agency as 'individual(s)-*acting*-with-mediational-means' (Wertsch, 1991), or 'individual(s)-*operating*-with . . .' [my italics] (Wertsch and Tulviste, 1996; Wertsch *et al.*, 1993; Wertsch, 1998). For Wertsch an important aspect of agency is the concept of teleological action: the notion that actors achieve their goals through decisions among alternative courses of action, choosing means that have the promise of being successful in the given situation and applying them in a suitable manner (Wertsch, 1991, p. 9). He maintains that the Bakhtinian construct of ventriloquism is useful 'because it reveals how agency cannot be reduced to an attribute of either the individual or the mediational means in isolation' (Wertsch *et al.*, 1993, p. 346). Beyond the classic example of the blind man with stick he has invoked the performance of the pole vaulter. This example illustrates the ways in which technological changes (the developments in materials from which a pole vaulter's pole is constructed) offer new possibilities for individuals acting with mediational means (ways of vaulting).

In *Mind as Action*, Wertsch (1998) makes ten claims about mediated action, bringing out the tension between agent and means. These claims explicate issues around the material nature of mediational means: their 'affordances' and constraints; the power and authority associated with them; and their use for action not anticipated by the producer. He deals with the multiple goals of action, its developmental paths, the transformation of action by means and the mastery and appropriation by the agent of means.

Wertsch (1998) argues that mediated action typically serves multiple goals and that these may often come into conflict with each other. For example, in many classrooms children are given what are ostensibly unambiguous tasks – such as problem solving in mathematics or science. However, when such problem solving is enacted it may take place in a context where complex matters of identity formation are in play. In some classrooms girls may not wish to present themselves as too adept at mathematics for fear of being positioned as socially unattractive. Boys may not wish to be seen to be trying too hard lest they be perceived as 'uncool'. However, whilst recognising the dynamic tension among the elements of mediated action, Wertsch also offers a rationale for looking at isolated elements of the system in order to analyse how changes in the mix affect the whole (Wertsch, 1998, p. 27). Wertsch's statement that cultural tools are in themselves powerless and only have impact when agents use them (Wertsch, 1998, p. 30), when presented starkly in this way could appear platitudinous. Nevertheless, the statement carries an important reminder about the focus and methods for research on learning resources. In his focus on the materiality of means (including speech) he underlines the way in which the material properties of tools can illuminate 'how internal processes can come into existence and operate' (Wertsch, 1998, p. 31).

Wertsch's ideas about the goals of mediated action are useful in the development of broadly based accounts of pedagogic practice. He suggests that agents have multiple purposes or goals that are often in conflict, that goals arise as part of the 'background framework' or context within which action is carried out and that there may be conflict between the goals of the agent and the embedded goals of the tools. He is interested also in how new forms of mediated action result from emergence of new means and 'unanticipated spin-offs'. Here he notes that tools can emerge in unpredictable ways through mis-use or borrowing from different contexts or through use for purposes different from those which designers intended.

Wertsch also considers issues of power and authority in respect of cultural tools and their use. He describes mediational means as 'differentially imbued with power and authority', 'privileging' and citing Goodnow, imbued with 'cognitive values' (Wertsch, 1998). The notion of cognitive values includes 'why it is that certain knowledge is publicly available and openly taught while other forms or knowledge are not' and why certain types of solutions are more highly regarded than others (Wertsch, 1998, p. 66). He suggests that the 'emergence of new cultural tools transforms power and authority' (Wertsch, 1998, p. 65) and that 'forces that go into the production of a cultural tool often play a major role in determining how it will be used' (Wertsch, 1998, p 142). He raises questions about how tools are manipulated by users and what tactics are used for employing others' tools.

In his work Wertsch has explored the relationship between social communicative and individual psychological processes, emphasising the dialogicality or multivoicedness of communication and examining linguistic dimensions of communicative acts. He has developed them through Vygtosky's ideas about sense and meaning, Bakhtin's ideas of heteroglossia, voice and dialogicality (Wertsch, 1985a) and Burke's pentadic approach to action (Wertsch, 1998).

Wertsch's exploration of Vygotsky's ideas about the way in which the inner word extends the boundaries of its own meaning illuminates some of the difficulties that are inherent in communication. He discusses the difficulties caused by scientific discourse aimed, as it is, at constancy across, and independence of contexts. In his development of Bakhtin's work he considers the dynamic tension between the dialogic and univocal functions of texts and the difference between monologic and dialogic models of communication, describing the transmission model (or conduit) as unidirectional and based on monologic assumptions. He draws on Lotman in suggesting that this function is fulfilled best when the codes of the speaker and the listener most completely coincide, which however, he makes clear is rare. In comparison, he returns to Bakhtin's idea of intermediation and Lotman's notion of the text as generative of new meaning, a 'thinking device' (Wertsch, 1991). In his examination of the practice of reciprocal teaching he supports the notion that 'reading involves active, dialogic engagement' (Wertsch, 1998, p. 130). Like Bakhtin, his work assumes that the addressee 'may be temporally, spatially, and socially distant' (Wertsch, 1991, p. 53).

Wertsch considers voice and multivoicedness as important dimensions of the socio-historical context for communication. He explores ideas about given and new information, about knowledge that is not held in common between speakers/writers, and about alterity, intersubjectivity and individual perspectives and how they help to explain how speakers understand or fail to understand each other (Wertsch, 1991, 1998). He considers the range of semiotic options open to a speaker and the reasons for choice of one over another and draws on linguistic theories in his examination of how the use of deictic, common and context-informative referents are associated with levels of intersubjectivity (Wertsch, 1985a).

In his later work Wertsch examines agency from the point of view of the roles that constituents play as revealed through their linguistic expression. His idea of 'discourse referentiality' is helpful in pointing to methods for investigation of communicative acts. This involves consideration of the 'relationship between unique, situated utterances and the contexts in which they occur' and 'how utterances function to presuppose the context of speech in which they occur, on the one hand, or act in a 'performative' capacity to create or entail the context, on the other' (Wertsch, 1998, p. 95). Specifically, he addresses issues to do with the presence/accessibility of the writer/reader in the text and reference to characters where their presence is assumed in the text (Wertsch, 1998).

Learning and development are dealt with by Wertsch and collaborators by building on an interpretation of Vygotsky's work on internalisation and externalisation and Bakhtin's notions of ventriloquism, alterity, resistance, mastery and appropriation (Wertsch and Stone 1985; Wertsch, 1991; Wertsch et al., 1993; Wertsch and Tulviste, 1996; Wertsch, 1998). Wertsch and Stone differentiate cognitive mastery from appropriation and use both terms in preference to internalisation, a concept which they argue implies a Piagetian model of transmission, assimilation and accommodation. They see the process of learning as involving construction, rather than copying and being dependent upon mastery of the cultural system of symbolic representation (Wertsch and Stone, 1985). Appropriation can involve resistance to the social setting which includes the cultural tool and Wertsch suggests that 'development often occurs through using a cultural tool before an agent fully understands what this cultural tool is or how it works' (Wertsch, 1998, p. 132). He regards conscious reflection as an important element in development within mediated action.

> Mediational means are often used with little or no conscious reflection. Indeed, it is often only when confronted with a comparative example that one becomes aware of an imaginable alternative. This conscious awareness is one of the most powerful tools available for recognising and changing forms of mediation that have unintended and often untoward consequences.
> (Wertsch, 1991, p. 126)

However, he argues that appropriation of the tool does not depend upon reflection though the degree and types of conscious reflection and voluntary use characterise particular instances of appropriation. Wertsch and Tulviste (1996) talk of creativity, as 'transformation of an existing pattern of action, a new use for an old tool', and Wertsch reminds us that individuals' histories with regard to cultural tools are an element in the development of mediated action. He argues that when Vygotsky uses the term 'mental function' he does so with reference to social interaction and to individual processes. In this sense mental functions may be seen to be carried by groups as well as individuals. Like Pea, he sees ability as the capacity to function with the tool and, citing Middleton, Bartlett, Resnick and Salomon, he also talks of mind being socially distributed, belonging to dyads and larger groups who can think, attend and remember together (Wertsch, 1991, 1998).

Wertsch's (1991) examination of speech genres includes discussion of the privileging of ways of thinking in certain settings; the emergence of particular sets of discourse and cognitive skills through 'exposure to the patterns of speaking and reasoning in formal instructional settings' (Wertsch and Tulviste, 1996), and the silence and distance that authoritative texts induce, compared with the dialogue and contact of internally persuasive discourse (Wertsch, 1998). He considers instructional contexts and the way in which questioning presupposes questions about 'the mastery, possession, and communication of knowledge' (Wertsch, 1998, p. 122). He cites Bruner when considering the importance of narrativity in organising and representing interrelationships of different kinds and as a key to the retention of information through integration of textual information in a coherent schema. Specifically, he sees narrative as a means for 'reflection', 'selection' and 'deflection' of reality (Wertsch, 1998).

Wertsch positions his work against the background of a debate within activity theory about the relative importance of the individual and the collective; relative emphases on the historical, cultural and social and choices that are made between the discourses and practices of the contributing disciplines. He argues that notions of dialogicality, speech genre and social language help 'make it possible to examine concrete intermental and intramental functioning without losing sight of how this functioning is situated in historical, cultural and institutional settings' (Wertsch, 1991, p. 122). Elsewhere he says:

> One of the most important characteristics of an activity is that it is not determined or even strongly circumscribed by the physical or perceptual context in which humans function. Rather, it is a sociocultural interpretation or creation that is imposed on the context by the participant(s).
>
> (Wertsch, 1985, p. 203)

He maintains that a 'focus on mediated action and the cultural tools employed in it makes it possible to "live in the middle" and to address the sociocultural situatedness of action, power and authority' (Wertsch, 1998, p. 65).

In sum, the analysis of mediated action is concerned with how humans employ cultural tools in social and individual processes. Because of its focus on the irreducible tension between agents and cultural tools which defines mediated action, this analysis stands in contrast with others that focus on individuals or on instruments in isolation. Many studies of mediated action are grounded in the ideas of Vygotsky, with the result that analyses of sociocultural situatedness and of language as a cultural tool have been particularly important. Contemporary analyses of mediated action are beginning to go beyond Vygotsky's formulation to examine issues such as the conditions that have given rise to cultural tools, and the constraints as well as affordances associated with them.

As I suggested above, analyses of distributed cognition focus on how humans working with instruments such as computers and how humans working in groups form integrated cognitive systems that cannot be understood by examining the elements of such systems taken separately (e.g. Hutchins, 1995). Analyses of mediated action pursue this line of reasoning by assuming that virtually any human mental process is distributed. Even an individual thinking in seeming isolation typically employs one or another set of linguistic or other semiotic tools, the result being that mediational means shape the performance at hand.

Activity theory

The terms praxis, or 'deyatelnost' in Russian, refer to the notion of practical social activity. Activity theorists seek to analyse the development of consciousness within such practical social activity settings. Their emphasis is on the psychological impacts of organised activity and the social conditions and systems which are produced in and through such activity. This concept has a long intellectual tradition. Lektorsky (1995) traces this heritage and Davydov (1990, 1995) reminds us that the term 'deyatelnost' refers to activity of long duration which has some developmental function and is characterised by constant transformation and change.

Cole (1996) discussed German, Scandinavian/Nordic, North American and Russian traditions in the development of activity theory along with theories which invoke notions of 'practice' (e.g. Giddens, 1979; Bourdieu, 1977) which he distinguished from approaches which had invoked the metaphors of ecology (e.g. Barker and Wright, 1968). This is not the place to engage in a detailed discussion of the similarities and differences within and between these theoretical fields. It is sufficient to note that these approaches have informed many of the developments in post-Vygotskian theory. They all seek to theorise the essence of Vygotsky's work, particularly his denial of the strict separation of the individual and the social. Probably through his reading of Spinoza, Vygotsky insisted that the individual and the cultural should be conceived of as mutually formative elements of a single, interacting system.

> Cultural activity and psychological phenomena depend on and sustain one another. There is no sharp division between them because they are intertwined together. The relationship is like a spiral, where each passes into and builds on the other. Psychological phenomena are the subjective processes of practical cultural activity, and cultural activity is the practical objectified side of psychological phenomena that compose organised social life. In this relationship, practical activity may be the more important moment because it inspires and organizes psychological phenomena. However, activity is never divorced from psychological phenomena.
>
> (Ratner, 1997, p. 114)

In his discussion of the concept of activity in Soviet Psychology, Kozulin (1998) considers the importance of the article written by Vygotsky under the title 'Consciousness as a problem of psychology of behaviour'. It was in this article that Vygotsky sought to restore the concept of consciousness as a legitimate and necessary element of psychology. It had been the subject of study through introspectionism and was deposed by the Russian behaviourists and reflexologists of the late nineteenth and early twentieth century. Vygotsky's distinction between 'subject of study' and 'explanatory principle' is central to his methodological oeuvre.

> If consciousness is to become a subject of psychological study, it cannot simultaneously serve as an explanatory principle. . . . Vygotsky suggested that sociocultural activity serves as such an explanatory source. He thus broke the vicious circle within which the phenomena of consciousness used

to be explained through the concept of consciousness, and similarly behaviour through the concept of behaviour, and established premises for a unified theory of behaviour and mind on the basis of sociocultural activity.

(Kozulin, 1998, p. 11)

Kozulin suggests that, in part, under the influence of philosophical trends which were dominant at the time, Vygotsky came to adopt and subsequently develop the concept of historically concrete human praxis as the explanatory principle. The development of this explanatory principle became one of the politically contested elements of his thesis in the years that followed Vygotsky's death. At times it appeared that the very concept of mediation itself was to be ripped from the framework of ideas which Vygotsky had struggled to put into place. In the hands of the command/control ideologues of the Stalinist era it appeared as though what was left of Russian Psychology would become a theory of determination rather than mediation. Thankfully, the essence of Vygotsky on mediation survived even if it had to be handled covertly at times. The heritage is, as Cole reminds us, of an activity theory within which mediation is a central concept.

The central thesis of the Russian cultural-historical school is that the structure and development of human psychological processes emerge through culturally mediated, historically developing, practical activity.

(Cole, 1996, p. 108)

Where Wertsch and his colleagues foreground the analysis of mediated action, activity theorists tend to foreground analysis of mind within activity systems. There is still some purpose in discussing these traditions as if distinct. However, in that those working within the field increasingly draw on both traditions – using one to compensate for the shortcomings of the other, the distinction is becoming increasingly blurred.

Leont'ev 'focused on those *activities* that eventually lead to the internalisation of external human actions in the form of inner mental processes' (Kozulin, 1996). The search for the appropriate unit of analysis, the 'minimal unit that preserves the properties of the whole' (Davydov and Radzikhovskii, 1985) characterises the divergence on what is the most appropriate focus for study between the various theorists working in activity theory and other sociocultural approaches.

Engeström (1999) discussed three generations of activity theory which have developed in the six decades that have passed since Vygotsky's death. In order to describe the first generation (as shown in Figure 3.1), he used the following representation of the mediated act to relate actors and their intentions to particular outcomes achieved using certain tools.

This first approach drew heavily from Vygotsky's concept of mediation. The triangle in Figure 3.1 represents the way in which Vygotsky brought together cultural artefacts with human actions in order to dispense with the

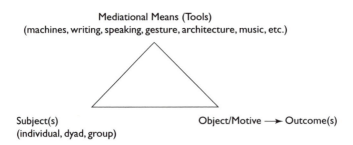

Mediational Means (Tools)
(machines, writing, speaking, gesture, architecture, music, etc.)

Subject(s)   Object/Motive ——► Outcome(s)
(individual, dyad, group)

Figure 3.1 First generation activity theory model.

individual/social dualism. This representation of a Vygotskian view of an activity system concurs with many of the features of the theory discussed in Chapters 1 and 2. During this period studies tended to focus on individuals. Perhaps more importantly they tended not to be grounded in an account of the social structures which themselves act to organise and constrain activity itself. Leont'ev (1978) developed a distinction between the concepts of 'activity' and 'action' which were underdeveloped by Vygotsky. Haenen (1996) provides a detailed discussion of this relationship.

Leont'ev's work on activity involved an elaboration of the notions of object and goal and the centrality of the object to an analysis of motivation. He established the idea that their objects distinguish different activities and that it is the transformation of the object/goal that leads to integration of elements of the activity system (Hakkarainen, 1999). Hood-Holzman (1985) notes the 'misreading' of the Soviet concept of activity with the Meadian concept of action. She acknowledges that at a superficial level there are many individual quotes that may be drawn from the writings of Mead and Vygotsky that appear to signify a general level of concordance. However, she argues that beyond a surface level of analysis lie significant conceptual differences. Wertsch and Lee (1984) also argue that many of the psychological accounts which attempt to discuss factors beyond the individual level of analysis 'tend to equate the social with the intersubjective'. For Engeström, activity is a collective, systemic formation that has a complex mediational structure. An activity system produces actions and is realised by means of actions. However, activity is not reducible to actions. Actions are relatively short-lived and have a temporally clear-cut beginning and end. Activity systems evolve over lengthy periods of socio-historical time, often taking the form of institutions and organisations.[1]

The main thing which distinguishes one activity from another is the difference of their objects (Leont'ev, 1978, p. 62). The shifting and developing object of an activity is related to a motive which drives it. Individual (or group) action is driven by a conscious goal. Although actions are aroused by the motive of the activity, they seem to be directed towards a goal . . . the one and the same action can serve different activities (Leont'ev, 1978, p. 64).

Automatic operations are driven by the conditions and tools available to the action, that is the prevailing circumstances.

> Apart from its (the action's) intentional aspects (what must be done) the action has its operational aspect (how it can be done), which is defined not by the goal itself, but by the objective circumstances under which it is carried out . . . I shall label the means by which an action is carried out its operations.
>
> (Leont'ev, 1972/1981, p. 63)

Leont'ev illustrates his proposed structure of activity (see Figure 3.2) through two well-known examples:

> When members of a tribe are hunting, they individually have separate goals and they are in charge of diverse actions. Some are frightening a herd of animals towards other hunters who kill the game, and other members have other tasks. These actions have immediate goals, but the real motive is beyond hunting. Together these people aim at obtaining food and clothing – at staying alive. To understand why separate actions are meaningful one needs to understand the motive behind the whole activity. Activity is guided by a motive.
>
> (Leont'ev, 1978, pp. 62–3)

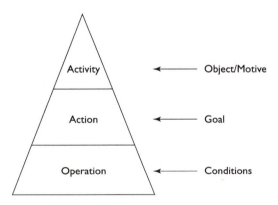

Figure 3.2 The hierarchical structure of activity.

He also offers the following example of learning to drive a car that illustrates the movement from one level of the structure of an activity to another.

> Initially every operation, such as shifting gears, is formed as an action subordinated specifically to this goal and has its own conscious 'orientation basis'. Subsequently action is included in another action, . . . for example,

changing the speed of the car. Shifting gears becomes one of the methods for attaining the goal, the operation that effects the change in speed, and shifting gears now ceases to be accomplished as a goal-oriented process: its goal is not isolated. For the consciousness of the driver, shifting gears in normal circumstances is as if it did not exist. He does something else: he moves the car from a place, climbs steep grades, drives the car fast, stops at a given place, etc. Actually this operation [of shifting gears] may, as is known, be removed entirely from the activity of the driver and be carried out automatically. Generally, the fate of the operation sooner or later becomes the function of the machine.

(Leont'ev, 1978, p. 66)

Arguing from a perspective that is influenced more by sociocultural theory than activity theory, Rogoff (1995) suggests that there are three inseparable, mutually constituting planes of analysis each of which is associated with specific forms of developmental processes.

Table 3.2 Rogoff's planes of analysis

Plane of analysis	Developmental process
Personal	Participatory appropriation
Interpersonal	Guided participation
Community processes	Apprenticeship

There are some parallels here with activity theory. However, the relationships between the planes of analysis are not made clear. The means by which transformation between levels may occur is not fully explicated although implicit in the outline. This transformation between levels is important in activity theory. Leont'ev makes clear his opposition to some 'frozen' notion of hierarchy within an activity structure. Continuous transformation between the three levels is envisaged. Despite all this emphasis on structure, albeit a structure embued with fluidity, there was little attempt to locate activity in rules and structures of the social world.

The second generation

Engeström advocates the study of artefacts 'as integral and inseparable components of human functioning' but he argues that the focus of the study of mediation should be on its relationship with the other components of an activity system (Engeström, 1999, p. 29).

Leont'ev distinguished between the material objective and affective motives of activity, seeing objective purpose as translating motive into a physical act, transforming the internal plane to the external world and driving activity through the formation of goals. After Hegel, he maintained that goals are determined in the course of activity (Engeström, 1999). Operations he saw as the external method used by individuals to achieve goals (Glassman, 1996, p. 323). He argued that motive can be collective but that goals are individual and he explored the idea of partial and overall goals, paving the way for Engeström's expanded version of activity.

In order to progress the development of activity theory Engeström has expanded the original triangular representation of activity systems that was used in the first generation. He did this to enable an examination of systems of activity at the macro level of the collective and the community in preference to a micro level concentration on the individual actor or agent operating with tools. This expansion of the basic Vygotskian triangle aims to represent the social/collective elements in an activity system, through the addition of the elements of community, rules and division of labour whilst emphasising the importance of analysing their interactions with each other. Nevertheless he acknowledges the methodological difficulty of capturing evidence about community, rules and division of labour within the activity system (Engeström, 1999).

In Figure 3.3 the object is depicted with the help of an oval indicating that object-oriented actions are always, explicitly or implicitly, characterised by ambiguity, surprise, interpretation, sense making, and potential for change (Engeström, 1999).

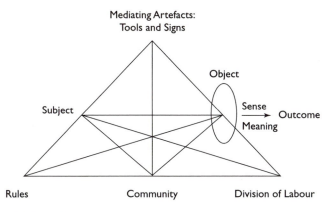

Figure 3.3 Second generation activity theory model.
The structure of a human activity system (Engeström, 1987, p. 78).

The importance of this second generation of activity theory was that it brought interrelations between the individual subject and his or her community into focus. At the same time Engeström drew on Il'enkov (1977) to emphasise the importance of contradictions within activity systems as the driving force of change and thus development.

The historical context of 1930s Russia was one in which social scientists did not regard the question of development as problematic. It was clear to someone such as Vygotsky, charged as he was with improving the lot of street children and other disadvantaged youth groups, that the notion of getting better was unambiguous. Cole (1996) amongst others has suggested that this position is also revealed in a deep-seated insensitivity of the second generation activity theory toward cultural diversity. Questions of diversity and dialogue between different traditions or perspectives have become increasingly serious challenges (Engeström, 1999)

Third generation

Engeström's discussion of the encapsulation of school learning led to his advocating the 'collective of learners' and 'advanced networks of learning' that 'transcend the institutional boundaries of the school' (Engeström, 1996). In a later paper on learning in work teams, Engeström raised the question of whether it is 'possible or desirable' to have a shared object in activity (Engeström, 1999a). Subsequently, in a contribution to the XMCA discussion list, he appeared to have clarified his view. He argued that the subject in collective activity is not always the same person: 'First, it is typically an individual (more seldom a group) who occupies the subject position in any given action. But in the next action (temporally or spatially seen) it may be a different individual member who is the subject.' He maintains that as goals are associated with actions (and thus with individuals), they are not attached to the activity as a whole.

> Activity is achieved through constant negotiation, orchestration and struggle between different goals and perspectives of its participants. The object and motive of a collective activity are something like a constantly evolving mosaic, a pattern that is never fully completed.
>
> (Engeström, 1999b)

He sees the attention of Wertsch and others to sign-mediated individual action in a sociocultural setting as an explicit distancing from 'ideas of historicity, object orientedness, and the collective nature of human activity' (Engeström, 1999b, p. 11). It is Engeström's view that

> artifact-mediated construction of objects . . . is a collaborative and dialogical process in which different perspectives . . . and voices . . . meet, collide and merge. The different perspectives are rooted in different communities and practices that continue to coexist within one and the same collective activity system.
>
> (Engeström, 1999a, p. 382)

Whilst Engeström holds that artefacts are structural to work practices, he and Middleton maintain that they are 'not just there'; they evolve or are replaced and 'there is an ongoing dialectic between what is taken to be structural or processual, stable or dynamic, representational or discursive forms in work practices' (Engeström and Middleton, 1996, p. 4). In his consideration of the mediating role of artefacts, Engeström includes both tools and signs but argues that it is more useful to categorise them by the processes involved in their use than by whether they are external, practical or internal, cognitive ones. He distinguishes between 'what' (naming and descriptive), 'how' (processual), 'why' (diagnostic and explanatory) and 'where to' (speculative or potentialising) artefacts (Engeström, 1999, pp. 381–2).

Engeström (1999) sees joint activity or practice as the unit of analysis for activity theory, not individual activity. He is interested in the process of social transformation and includes the structure of the social world in analysis, taking into account the conflictual nature of social practice. He sees instability (internal tensions) and contradiction as the 'motive force of change and development' (Engeström, 1999, p. 9) and the transitions and reorganisations within and between activity systems as part of evolution; it is not only the subject, but the environment, that is modified through mediated activity. He views the 'reflective appropriation of advanced models and tools' as 'ways out of internal contradictions' that result in new activity systems (Cole and Engeström, 1993, p. 40).

The third generation of activity theory as proposed by Engeström intends to develop conceptual tools to understand dialogues, multiple perspectives and networks of interacting activity systems. He draws on ideas of dialogicality and multivoicedness in order to expand the framework of the second generation. The idea of networks of activity within which contradictions and struggles take place in the definition of the motives and object of the activity calls for an analysis of power and control within developing activity systems. The minimal representation which Figure 3.4 provides shows but two of what may be a myriad of systems exhibiting patterns of contradiction and tension. Engeström (1999b) provides the following example of such a minimal system.

Object moves from an initial state of unreflected, situationally given 'raw material' (object 1; e.g. a specific patient entering a physician's office) to a collectively meaningful object constructed by the activity system (object 2; e.g. the patient constructed as a specimen of a biomedical disease category and thus as an instantiation of the general object of illness/health), and to a potentially shared or jointly constructed object (object 3; e.g. a collaboratively constructed understanding of the patient's life situation and care plan). The object of activity is a moving target, not reducible to conscious short-term goals.

(Engeström, 1999b)

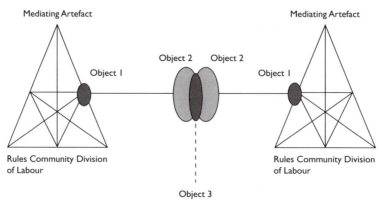

Figure 3.4 Third generation activity theory model.

Engeström has maintained that goals of actions are 'reformulated and revised as one acts, and they are commonly explicated clearly only retrospectively'; he saw the construction and redefinition of the object, as related to the 'creative potential' of activity (Engeström, 1999a, p. 381).

As a theoretical underpinning for analyses of innovative learning Engeström sees the characteristics of activity theory as:

* firstly, 'contextual and oriented at understanding historically specific local practices, their objects, mediating artifacts, and social organization';
* secondly, 'based on a dialectical theory of knowledge and thinking, focused on the creative potential in human cognition'; and
* thirdly, 'a developmental theory that seeks to explain and influence qualitative changes in human practices over time' (Engeström, 1999a, p. 378).

He maintains that it is important to extend beyond the singular activity system and to examine and work towards transformation of networks of activity. To this end he sees potential in the exploration by some activity theorists of 'concepts of *boundary object, translation, and boundary crossing* to analyze the unfolding of object-oriented cooperative activity of several actors, focusing on tools and means of construction of boundary objects in concrete work processes' (Engeström, 1999, p. 7).

Cole and Engeström represent cognition as the 'emergent new state of the subject's knowledge' resulting from the 'analysis and synthesis of (at least) two sources of information in real time', the two being the object already held by the subject and the object as represented through the medium (Cole and Engeström, 1993, p. 7). They posit an 'expansive cycle' which represents a cyclical relationship between internalisation and externalisation within activity that is constantly changing. Their thinking reflects a cultural theory of mind in which cognition is redistributed; there are 'new forms of joint-activity-at-a-distance' and 'thinking occurs as much among as within individuals' (Cole and Engeström, 1993, p. 43). Engeström sees internalisation as related to reproduction of culture and externalisation as the production of new cultural artefacts and he quotes Bhaskar:

> It is no longer true to say that human agents create it [the society]. Rather we must say they reproduce or transform it.
>
> (Engeström, 1999b, p. 10)

Engeström suggests that an expansive cycle 'begins with the questioning by individuals of accepted practice, and it gradually expands into a collective move- ment or institution', though he acknowledges that a full expansive cycle is not common (Engeström, 1999a, p. 383). Conflict and questioning or dissatisfaction are central to his notion of development; out of them, he argues, transformation of practice grows. This is a position that has particular relevance to the examination of practice that centres on the lay/professional relationships.

The notion that there is a historical dimension to learning activity is related to the fact that Engeström sees its object as being 'social productive practice, or the social life-world, in its full diversity and complexity'. He maintains that productive practice 'exists in its present dominant form as well as in its historically more advanced and earlier, already surpassed forms' and that learning activity is directed towards the interaction of these forms (Miettinen, 1999, p. 331).

Much of Engeström's work involves developmental intervention based research. He argues that research has a dialectical, dialogic relationship with activity and he focuses on contradictions as causative and disturbances as indi- cators of potential. He sees interventions as enabling the construction of new instrumentalities, and the bringing about through externalisation the 'trans- formative construction of new instruments and forms of activity at collective and individual levels' (Engeström, 1999b, p. 11). He suggests that activity theory may be summarised with the help of five principles. They stand as a manifesto of the current state of activity theory:

> The first principle is that a collective, artifact-mediated and object-oriented activity system, seen in its network relations to other activity systems, is taken as the prime unit of analysis. Goal directed individual and group actions, as well as automatic operations, are relatively independent but subordinate units of analysis, eventually understandable only when interpreted against the background of entire activity systems. Activity systems realize and reproduce themselves by generating actions and operations.
>
> The second principle is the multi-voicedness of activity systems. An activity system is always a community of multiple points of view, traditions and

interest. The division of labour in an activity creates different positions for the participants, the participants carry their own diverse histories, and the activity system itself carries multiple layers and strands of history engraved in its artifacts, rules and conventions. The multi-voicedness is multiplied in networks of interacting activity systems. It is a source of trouble and a source of innovation, demanding actions of translation and negotiation.

The third principle is historicity. Activity systems take shape and get transformed over lengthy periods of time. Their problems and potentials can only be understood against their own history. History itself needs to be studied as local history of the activity and its objects, and as history of the theoretical ideas and tools that have shaped the activity. Thus, medical work needs to be analysed against the history of its local organization and against the more global history of the medical concepts, procedures and tools employed and accumulated in the local activity.

The fourth principle is the central role of contradictions as sources of change and development. Contradictions are not the same as problems or conflicts. Contradictions are historically accumulating structural tensions within and between activity systems. The primary contradiction of activities in capitalism is that between the use value and exchange value of commodities. This primary contradiction pervades all elements of our activity systems. Activities are open systems. When an activity system adopts a new element from the outside (for example, a new technology or a new object), it often leads to an aggravated secondary contradiction where some old element (for example, the rules or the division of labor) collides with the new one. Such contradictions generate disturbances and conflicts, but also innovate attempts to change the activity.

The fifth principle proclaims the possibility of expansive transformations in activity systems. Activity systems move through relatively long cycles of qualitative transformations. As the contradictions of an activity system are aggravated, some individual participants begin to question and deviate from its established norms. In some cases, this escalates into collaborative envisioning and a deliberate collective change effort. An expansive transformation is accomplished when the object and motive of the activity are reconceptualized to embrace a radically wider horizon of possibilities than in the previous mode of the activity. A full cycle of expansive transformation may be understood as a collective journey through the zone of proximal development of the activity.

(Engeström, 1999b, pp. 4–5)

Conclusion

In this chapter I have discussed four of the many approaches to the discussion of the social formation of mind that have developed on the basis of Vygotsky's work. They are not discrete positions in that they tend to inform each other. They tend to emphasise particular aspects of the theoretical legacy that was bequeathed by Vygotsky. Within each of these broad fields of writing there are, of course, many differences, debates and disagreements. I am aware that this short review cannot do justice to the entire range. My purpose has been more to sketch the outline in order to provide a framework for the consideration of applications. In this way the focus on situated learning, or distributed cognition, on mediated action or activity as the means of mediation within the analysis of classroom practice becomes rooted in the prior assumptions and dilemmas within the theoretical field. In Chapter 5 I will take the discussion a little further when I outline my own suggestions for the extension of some of these ideas with a specific reference to the expanded definition of pedagogy that I outlined in Chapter 1. This discussion will focus on some of what I regard as the constraints of some aspects of activity theory when it is applied to pedagogic practice. In Chapter 4 I will consider some of the pedagogic applications of these theories that have been developed in recent years.

Note

1 http://www.helsinki.fi/~jengestr/activity/6a.htm

Applications of sociocultural and activity theory to education

In this chapter I will discuss some recent pedagogic applications of post-Vygotskian theory. There are two main points of departure in this discussion. The first is concerned with the analysis of knowledge content within pedagogic exchange. This section is influenced by the distinction between scientific and everyday concepts. The second section takes the concept of the Zone of Proximal Development (ZPD) as the starting point of a discussion of interaction and process. I recognise that this is a somewhat artificial way of categorising the myriad of applications of Vygotsky's work. I am using it as a way of identifying the strengths and limitations of the work.

Content based approaches

Nelson (1995) argues for three levels of knowledge organisation in human thought. One level is constructed through direct experience without the intervention of language. The second level involves the use of language in particular community. This is culturally organised knowledge that is distinguished from formally organised theoretical knowledge. The former is acquired informally, the latter has to be 'mastered as an abstract system' (Nelson, 1995, p. 245). This three-level model contains a direct reference to the scientific/everyday distinction that I discussed in Chapter 2. The linkage between the nature of knowledge and the form of acquisition is of particular significance to the discussion of pedagogy. The Russian academic, V.V. Davydov is often associated with the development of an approach to teaching and learning within which the analysis of theoretical knowledge is central. As Hedegaard and Chaiklin (1990) remind us, this body of work identifies the general developmental potential of particular forms of teaching as well as its specific microgenetic function.

> First, following Vygotsky, Davydov argues that teaching plays an essential role in the mental development of the child. That is, not only should formal instruction contribute to the acquisition of special abilities and knowledge but it should also contribute to children's general mental development.

Good teaching develops a capacity for relating to problems in a theoretical way, and to reflect on one's thinking. Second, Davydov develops an extensive analysis of theoretical knowledge grounded in a materialist-dialectical philosophy. This concept contrasts with the concept of knowledge and thinking used by the cognitive and Piagetian traditions because it emphasises that knowledge is constituted by the relations between the object of knowledge and other objects, rather than some essential properties or characteristics that define the object. Third, Davydov describes in theory and in practice how to use this theory of knowledge in specific teaching programs.

(Hedegaard and Chaiklin, 1990, p. 153)

Davydov (1988, 1990, 1995) insisted that the tradition of teaching empirical knowledge should be changed to a focus on teaching theoretical knowledge and he developed a 'Developmental Teaching' programme which pursued this goal. The connection between the spontaneous concepts that arise through empirical learning and the scientific concepts that develop through theoretical teaching is seen as the main dimension of the ZPD. The process of 'ascending from the abstract to the concrete' which formed the core of Davydov's early work has been extended by Hedegaard into a conceptualisation of teaching and learning as a 'double move' between situated activity and subject matter concepts. When working within this approach, general laws are used by teachers to formulate instruction and children investigate the manifestations of these general laws in carefully chosen examples which embody core concepts. These core concepts constitute the 'germ cell' of subsequent developments. In practical activity children grapple with central conceptual relations which underpin particular phenomena. In this way the teaching focuses directly on the scientific concepts that constitute the subject matter. Kozulin's description of the general approach perhaps underplays the significance of the term 'development of thinking'.

Content-based programs presuppose that teaching thinking should be firmly embedded in the content material. In its most consistent form, content-based cognitive education was realized by Davydov (1988) and other neo-Vygotskians in the Soviet Union and Eastern Europe. These neo-Vygotskians argued that in a properly designed and implemented curriculum, the development of thinking should be the inherent and, therefore, internal element. This thesis is based on the assumption of the theoretical nature of formal learning.

(Kozulin, 1998, p. 81)

Cole and Griffin (1983) make an important distinction between skills and activity in the context of an extended discussion concerning that content which may be regarded as basic within the curriculum. They draw on an interpretation of Vygotsky which insists that he proposed a holistic approach within which the unit of study must be psychological activity in all its complexity. The key point is that the unit of study must retain the meaning of the activity. The emphasis in their writing is placed on the teaching and acquisition of skills within authentic and meaningful events. The importance of the interplay between the scientific concepts derived in theoretical learning and the spontaneous concepts formed in empirical learning is central to this account of development. If the two forms do not 'connect' then true concept development does not take place. Thus, theoretically driven content based teaching which is not designed to connect with learners' everyday empirical learning will remain inert and developmentally ineffective. The importance of this distinction between teaching which serves an ontogenetic purpose and teaching which remains valuable at the microgenetic level alone was discussed in Chapter 2.

Ivic (1989) insists that Vygotsky's emphasis was not on the transmission and acquisition of a body of information alone. He was concerned with the provision through education, of the tools, techniques and intellectual operations that would facilitate development. He was critical of many forms of education that seemed to remain content with the transmission of knowledge.

> School does not always teach systems of knowledge but in many cases overburdens its pupils with isolated and meaningless facts; school curricula do not incorporate tools and intellectual techniques, all too often schools do not provide a setting for social interactions conducive to knowledge construction.
>
> (Ivic, 1989, p. 434)

This position was clearly established in some of Davydov's later writing. It is important to note that this text was written some five years after the fundamental changes had taken place in the former Soviet Union. There were many points in his career when Davydov fell foul of the political scrutiny that existed under the former regime. His emphasis on creativity in the following extract may well have proved somewhat difficult for his political masters at a time when the place of the individual and subjectivity was undervalued and even repressed within the command control consciousness of the past. Here he discusses his pedagogic contribution to the reform of the Soviet system of education. The key references here are to:

- the development of the whole personality, which as discussed in Chapter 2, always retains a profoundly social characteristic in the Russian language and culture;
- creative potential – thus signalling a profound distance from ideologies of determination;
- the emphasis on values;
- the facilitative rather than dominating role of the pedagogue;
- and lastly, the need to respond to the diversity of learners with an appropriately diverse range of approaches.

For the contemporary reform of Russian education, the following general ideas of Vygotsky are basic, ideas that have been set forth and made more precise by his students and followers. The first idea is that education, which includes both human teaching/learning and upbringing, is intended first of all to develop their personalities. The second idea is that the human personality is linked to its creative potentials; therefore, the development of the personality in the education system demands first of all the creation of conditions for discovering and making manifest the creative potentials of students. The third idea is that teaching/learning and upbringing assume personal activity by students as they master a variety of inner values; the student becomes a true subject in the process of teaching and upbringing. The fourth idea is that the teacher and the upbringer direct and guide the individual activity of the students, but they do not force or dictate their own will to them. Authentic teaching/learning and upbringing come through collaboration by adults with children and adolescents. The fifth idea is that the most valuable methods for students' teaching/learning and upbringing correspond to their development and individual particularities, and therefore these methods cannot be uniform.

(Davydov, 1995, p. 13)

In the recently published *Educational Psychology*, Vygotsky announced that 'the fundamental prerequisite of pedagogics inevitably demands an element of individualisation, that is, conscious and rigorous determination of the individualised goals of education for each pupil' (Vygotsky, 1997b, p. 324). This suggestion of responsiveness to diversity rather than imposition of 'sameness' in learning and development has still to permeate many practices in the field. Davydov's programme advocates pedagogic responsiveness to an individual learner within a framework that is supported by concepts of theoretical knowledge. This framework has a distinctly Russian cultural emphasis. Alternatives have developed outside the former Soviet Union. Bruner (1996) is one of many commentators who have drawn attention to the broad range of approaches that attract the label 'metacognitive'.

Modern pedagogy is moving increasingly to the view that the child should be aware of her own thought processes, and that it is crucial for the pedagogical theorist and teacher alike to help her to become more meta-cognitive – to be as aware of how she goes about her learning and thinking as she is about the subject matter she is studying. Equipping her with a good theory of mind . . . is one part of helping her to do so.

(Bruner, 1996, p. 64)

In a paper that provides what is essentially a geographically and politically boundaried account of the development and implementation of the concept of mediation, Karpov and Haywood (1998) distinguished between metacognitive mediation and cognitive mediation. Metacognitive mediation refers to children's acquisition of semiotic tools of self-regulation, self-planning, self-monitoring, self-checking and self-evaluating. They summarise Vygotsky's ideas on the development of self-regulation in children as follows: (a) someone regulates the child's behaviour by the use of external speech; (b) the child regulates someone else's behaviour by the use of external speech, and regulates his or her own behaviour by using egocentric speech; (c) the child regulates his or her own behaviour by inner speech. Here children's use of semiotic tools, such as speech, for regulating the behaviour of others in the course of joint activity is itself a powerful facilitator of the child's acquisition of those tools. Karpov and Haywood define cognitive mediation in terms of the child's acquisition of cognitive tools that are necessary to solving subject domain problems.

Serpell (1999) suggests that the emphasis in North American writing on what Karpov and Haywood term 'metacognitive mediation' has arisen from a dissatisfaction with Piaget's emphasis on the child's direct interaction with the physical world. He argues that many neo-Vygotskian analyses in the US have focused on how the focal child interacts with adults and older children in learning about the physical world. Vygotsky's writing is thus taken as a justification for understanding the child's developing cognition within a social context. The theoretical move to Vygotsky was invoked to counter the conception of individual mind in isolation, and the tendency to objectify scientific knowledge. Serpell asks why this emphasis was not present in the Soviet setting and suggests that such assertions were deeply embedded assumptions which did not require explicit attention within the cultural circumstances that obtained at that time.

Karpov and Haywood argue that, in their enthusiasm for elaborating Vygotsky's other type of mediation (termed 'cognitive') into a 'theoretical learning' approach to the design of instruction, Russian researchers have 'underestimate(ed) . . . the role of students' collaborative problem-solving activity' (Karpov and Haywood, 1998, p. 33). As Serpell notes, their interpretation of the Soviet work relies heavily on unproblematised use of the concept of 'internalisation'.

Wells (1994a, b) identifies one of the many criticisms that have frequently been levelled against Vygotsky's theory of school instruction. This is the suggestion that it is more concerned with cultural transmission than it is with cultural renewal and the encouragement of innovation and diversity. This is certainly the tone of the article by Cobb et al. (1996) who, along with Steffe (1996), argue that a reconciliation of sociocultural theory with Piaget's genetic epistemology could be one way of bringing together the supposedly 'macro' activity theory with the 'micro' constructivist classroom level analysis which privileges the study of the detail of interaction. From my perspective this would entail developing models of description of the 'macro' which could be directly related to predictions for the 'micro'. Of the many descriptions of 'constructivism' that abound it is possible to find those which espouse some form of neo-Kantian inevitability at the level of the individual as well as those which appear as some form of social determinism. It would seem to me that the very essence of Vygotsky's work is to assert that neither is appropriate. The key would seem to lie in asking questions about the social constraints and affordances that create the possibilities for the construction of individual understanding. As discussed in Chapter 2, Valsiner's work on a refined model of the ZPD is one way of approaching this issue. As yet we are without ways of describing and analysing the types of social circumstances, as for example in Valsiner's extended model of ZPD, that give rise to the possibility of specific forms of individual develop-ment. The connections that Cobb *et al.* discuss may or may not be referenced to predetermined developmental pathways which may be followed as individuals construct understandings with the benefit of experience in particular socio-cultural contexts. If connections are to be made between sociocultural circumstances and individual development which is not constrained by some form of logico-mathematical route map, then much more needs to be done to articulate the structuring of the social circumstances which will allow us to consider the probabilities and possibilities for individuals.

Wells (1994a, b) also argues that, in its emphasis on the immediate context of interpersonal interaction, Vygotsky's theory ignores the larger cultural and historical context of the activity systems and ideologies, both local and societal, within which this interaction occurs. The activity theorists, as noted in Chapter 2, robustly refute this criticism. Chapter 5 will explore the extent to which the broader pedagogic implications of the theory have been truly exploited. Wells (1994a) further suggested that the learning of school knowledge, and specifically the development of scientific concepts, tends to be treated as an end in itself. He proposes rather it should be understood as the appropriation and further development of a set of tools that is used for problem solving in the achievement of goals that the students find personally significant. As is clear from my references to his work, Davydov's (1995) paper attempts a response to this challenge.

Kozulin (1998) provides a number of clear examples of approaches to 'cognitive education' which have some basis in Vygotsky's work. He includes the mediating learning experience/instrumental enrichment thesis developed by Reuven Feuerstein within this portfolio of examples. This, almost clinical, approach contrasts with the emphasis to be found in the essay that Kozulin (1998) offers on literature as a psychological tool in chapter six of his book. Feuerstein's work may be characterised by its abstract nature. It represents one of many attempts to identify and analyse those aspects of upbringing, or to use his term 'mediated learning experience', which may be provided in a decontextualised format to those who have not acquired specific skills and orientations through their own everyday experience. On the other hand, Kozulin's work on literature presents a strong case for a very rich understanding of the formative and shaping effect of cultural artefacts, such as books and plays, in social life. Here the emphasis is on literature as mediational means. Vygotsky's insistence that it is not words in and of themselves that are important but the capacity for carrying and shaping meaning that has a formative effect is pertinent

Knowledge, knowledge production and knowing

In a recent book Wells (1999) asks what we mean by knowledge and under what conditions are children best able to construct it. He suggests that in order to understand the nature of knowledge we should focus on the activity of knowing. Here knowing is defined as

> the intentional activity of individuals who, as members of a community, make use of and produce representations in the collaborative attempt to better understand and transform their shared world.
>
> (Wells, 1999, p. 76)

Scardamalia and Bereiter (1991, 1996) suggest that the kind of education that will best prepare students for life in a knowledge society should foster:

- flexibility;
- creativity;
- problem-solving ability;
- technological literacy;
- information-finding skills; and
- a lifelong readiness to learn.

As Scardamalia and Bereiter argue, the idea of students as participants, along with teachers and perhaps others, in a collaborative enterprise, has been around at least since Dewey, but it has been taking a more definite shape over the past decade in various experimental programmes. The new approaches are all to some extent based on the model of the scientific research team.

Brown and Campione (1990, 1994) have used the term 'fostering communities of learners' to characterise the very impressive approach they have developed. In it, teaching and learning are closely intertwined. In a typical activity, different groups of students research different aspects of a topic and then prepare materials that they use to instruct the members of the other groups. A robust application of the scientific research team model is in what Bereiter and Scardamalia call 'collaborative knowledge building' (after Scardamalia *et al.*, 1994; Scardamalia and Bereiter, 1991, 1996).

Therefore, if the future lies in schools as knowledge-building organisations we need to rethink teaching by examining the relationships between cognition and context and between learning and knowledge production. In a recent discussion of this area of work my colleagues in the SAT centre, Anne Edwards and Stewart Ranson, suggest that the following become points for consideration when such developments are being planned:

1   *Learning occurs through engaged participation in the activities of knowledge communities.* Participation involves both the use and production of knowledge and a disposition to engage. The current policy agenda, aimed at social

inclusion through economic participation in a knowledge-based economy, calls for a pedagogy which addresses students' self-beliefs and knowledge use and production in and out of school (Osin and Lesgold, 1996; Bentley, 1998).

2   *Teaching involves informed interpretations of and responses to students' orientations to knowledge.* Teaching is therefore a complex activity which demands that teachers interpret students' constructions of opportunities for engagement and select responses which assist that engagement. Effective teaching is informed by knowledge of pupils, knowledge of disciplines and knowledge of pedagogy. But how that knowledge is used and produced remains contested (Wells, 1999). While in discussions of pedagogy, we lack those 'middle level concepts' with which teachers' knowledge might be shared, used and developed. However, if these middle level concepts are to be developed, this is most likely to occur at the sites of practice in conversations about practice (Greeno *et al.*, 1996; Hirst, 1996).

3   *Schools as sites of teachers' knowledge use and production need to understand the range of orientations to knowledge held within them and how they originated.* Understanding relationships between historically formed institutional knowledge and the pedagogies of practitioners will assist the implementation of innovatory practices. We therefore need to know more about how schools interpret and respond to the situational affordances of their internal and their wider communities as they work to engage students as learners. It is clear that pedagogies which respond to the shifting demands of a fast-moving knowledge economy will best be developed in schools which are capable of using and producing new knowledge (Edwards *et al.*, 2000).

According to Scardamalia and Bereiter (1996) the primary function of schooling should become construction of collective knowledge in 'problem-based learning' and 'project-based learning'. They place emphasis on the distinction between knowledge content residing in people's minds and knowledge as resource or knowledge as product. This could be interpreted, erroneously, as a call for the 'project based' approach that typified much of what was termed the 'progressive' teaching within which empirical learning was not always connected with the power of culturally powerful scientific concepts. Bereiter's (1997) critique of situated cognition theory cautions against the treating all knowledge as situated and denying or ignoring the possibility of the existence of knowledge objects. His approach to knowledge building retains an emphasis on working with knowledge objects. Wells (1999) places more emphasis on the processes of coming to know that transcend particular forms of knowing.

One way of describing the difference in emphasis that is to be seen in the work of Wells and that of Bereiter is between dispositions and knowledge objects. Both refer more or less explicitly to both matters. Bereiter foregrounds knowledge objects:

> The knowledge that is being worked with is not situated knowledge. It is knowledge that has been transformed into objects that can be treated or used in an unlimited variety of situations. Thus, knowledge is no longer bound to the situations in which it was constituted.
>
> (Bereiter, 1997, p. 298)

He also refers to 'unnatural cognitive actions performed by logic machines' which should not be seen as a reference to disposition but is most certainly a reference to the practice of knowledge building.

> In order to work effectively with knowledge objects, people have to master the practices of nonsituated cognition. This means learning to carry out the sorts of unnatural cognitive actions performed by logic machines. This does not mean becoming less human; it means acquiring a special set of skills to use wisely or unwisely, imaginatively or ploddingly, as we do with the many other intellectual, practical, and social skills that constitute human competence.
>
> (Bereiter, 1997, p. 298)

Wells (1999) appears to suggest that the pedagogic task is to ensure that participants acquire dispositions that transcend contexts.

> The manner in which classroom activities are selected and organized should not only lead students to construct a personal understanding of the topics involved that equips them to participate effectively and responsibly in similar and related activities beyond the classroom, but it should also encourage the development of the disposition and the necessary strategies to adopt the same stance independently in new and unfamiliar situations.
>
> (Wells, 1999, p. 91)

The difference here is on the emphasis that is placed on what it is that is acquired that permits the learner to operate outside the immediate pedagogic context.

Wells (1999) brings this debate back to a Vygotskian root in his reference to the complex relationship between inner and outer speech and, ultimately, sense and meaning. He proposes a model in which modes of knowing (procedural, substantive, aesthetic, theoretical, meta) are seen in relation to the different opportunities that are available for making meaning (experience, information, knowledge building, understanding).

> Information and knowledge building involve public meanings and representations mediated by culturally conventional semiotic systems; they are oriented outward, as it were, to the social world of discursive interaction. Experience and understanding, by contrast, are inner oriented; they are

concerned with the individual's more direct and intuitive involvement in the world as encountered in the particularities of his or her own life trajectory. Thus, if we were to superimpose Vygotsky's distinction between 'social' and 'inner' speech on this model, social speech would be associated with information and knowledge building, whereas it is with experience and understanding that the idiosyncratic, sense-imbued nature of inner speech and imaging would be most closely related.

(Wells, 1999, p. 87)

There are a number of interventions that are seen as having a Vygotskian root. Some were initiated from a clear theoretical base and others have, as it were, 'grown into' the theory. Equally, some make claims to such inspiration, which are quite hard to detect. The distinctions between knowledge, knowledge production and modes of knowing constitute significant areas of contestation within modern pedagogic theory. The differences of emphasis on knowledge objects, disposition or knowledge building actions and skills should not detract from the importance of rethinking learning in the context of knowledge building. Bringing this emphasis to bear on the important insights that Vygotsky's work on scientific concepts has raised remains a challenge. If knowledge building results in only empirical learning then the Vygotskian thesis will have been used to defeat itself.

Having outlined some of the debates in the selection of content and perspectives on knowledge I will now move to consider some of the issues that are raised when one adopts a Vygotskian perspective on the notion of support for learning which either explicitly or implicitly refers to the ZPD model.

Scaffolding

In the following section I will discuss a number of interventions such as 'scaffolding' and 'reciprocal teaching' which have much in common. However, their commonality has been achieved through somewhat different trajectories.

Because of Vygotsky's influence, we are now hearing more about such concepts as cognitive apprenticeships (Collins *et al.*, 1989), reciprocal teaching (Palincsar and Brown, 1984), and situated learning (Lave and Wenger, 1991). In all of these cases, the teacher (or more capable adult or peer) plays a critical role in guiding the child's participation in activities intended to increase his or her understanding of a particular concept.

(Emihovich and Souza Lima, 1995, p. 378)

In an important review of the field, Stone (1998) notes that the term 'scaffolding' was originally used as an instructional metaphor in a largely pragmatic and a theoretical manner. He suggests that Cazden (1979) was the first writer to make an explicit reference to Vygotsky's work in connection with the term. Wood *et al.* (1976) had previously defined scaffolding as a form of adult assistance that enables a child or novice to solve a problem, carry out a task or achieve a goal which would be beyond his unassisted efforts. They envisaged a process whereby the adult controlled those elements of the task that were initially beyond the learner's capacity, thus allowing the learner to complete those that were within existing capabilities. The overall emphasis here is on the creation of a pedagogic context in which combined effort results in a successful outcome.

The way in which this combined effort is conceptualised varies as a function of the theoretical metaphors which guide particular authors. For example, Cole and Engeström (1993) invoke the terms of distributed cognition in their portrayal of the requirements for the teaching of reading. They present an image of a teaching system which is 'stretched across' other things and people.

(a) the cognitive processing involved in learning to read is not an individual matter; the requisite cognitive processes are distributed among teacher, pupil, other students, and the cultural artefacts around which they co-ordinate in the activity called teaching/learning to read;
(b) The expected future state, mature reading, must somehow be present at the beginning of instruction as constraints enabling the development of the to-be-acquired new system of mediation, mature reading . . . the combined child-adult system . . . can co-ordinate the child's act of reading before the child can accomplish this activity for him-her self.
(Cole and Engeström, 1993, pp. 23–4)

The scaffolding approach has tended to concentrate rather more on distribution across people rather than artefacts or things. Crucially scaffolding involves simplifying the learner's role rather than the task. More recently Bruner (1997) has provided an elaborate sketch of the term scaffolding and placed it in direct relation to the Vygotskian concept of the ZPD.

The ZPD is where pedagogy and intersubjectivity enter the Vygotskian picture. But how does pedagogy work? Through shielding a learner from distraction, by fore fronting crucial features of a problem, by sequencing the steps to understanding, by promoting negotiation, or by some other form of 'scaffolding' the task at hand (Brown and Campione, 1990; Bruner *et al.*, 1997; Tharp and Gallimore, 1988a, b; Tomasello *et al.*, 1993, Wood *et al.*, 1976)? How does the helper/tutor know what the learner needs? Here, intersubjectivity enters – alas, more implied than explicated. Most important, however, the ZPD poses specific questions as to how culture gets internalised by the mediation of others (Shore, 1996). As Tomasello *et al.* (1993) point out, the very transmission of culture depends upon (a) some principled concordance between a learner's capabilities and what the culture had on offer; (b) some person in the culture, a tutor, who can sense what a learner needs and delivers it, and (c) some shared agreement about how such

> an intersubjective arrangement is supposed to work canonically in *this particular culture*, as in Rogoff *et al.*'s (1993) recent comparative study of Salt Lake City middle-class 5 year olds and their mothers in contrast to their counterparts in a Guatemalan Mayan Indian town. To put it bluntly, the ZPD recognises that *Homo* is the only species that uses teaching in any systematic way and asks what it takes for somebody to teach or be taught by another.
>
> (Bruner, 1997, p. 69)

This way of conceptualising adult–child interactions provides important tools for analysing such interactions and enhancing their formative potential. Following Stone (1998), I will discuss studies that illustrate the application and development of the scaffolding concept in studies of parent–child interaction as well as teacher–student interaction. These studies tend to focus on speech as the means by which tutors provide support for learners. Mehan (1997) reported ethnomethodological studies of interactional activities and normative procedures which sustain interaction, and the skills and abilities that students must use to appear competent in a classroom. This research serves as an important reminder that non-verbal modalities are functional in scaffolded instruction.

Descriptive studies such as those of Bruner (1975) reported a variety of examples of instructional strategies used by parents. David Wood and his colleagues moved the field forward through attempts to conduct experimental manipulation of instructional interaction. These early studies, such as Wood *et al.* (1976) and Wood *et al.* (1978), which also involve the development of definitions, have been extended more recently to form one of the most influential contributions to the field.

Wood and Wood (1996a, b) and Wood (1998) have developed an approach to tutoring which is based on an interpretation of the ZPD. The two principles of *uncertainty* and *contingency* form the central features of the approach. It is suggested that uncertainty makes learning more difficult. When a learner is uncertain or unfamiliar with the relevant features of a task then motivation, task orientation and memory of the task itself is reduced. This suggestion echoes that of Greeno (1991) concerning 'learning the landscape' of a task or task environment. For Greeno an expert is, in part, someone who is familiar with the task terrain, its features and demands. Thus, an expert is someone who has reduced the uncertainty in a task situation. Learners for whom uncertainty is high require support in the process of reducing the uncertainty or 'learning the landscape' of the task.

The second key principle of the Woods' approach is that support offered within the ZPD of a learner whose uncertainty concerning a task is high is that it (the support) should be *contingent* upon the responses of the child. Within the ZPD of the learning/tutorial situation envisaged by Wood, five levels of increasing control are suggested. These prompts range from minimal control – the tutor prompts the learner with a general question, such as 'What might be done here?' – to highly controlled situations, in which the tutor actually demonstrates the steps needed to fulfil the requirements of the task:

- Level 0: no assistance;
- Level 1: a general verbal prompt ('What might you do here?');
- Level 2: specific verbal ('You might use your computer tools here');
- Level 3: indicates materials ('Why not use a graph plotter?');
- Level 4: prepares materials (selects and sets up tool);
- Level 5: demonstrates use.

Every time the learner makes a correct move or action, Wood's principle of contingency suggests that the tutor reduces the level of control. If the learner makes a mistake the level of control is raised. The level of support is thus contingent on the learner's progress within the interaction between the tutor and the tutee. The tutor's task is to seek to ensure progress whilst at the same time reducing the level of control. Ideally the learner actually decreases the level of dependence upon the support structure as the learning sequence progresses.

Day and Cordon (1993) have compared 'scaffolded' and 'non-scaffolded' instruction and found that scaffolded instruction resulted in faster and better maintenance of learning. They took measures of individual differences such as impulsivity, achievement orientation and verbal intelligence within the experimental groups of American third grade pupils and demonstrated that such differences played a greater role in predicting learning success for the children who did *not* receive the scaffolded instruction (Stone, 1998).

Cazden's (1979) study drew attention to the parallels that exist between parent–child language games and some of the forms of discursive practice that take place in classrooms The promotion of parent–child interaction as a model for teacher–child interaction was also advocated by Langer and Applebee (1986) who identified five key factors in what they considered to be effective scaffolding:

- *ownership* (of the activity to be learned);
- *appropriateness* (to the student's current knowledge);
- *structure* (embodying a 'natural' sequence of thought and action);
- *collaboration* (between teacher and student);
- *internalisation* (via gradual withdrawal of the scaffolding and transfer of control).

It would seem that not all these factors are realised in what may be the dominant forms of classroom practice. Bliss *et al.* (1996) set out to explore and identify scaffolding strategies in three specific primary schooling contexts: design and technology, mathematics and science. Their claim is that scaffolding specialist knowledge is very difficult in some classrooms. One interpretation of their findings is that much attempted 'scaffolding' takes place in a context where there is insufficient understanding of the distinctions that Davydov and Hedegaard make between forms of knowledge. In terms of the original theory, their suggestion is that manipulation of assistance within a ZPD without an understanding of the distinction between scientific and spontaneous concepts is of limited value.

> To imagine that socially constructed knowledge in areas like science, technology or mathematics is everyday knowledge is to misunderstand the purpose of schooling, which is the pupil's initiation into grappling with the theoretical objects of these domains.
>
> (Bliss *et al.*, 1996, p. 60)

This echoes Kozulin's (1998) claim that entering formal schooling requires a repositioning with respect to knowledge on the part of the pupils. The skills required for sensitive pedagogic assistance and the understanding of the scientific concepts which constitute the knowledge domain become necessary features of effective teaching and learning which makes claims to a Vygotskian root.

Reciprocal teaching

There are similarities here with the work of Brown and Palincsar (1989) and Palincsar and Brown (1984) who have developed a co-operative learning system for the teaching of reading, termed *reciprocal teaching*. The teacher and learners assemble in groups of two to seven and read a paragraph together silently. A person assumes the 'teacher' role and formulates a question on the paragraph. The group, whose members are playing roles of producer and critic simultaneously, addresses this question. The 'teacher' advances a summary, and makes a prediction or clarification, if any is needed. The role of teacher then rotates, and the group proceeds to the next paragraph in the text. The reciprocal teaching method uses a combination of modelling, coaching, scaffolding, and fading to achieve impressive results, with learners showing dramatic gains in comprehension, retention, and far transfer over sustained periods.

The reciprocal teaching approach then involves:

1   Summarising: identifying and paraphrasing the main idea in the text.
2   Question-Generating: self-questioning about the type of information that is generally tapped on tests of comprehension and recall.
3   Clarifying: discerning when there has been a breakdown in comprehension and taking the necessary action to restore meaning (e.g., reading ahead, rereading, asking for assistance).
4   Predicting: hypothesising what the structure and content of the text suggest will be presented next (from Palincsar and Brown, 1988).

Palincsar and Brown (1988) give the following example of scaffolding with respect to a text concerned with aspects of geology.

The text being discussed is as follows: 'Below the crust is a large layer called the mantle. It is a much heavier layer. The part of the mantle just below the crust is a strange place. Pressure there is very great and the temperatures are very high.

Doug:	This told about the second layer of the earth, the one that is under the first one . . .
Sara:	The one under the crust.
Doug:	Yeah, the crust. It told about what it is like, like how heavy it is and what the temperature is. My prediction is that they will tell us about the next layer because this picture shows another one, and I'll bet it will be cooler because dirt gets colder when you dig.
Chris:	That doesn't make sense to me because, because as it's been goin' down, it's been getting hotter.
Stephanie:	And heavier too.
Chris:	Pretty soon, we'll get to the gooey stuff and it's real hot.
Sam:	That's the lava.
Teacher:	Well, let's read on and see who's right in their predictions. What will the next layer be like? Who will be the teacher?'

(Palincsar and Brown, 1988, p. 57)

Palincsar and Brown suggest that strategies such as predicting, questioning, summarising, and clarifying help readers to anticipate information they will encounter, to integrate what is presented in the text with prior knowledge, to reconstruct prior knowledge, and help teachers to monitor for understanding. In the transcript Doug starts with an attempt at a summary. He then moves to prediction on the basis of an interpretation of the text and prior knowledge (because dirt gets colder when you dig). Chris then questions this and proposes an alternative theory (because as it's been goin' down, it's been getting hotter). As the episode proceeds the children support each other's thinking through the application of the elements of reciprocal teaching. The skills that promote thinking are the object of teaching. Once the children become expert in the use of these skills they will be of general value in a wide range of contexts. A central issue here is not just that the children are instructed in these skills but also that they may enact them in a context in which particular forms of communication take place. The intervention depends on a broader form of social organisation within the classroom for success.

> Theory and research suggest that these thinking skills be instructed in a manner that promotes expert scaffolding and guided practice in a supportive and collaborative context. Such a context is created when teachers and their students engage in dialogue about text.
>
> (Palincsar and Brown, 1988, p. 58)

This type of approach may be thought of as one in which pupils are required to externalise their self-regulatory practices in order to open them to instruction and development. Palincsar and Brown (1988) achieved this in the context of acting out problem solving with pupils. Schoenfeld, who reports teaching in higher education in which the teacher thought aloud as mathematical problems were being solved, has also used this approach. By drawing attention to the problem-solving procedure being used he was providing a model for his undergraduate students to use in their own problem-solving processes.

> What do you do when you have a problem like this? I have no general procedure for finding the roots of a polynominal, much less for comparing the two roots of them. Probably the best thing to do for the time being is to look at some simple examples and hope I can develop some intuition for them. Instead of looking at a pair of quadratics: at least I can solve those. Now what happens if . . .
>
> (Schoenfeld, 1985)

In this way Schoenfeld was making visible that which was hidden. Far too often novice learners get the wrong idea about the ways that experts perform tasks. For example, many pupils in schools seem to have little understanding of the way their teachers write. The process of drafting and sculpting text is lost and replaced by the mistaken idea that one starts an essay at the beginning and finishes at the end with no crossing out or frustration at getting stuck. Similar perceptions of adults' and more able peers' abilities in mathematical problem solving may mask 'natural' procedures and inhibit learners in their apparently 'clumsy' efforts.

Pedagogies which do not attend to ways in which understanding develops may, in practice, reconstruct the curriculum subject in a way that makes real learning more difficult. The scientific concepts of the curriculum subject may be hidden from instruction that is aimed at the production of particular 'performances'. Practices such as reciprocal teaching aim to make explicit those aspects of the curriculum that too often remain tacit for too many learners. Wilson, Teslow and Taylor (1993) argue this case with respect to mathematics.

> Exposure to multiple ways of accomplishing a task of varying degrees of skill helps the learner to recognize that there is no one embodiment of expertise and encourages him/her to view learning as a continuing process (Vygotsky, 1978). In addition, it requires the learner to adopt the culture of a discipline such as mathematics rather than to merely use its tools.
>
> (Wilson et al., 1993, p. 82)

Pupils may co-operate with teachers or more able peers in an activity that is more complex than they can understand when working on their own.

Characterizing a relationship as *horizontal* does not exclude the possibility that some members are more capable than others at some given moment. It only means that roles among members are changeable in interaction. Thus the vertical horizontal distinction should be taken as a continuum rather than a dichotomy.

(Hatano and Inagaki, 1991, p. 333)

In reciprocal teaching the child works with the teacher's understanding without necessarily being directly taught. Newman *et al.* provide an important account of the process of social mediation in learning to divide. They studied division because it provides a clear example of learning in which responsibility is transferred from teacher to learner and then back from learner to teacher in a series of cycles of increasing understanding and learning control.

The problem facing the student can be phrased as follows: the student must acquire the concept, 'gazinta' (goes into). At the outset, the child is confronted with the confusing request to say how many times '5 gazinta 27'. Before this time in the arithmetic curriculum, the child has worked on 'number facts', viz., 'five 5s are 25; five 6s are 30' and only 'three 9s' or 'nine 3s' are 27. So, how can 5 'go into' 27? Five can 'go into' 25 or 30; but only 3 or 9 can 'go into' 27! Expert skill in carrying out the procedure actually calls for an initial estimate of the quotient, which is then checked and adjusted in the subsequent steps., the initial step of estimating is a very difficult thing to explain to the novice who does not yet know what it is that one is attempting to estimate!

(Newman *et al.*, 1989)

Prolepsis may occur in reciprocal teaching and many other pedagogic settings. The term refers to a communication that leaves implicit some information that may be provided subsequently.

Vygotsky's views on the role of social experience in shaping learning and development, frequently through the mechanism of proleptic instruction, point to the importance of a careful analysis of the social and communicational dynamics within instructional settings.

(Reid and Stone, 1991, p. 9)

Proleptic instruction also suggests instruction that takes place in anticipation of competence. Thus, a learner may be encouraged to participate in an activity which as yet they cannot perform alone. This assumption or anticipation of competence in a social context supports the individual's efforts and encourages the learner to make sense of the situation in a powerful way. As Reid and Stone (1991) note, what is meant is not only determined by the physical context, however, but also depends on the social context of the *adult's intended goal*.

Thus, the child is led to infer a new perspective, one that is the *joint product* of the child's own initial perspective and that of the adult.

> The expert, then (a) models appropriate comprehension activities, (b) makes the usually covert strategies overt, (c) engages in an 'on–line' diagnosis of difficulties and monitors understanding, and (d) gives appropriate feedback and asks a little more of the child as the child acquires competence. The novice, in contrast (a) participates at his or her own current cognitive level, (b) makes current competence overt, (c) receives feedback that rewards and stretches, and (d) gradually progresses to competence.
>
> (Reeve *et al.*, 1987, p. 128)

There is a danger with the use of the term scaffolding that it could become applied so widely and frequently that it loses any meaning beyond some reference to teaching and learning. Given that the term came into use without reference to a particular set of theoretical assumptions it runs the risk of being appropriated and transformed by almost any set of pedagogic and/or psychological assumptions.

Stone (1998) identifies four key features of the use of scaffolding that also typify reciprocal teaching. These are useful in that they at minimum place some sort of boundary around the use of the term. They are:

1 The recruitment by an adult of a child's involvement in a meaningful and culturally desirable activity beyond the child's current understanding or control.
2 The titration of the assistance provided utilising a process of 'online diagnosis' of the learner's understanding and skill level and estimation of the amount of support required.
3 The support is not a uniform prescription – it may vary in mode (e.g. physical gesture, verbal prompt, extensive dialogue) as well as amount.
4 The support provided is gradually withdrawn as control over the task is transferred to the learner.

Alongside the concern that the term 'peer support' has become overextended in its use there are a number of others that require consideration. Firstly, much of the literature focuses on adults, whether they are parents or teachers, as 'scaffolders'. The literature on peer tutoring suggests that this is a serious omission.

> Only in a few (and, incidentally, the most powerful) articulations of scaffolding, have researchers paid attention to students' activity and entered into dialogues that allow students to exercise some control over the dynamics of the instructional situation, and to negotiate the instructional interaction, given their evolving intellectual potential. Palincsar was perhaps the first to pursue this line of study.
>
> (Reid, 1998, p. 389)

However, it is also clear that peer tutoring is only effective in specific circumstances. Jonathan Tudge and his colleagues have done much to clarify the potential for peer tutoring within a Vygotskian approach to teaching and learning. Tudge and Rogoff (1989) argue that social interaction does not carry 'blanket benefits' and that the circumstances in which social interaction facilitates development need to be carefully specified. They suggest that changes of perspective may be brought about in the free verbal interchange that typifies peer interaction. The central characteristic of effective interaction was seen to be the establishment of intersubjectivity irrespective of whether adults or peers were involved and irrespective of whether the situation was one which embodied cognitive conflict (following Piaget) or joint problem solving (following Vygotsky).

Dixon-Krauss (1995) reports a classroom action research programme using peer social dialogue integrated with teacher support to develop children's reading, writing and abstract thinking in story reflection and sense of audience. In this study she paired twenty-four first and second grade pupils for a six-week partner reading and writing activity. This pairing was intended to provide peer social dialogue through partner storybook reading, discussion, and dialogue journal writing. In addition, teaching on verbal story reflection added support to the partner instructional activity. Most improvement was witnessed in word recognition.

Results from a study of 162 children involved in solving mathematical balance beam tasks led Tudge (1992) to suggest that Piagetians may have overemphasised the benefits of collaboration by confounding confidence with competence. His findings also suggest that, even when intersubjectivity is achieved, positive outcomes may not result. Peer collaboration may, in some circumstances, have negative effects on learning!

Tudge et al. (1996) demonstrated that children whose partner exhibited higher-level reasoning were far more likely to benefit from collaboration than those whose partner did not, provided that the pair achieved shared under-standing. They formulate conclusions for the benefit of teachers who are interested in encouraging pair or group work:

- Simply pairing children, even if they bring different perspectives to bear on the task, will not necessarily lead to cognitive advance. It is more likely to do so if the problem to be solved is potentially within reach. Being 'within reach' is conditioned by: problem difficulty; the ease with which the 'teacher' can provide feedback; and partner ability.
- Providing problems that are potentially within a child's zone or incorporate an optimal mismatch may be necessary but not sufficient for development. Encouragement to share the goal of collaboration to reach a solution, support for problem solution, and strategy discussion are all offered as potential supports.
- Having a partner may bring benefits as well as distractions.

- Having a more capable partner is more beneficial than working alone in the absence of contingent feedback from an adult tutor.

(Adapted from Tudge *et al.*, 1996, pp. 2906–7)

Social contexts for learning

The term 'cognitive apprenticeship' has been used by Collins (1991) and Collins *et al.* (1989) amongst others, to refer to an instructional model informed by the social situation in which an apprentice might work with a master craftsperson in traditional societies. It is also informed by Rogoff and Lave's (1984) work on the way that learning takes place in everyday informal environments. One of the limitations of this model is with respect to the modelling of 'ideal' learning environments that may not be attainable within the institutional constraints of schooling.

The cognitive apprenticeship approach proposes that learners should engage in meaningful learning and problem solving whilst working with authentic problems. This question of authenticity seems to raise key problems. Vygotsky's distinction between the everyday and the scientific would lead to the suggestion that if 'authentic problems' in 'authentic settings' are to form the content of a curriculum then they should be selected very carefully. Following Davydov and Kozulin they should be problems which lead to theoretical learning. Following Bernstein's (1999b) distinction between horizontal and vertical discourses we should be wary of providing learners with experiences which lead to their positioning within what he terms a segmented horizontal discourse, whereby participants are unlikely to access the analytical power or certainly the 'cultural capital' of scientific concepts. The radically situated account of knowledge and learning must be placed within a political analysis of power and control. If not, those who are situated in advantaging contexts will be further advantaged. The cognitive apprentice approach opens the question of the relationship between the schooled and the everyday and yet seems to close the question by attempting to place the schooled in the everyday. This seems to ignore the suggestion that schooling may be capable of helping to transcend the constraints of the everyday. Both scientific and everyday concepts are a necessary part of development. Hedegaard notes it is in the connection between the two that the business of development is enacted.

> The integration of subject matter knowledge and everyday knowledge is important for children's conceptual development. Everyday knowledge is a precondition for children's learning of subject matter knowledge, but development of everyday knowledge does not stop being important. On the contrary, subject matter knowledge contributes to the development through integration with children's everyday activity. Thereby, the children's everyday knowledge can develop to more complex levels.

(Hedegaard, 1998, p. 123)

In a discussion of ways in which 'real life' can be brought to the classroom Wardekker (1998) offers two approaches.

> If we understand schools as places where pupils are introduced to the participation in socio-cultural practices this introduction is better when 'virtual practice' as set up in the school retains the essential characteristics of the actual practice and . . . the motivation needed to engage in the work of constructing genuine concepts depends on being able to see what you are learning for and in what practices you will be able better to participate.
>
> (Wardekker, 1998, pp. 147–9)

Hedegaard extends this argument and proposes three key 'anchor' or reference points: (a) everyday life situations that are characteristic to the community; (b) subject matter areas (problem areas that are relevant for society life and that have dominated the different sciences through time and develop central concepts and procedures of science); and (c) the learning subjects and their development (Hedegaard, 1998, p. 117).

In their work on instructional conversations Tharp and Gallimore (1988a, b) propose that teachers should act to 'weave together everyday and schooled understanding'. The skilled teacher brings, or weaves, together pupil perspectives and understandings with those that she seeks to promote in the classroom. This process builds upon pupil prior knowledge and understanding with the ideas and concepts the teacher wishes to explore with them. Here instruction and conversation are woven together. Tharp (1993) has provided a summary of the types of instruction which have been seen to provide assistance to 'bring the performance of the learner through the ZPD into an independent capacity' where the 'means of assistance are woven into a meaningful dialogue'.

The seven means of assisting performance and facilitating learning identified by Tharp (1993) are as follows:

1   Modelling: offering behaviour for imitation. Modelling assists by giving the learner information and a remembered image that can serve as a performance standard.
2   Feedback: the process of providing information on a performance as it compares to a standard. Feedback is essential in assisting performance because it allows the performance to be compared to the standard and thus allows self-correction. Feedback assists performance in every domain from tennis to nuclear physics. Ensuring feedback is the most common and single most effective form of self-assistance.
3   Contingency management: application of the principles of reinforcement and punishment to behaviour.
4   Instructing: requesting specific action. It assists by selecting the correct response and by providing clarity, information and decision making. It is most useful when the learner can perform some segments of the task but

cannot yet analyse the entire performance or make judgements about the elements to choose.

5 Questioning: a request for a verbal response that assists by producing a mental operation the learner cannot or would not produce alone. This interaction assists further by giving the assistor information about the learner's developing understanding.

6 Cognitive structuring: 'explanations'. Cognitive structuring assists by providing explanatory and belief structures that organise and justify new learning and perceptions and allow the creation of new or modified schemata.

7 Task structuring: chunking, segregating, sequencing, or otherwise structuring a task into or from components. It assists learners by modifying the task itself, so the units presented to the learner fit into the ZPD when the entire unstructured task is beyond that zone.

(Tharp, 1993, pp. 271–2)

In the instructional conversation approach parents and teachers are asked to engage in a meaningful instructional dialogue with the child and to help connect their existing understanding with the knowledge and understanding that holds sway in schooling.

Moll and his colleagues (e.g. Moll and Greenberg, 1990; Moll, 1990; Moll, 2000) have taken a similar tack in that they seek to enrich academic understanding with those understandings that have been acquired through participation in communities which have accrued 'funds of knowledge'. Moll argues that schools should draw on the social and cognitive contributions that parents and other community members can make to children's development. Through anthropologically driven studies of learning in clusters of households much has been learned about the ways in which knowledge is built and acquired in such settings. After-school clubs are used as settings in which the richness of the community knowledge funds can be brought together with the academic purposes of the teaching. The after-school clubs were designed so that multiple goals could be pursued: the children engaged in meaningful activities in which valued outcomes were achieved. Teachers ensured that academic progress was facilitated in the context of these activities.

In a statement that in some ways echoes the position of Cole and Griffin (1983) on basic skills, Moll and Greenberg (1990) argue for connections to be made between the intellectual resources of home and school.

Vygotsky (1987) wrote that in 'receiving instruction in a system of knowledge, the child learns of things that are not before his eyes, things that far exceed the limits of his actual and even potential immediate experience' (p. 180). We hardly believe that rote instruction of low-level skills is the system of knowledge that Vygotsky had in mind. We perceive the students' community, and its funds of knowledge, as the most important resource for reorganizing instruction in ways that 'far exceed' the limits of current schooling. An indispensable element of our approach is the creation of meaningful connections between academic and social life through the concrete learning activities of the students. We are convinced that teachers can establish, in systemic ways, the necessary social relations outside classrooms that will change and improve what occurs within the classroom walls. These social connections help teachers and students to develop their awareness of how they can use the everyday to understand classroom content and use classroom activities to understand social reality.

(Moll and Greenberg, 1990, pp. 345–6)

Brown *et al.* (1996) report the development of the Community of Learners project (e.g. Brown and Campione, 1990, p. 94). This has developed to meet the needs of inner city children as they engage in science education. The project has been concerned with what should be taught, when it should be taught and how it should be evaluated. In doing so they have drawn on both Vygotsky and Piaget. Piaget's work has informed the design of a developmental science curriculum. They draw on the later functionalist period of Piaget's work rather than the earlier structuralist work which they see as having led to a consistent underestimation of young learners' capability (Piaget, 1978). Vygotsky's work has informed the design of social contexts for learning. They suggest that five main principles derived from neo-Vygotskian work have influenced their design of instructional environments. These are:

- classrooms invoke multiple zones of proximal development;
- a community of academic and eventually scientific discourse is developed;
- meaning is negotiated and refined;
- ideas are seeded and appropriated; and
- common knowledge and distributed expertise are both essential.

They understand a learning community as a context within which multiple zones of proximal development are in place at the same time. It is envisaged that each learner can pursue different sequences and progress through different routes each at their own pace. Thus the classroom is seen as a setting in which multiple, overlapping zones of proximal development are supported. This support is made available through the system of practices that make up the Community of Learners.

Many contemporary post-Vygotskian writers have sought to associate specific practices with specific discourses.

Rather than language being understood as a 'generalised or abstract system that mediates activity interaction, and thought' it should be treated as 'a multitude of distinct speech genres and semiotic devices that are tightly linked with particular social institutions and practices'. In schools 'there are many speech genres that mediate specific forms of social and psychological life in distinct ways'.

(Minick *et al.*, 1993, p. 6)

The Community of Learners project seeks to promote the development of discursive practice that is typical of academic discourse in general and scientific discourse in particular. This involves the active promotion of discourse that features constructive discussion, questioning and criticism as part of its expected and familiar practice. Dialogic participant structures are maintained and supported in face-to-face activities; through print or electronic mail. Importantly the project seeks to promote the appropriation of such discursive tools in that it is intended that they become part of the thought processes of community members. Minick *et al.* (1993) argue that within a Vygotskian framework modes of thinking are seen to evolve as integral systems of motives, goals, values and beliefs that are closely tied to concrete forms of social practice. Brown *et al.* (1996) suggest that within the Community of Learners project dialogues provide the format for novices to adopt the discourse structure, goals, values and belief systems of scientific practice and that over time, the community of learners adopts a common voice and common knowledge base, a shared system of meaning, beliefs, and activity.

Communities of learners within which communities of discourse evolve are contexts for the constant negotiation of meaning. Brown *et al.* (1996) also argue that scientific modes of speculation, evidence, and proof become part of the common voice. It is here that they invoke a version of Vygotsky's views on the relationship between scientific and everyday concepts.

Successful enculturation into the community leads participants to relinquish everyday versions of speech activities having to do with the physical and natural world and replace them with discipline embedded special versions of the same activities.

(Brown *et al.*, 1996, p. 162)

They suggest that through mutual appropriation ideas and concepts migrate throughout the community. These ideas may be introduced by any of the participants and may or may not become established within the community. In this way Brown *et al.* (1996) describe an intervention which has sought inspiration from Vygotsky for the design and theory of communication and participation. Vygotsky is seen as the inspiration for the design of social sites for learning rather than the formulation of the content of the curriculum.

Bentley (1998) has proposed that the educational system should look beyond the classroom for social sites for learning. Whilst well intentioned, this approach awaits reconciliation with the questions that Vygotsky raised about forms of learning and conceptual development. Moll, Tharp and Gallimore have moved some way towards an answer through seeking to connect the everyday with the schooled. Their focus has not been on what should count as the 'scientific concepts' of schooling. This is the question which Davydov (1988) and Hedegaard (1990) raise as to what sort of content will seek to promote development. The primary distinction is between tasks in which microgenetic progress may be witnessed and assessed and those activities which serve a genuinely ontogenetic function. One of the many problems associated with this position is that whilst much time may be expended connecting the everyday with the schooled, that which constitutes the schooled may not embody scientific concepts or the potential for the development of scientific concepts. The development of the content, sequence and criteria of evaluation of the curriculum in school may be subject to many influences and pressures. These pressures may serve immediate political purposes and/or reiterate historical traditions. The extent to which cultural artefacts such as the school curriculum are structured with principles of learning and development in mind is open to speculation.

In arguing the case for curriculum design that is informed by Vygotsky's position on conceptual development I echo the imperatives announced by writers such as Hedegaard and Davydov. The challenge that they in turn face is in finding settings and circumstances in which learners will best participate in appropriate learning experiences. I will now move to describe two interventions that make a significant contribution to ideas concerning learning outside the school and inside the school respectively.

Michael Cole's work on the after-school educational programme which he has named the Fifth Dimension is a good example of an intervention which aims to create sustainable forms of educational activity through collaborative learning with a strong emphasis on play and imagination. The Fifth Dimension has been implemented at several sites in the USA – notably California – as well as in several other countries such as Sweden and Mexico (Cole, 1997). The approach has also been implemented using the medium of Spanish at La Clase Magica, Solana Beach, California. The Fifth Dimension aims to sustain a context which can, through the promotion of collaborative learning, create possibilities for children to become motivated and actively involved in their own development. A Fifth Dimension site has a space in which a number of computers are available. Computer games and activities are organised into a system which is presented as a maze. Learners make their own way through this maze of activities and games and represent their progress as models on a physical representation of it. The system is rule bound. Children, working in small groups, work their way through the maze in negotiation with a mythical figure, referred to as the 'Wizard' who encourages reflection on progress and process. Different levels of task and sequences allow each child to adopt their own route. Completion of passage through the maze leads to the possibility of becoming a 'Wizard's Assistant' who acts to support others and extend their own activities.

The Fifth Dimension aims to promote a culture of collaborative learning within a system of shared rules. Playing in the maze is, as with all forms of play, rule governed. In order to participate children must acquire an understanding of the possibilities that the rules afford. Cole has demonstrated how differences in culture between Fifth Dimension sites give rise to differences in outcome. The broader contexts of learning revealed differences in the degree of social cohesion and these differences lead to differences in the form that the activity assumed.

> The culture of the site, understood as a collective reality – as an activity *system* – is thus the key explanatory factor in accounting for the different patterns of generation and accumulation of knowledge bound up with a particular activity. The same task–activity evolves differently and comes to be imbued with different meaning within two different sociocultural contexts.
>
> (Nicolopoulou and Cole, 1993, p. 306)

Nicolopoulou and Cole (1993) suggest that the set of tools that are to be found in sociology offer a way forward in studying such sociocultural differences. The challenge lies in the ways in which the tools and accounts of post-Vygotskian psychology can be brought into productive interplay with an appropriate form of sociology.

> We will end on a more general theoretical note. Several writers have recently suggested that developmental psychology should draw on sociology to extend and enrich its understanding of individual development.
>
> (Nicolopoulou and Cole, 1993, p. 311)

Thus, sociocultural differences between contexts for learning require investigation. This points to the need to consider the concept of pedagogy at a level beyond the interpersonal. The broader sociocultural and/or institutional dimensions of pedagogy are often omitted from the analysis and hence the formulation of what is appropriate. Nicolopoulou and Cole have shown how notionally the same intervention manifests in different ways as a function of broader cultural differences. Yet so much of the post-Vygotskian approach to pedagogy is truncated to operate at the interpersonal level only. Even within one sociocultural setting, some children may need to achieve a balance between different priorities. Different sociocultural contexts may evoke different balances in priority. This issue was explored by Rueda and Mehan (1986) who sought to understand the ways in which the performance of students with learning disabilities varied as a function of instructional context.

> The situational variability in performance seems to arise because students with learning disabilities are working on two tasks at once: managing their identities and managing an intellectual task. They employ strategies directed at avoiding the task presented to them and managing the situation so as to

appear competent. . . . In negotiating a tarnished identity, as well as when attempting to solve a memory task, one makes strategic choices among courses of action, contemplates the nature of the problem to be solved, considers the potential for the success of any given strategy, and monitors and adjusts strategic behaviour based on the contextual information available.

Rueda and Mehan, 1986, pp. 158–9)

The focus on rules for participation within the Fifth Dimension raises interesting questions concerning the rules for participation inside schools. Mercer, who has sought to explicate rules for communicating inside classrooms, has also explored this issue. Mercer (2000) suggests explaining children's development as *interthinkers*. He draws on work of Lave and Wenger (1991) and the situated learning concepts of 'legitimate peripheral participation' and 'guided participation' in his proposal that we should seek to understand how more experienced members of communities act as '*discourse guides*' as children are supported in their appropriation of collective thinking. He invokes the established sociocultural position that specific activities produce and require specific forms of discursive practice and that these ways of linguistic being are associated with collective ways of thinking. Experts in such settings are those who recognise the linguistic landscape (Greeno, 1991) and are thus able to act appropriately and become seen as competent communicators. For Mercer the genres associated with specific activities help participants in activities to interpret sense data. He offers insights into how such participation may be supported in the classroom.

Through extended and meticulously detailed research he identified the following characteristics of effective teachers.

1. *They used question-and-answer sequences not just to test knowledge, but also to guide the development of understanding.* These teachers often used questions to discover the initial levels of students' understanding and adjust their teaching accordingly, and used 'why' questions to encourage students to reason and reflect on what they were doing.

2. *They taught not just 'subject content', but also procedures for solving problems and making sense of experience.* This included teachers demonstrating to children the use of problem-solving strategies, explaining to children the meaning and purpose of classroom activities, and using their interactions with children as opportunities for encouraging children to make explicit their own thought processes.

3. *They treated learning as a social, communicative process.* This was represented by teachers doing such things as organizing interchanges of ideas and mutual support amongst students, encouraging students to take a more active, vocal role in classroom events, explicitly relating current activity to past experience and using students' contributions as a resource for building the 'common knowledge' of the class.

(Mercer, 2000, p. 160)

This research involved the development of a 'Talk Lessons' programme within which teachers were supported in their attempts to create classroom based communities of enquiry in which 'intermental development zones' (IDZ) operate. Mercer suggests that as his interest lies in 'the quality of teaching and learning as an "intermental" or "interthinking" process' the concept of an IDZ is more appropriate than the ZPD concept that he understands in terms of assessment practices. The discussion available in Chapter 2 outlines the tensions that exist in the operational definition of ZPD and its functional capacities. Mercer states the importance of the IDZ as follows:

> For a teacher to teach and a learner to learn, they must use talk and joint activity to create a shared communicative space, an 'intermental development zone' (IDZ) on the contextual foundations of their common knowledge and aims. In this intermental zone, which is reconstituted constantly as the dialogue continues, the teacher and learner negotiate their way through the activity in which they are involved. If the quality of the zone is successfully maintained, the teacher can enable a learner to become able to operate just beyond their established capabilities, and to consolidate this experience as new ability and understanding. If the dialogue fails to keep minds mutually attuned the IDZ collapses and the scaffolded learning grinds to a halt.
>
> (Mercer, 2000, p. 141)

Mercer has developed an initiative called the 'Talk Lessons' programme that involves teachers as creators of communities of enquiry within which they establish IDZs with pupils. In these sessions they talk about the purposes of lessons with pupils with particular reference to the kind of talk that is seen as desirable and productive. The following rule sets are examples of outcomes of such project work.

OUR GROUND RULES FOR TALK
We have agreed to:
Share ideas
Give reasons
Question ideas
Consider
Agree
Involve everybody
Everybody accepts responsibility

OUR TALKING RULES
*We share our ideas and listen to each other
*We talk one at a time
*We respect each other's opinions

★We give reasons to explain our ideas
★If we disagree we ask 'why'?
★We try to agree in the end

(Mercer, 2000, p. 161)

Wells (1993) draws on the work of Christie and Lemke to suggest that the notion of curriculum genre may be seen as a type of action within the 'activity/action/operation' model of activity systems. The tacit rules of the curriculum genre must be acquired if successful participation is to be assured. Mercer's work may be seen as an approach to explicating the tacit demands of one particular form of participation.

Mercer's use of genre within a sociocultural framework has some similarities with Kozulin's discussion of literature as a psychological tool. Here the notion of rule becomes extended to a more diffuse concept of historical, cultural and social guidance. It also links with what Bruner has suggested about the ways in which we write rules for ourselves through the narratives we create about who we were, who we are, and who we can be. He suggests that the 'stories' we tell ourselves act to transform our own experiences.

> Eventually the culturally shaped cognitive and linguistic processes that guide the self-telling of life narratives achieve the power to structure perceptual experience, to organize memory, to segment and purpose-build the very 'events' of the life. In the end, we become the autobiographic narratives by which we 'tell about' our lives.
>
> (Bruner, 1987, p. 15)

The novel, seen as form of cultural artefact, can function as a part of the apparatus that shapes personal narratives. The notion of narrative forms of thinking has been explored over some time. Michaels (1990) writes of ways in which such forms of thinking can serve the 'connecting' function between home and school.

> Narrative forms of thinking are well developed in even very young school aged children and reflect the traditions of meaning making through talk that one develops in the family and community. . . . In charting occurrences of narrative discourse and its transformation in school, we can see the ways that home and school worlds connect, mingle, or conflict. We can also see, over time, how certain forms of discourse, certain ways of making and displaying meaning, often not narrative in nature, come to be privileged, promoted, and 'taken' in the Vygotskian terminology associated with the scaffolding metaphor: appropriated into children's talk and writing.
>
> (Michaels, 1990, p. 306)

Brice Heath (1983) showed how forms of narrative may act as bridges or barriers in the connection between conceptual understandings of the home and the school. Running through this work is an implicit account of the dynamic interplay between socially established cultural artefacts and personal meanings. This position is rehearsed in Holland and Cole (1995) although rather more through the metaphors of cognitive psychology and anthropology than literary theory. As mentioned in Chapter 2, they use discourse and schema theory to show the psychological possibilities for activities with cultural artefacts. They seek to understand the process by which personal representations are shaped by socially shared representations and vice versa. Prompted by his understanding of the formative power of the novel in Russian society and his analysis of the processes which Holland and Cole and Bruner suggest, Kozulin makes proposals for the place of literature and literary activity in education. He suggests that more attention should be paid to the literary creative process as a paradigm of human understanding and that students should be made aware of the connection between classical 'autonomous texts' and the form of verbal reasoning they are using (Kozulin, 1998, pp. 141, 145). His emphasis is not simply on novels and texts more generally as repositories of socially sedimented rules; he takes a view that creative literary processes are a necessary part of preparation for an unknown future.

> Traditional education was essentially retrospective. The universal model and the cultural tradition were given, and the task of a student was to absorb this tradition and the intellectual tools associated with it. Thus a student was taught to deal with problems that reproduced past cultural patterns. Under the dynamic conditions of modernity the necessity for prospective, rather than retrospective, education became obvious. Prospective education implies that students should be capable of approaching problems that do not yet exist at the moment of his or her learning. To achieve this capability, the student should be oriented toward productive, rather than reproductive, knowledge. Knowledge should thus appear not in the form of results and solutions but rather as a process of authoring.
>
> (Kozulin, 1998, p. 151)

This suggestion extends the analysis of knowledge building proposed by Bereiter and Scardamalia but does not contradict their basic premise. To practise the production of knowledge through authoring would become a basic activity within education. Authoring does not always require the battery of skills that are currently pronounced as basic and seen as necessary priors to creative literary activity. This is *not* an argument against the importance of being able to read and write; rather it is a caution against denying access to an important educational activity.

Kozulin further suggests that the dialogical type of learning characteristic of the humanities could be extended to teaching science. 'Through this, the inter-textual and conceptual decontextualized types of cognition can be successfully combined' (Kozulin, 1998, p. 152). Thus, Kozulin advocates an emphasis on literature as a pysychological tool and the use of literary practices in the development of pedagogies that involve understanding and changing the narratives that we use to understand ourselves and others.

Holland and Cole (1995) used the term scripts, as developed in cognitive psychology and discourse theory, in order to discuss the relationship between personal and social meaning. Gutierrez and Stone (2000) have used the term script in the analysis of classroom discourse. Their concern is with the way in which official scripts and counterscripts affect learning in the classroom. They are particularly interested in the way in which the discourse of subversion takes place and results in a resistant discourse which serves to create alternative goals and tasks for students who feel marginal within the official script. Using an activity theory approach they analyse the possibilities for a 'third space' in which conflict and difference is brought into productive play. Theirs is an attempt to examine the relationship between the interpersonal and the larger community. Lee's (2000) work is suggestive of where this way of conceptualising the pedagogic task may lead. She has developed an instructional intervention which she terms 'Cultural Modelling' which aims to provide students with explicit strategies for engaging with problems such as those of irony, symbolism and points of view. Through this modelling the use of language known as 'signifying' used in fractions of the African American community can be harnessed to provide support for the development of complex skills in the interpretation of literature. Through such modelling a connection is made between everyday and scientific concepts in what may be seen as a 'third pedagogic space'.

In very different ways Mercer and Lee are making explicit that which is tacit in the rule systems that regulate and typify patterns of communication and participation in classrooms. They are designing pedagogic moves which refer to demands which lie beyond the immediate criteria of evaluation of a specific task.

Forman and McPhail (1993) seem to share this broader pedagogic perspective in that they argue that successful peer collaboration requires a shared means of communication. Here they associate specific forms of communicative competence with specific pedagogies. The irony is that these competencies are rarely taught but remain crucial elements of successful performance.

> Their discourse depends on the selection of appropriate semiotic devices, such as speech registers, which are supplied by particular cultural practices. School introduces children to aspects of the mathematical and scientific register (e.g., vocabulary items) but provides them with relatively few opportunities to practice these registers. It is due, in part, to the predominance of the recitation model of classroom instruction that requires students to restrict their conversation to responses to the teacher's questions. . . . Collaborative problem solving is one activity in which children can use these academic registers in a meaningful fashion: to engage in logical arguments, to share their ideas and to work together in the pursuit of common goals.
>
> (Forman and McPhail, 1993, p. 226)

O'Connor and Michaels (1993) argue that a shared classroom culture is a basic requirement of a context in which students learn to take themselves seriously as learners and see all other students as fellow learners, while fully engaging with the relevant academic content. The creation of such a culture must therefore be a pedagogic intention, which lies beyond a narrow and constrained view of the immediate task demand. It involves the teachers in detailed and demanding co-ordination of the academic task and social participation structure. Reid summarises his concerns about the limitations of narrowly construed scaffolding approaches in terms of the wider pedagogic differences that may distinguish between classrooms and schools.

> Careful analyses of the participation structures teachers create in schools not only would reveal the strengths and weaknesses of our scaffolding techniques for bringing about achievement, but also would alert us to possible unintended outcomes, such as the ones just mentioned – disadvantaging students who are unfamiliar with, and unpracticed in using, the particular participation structure; controlling students' responses in ways that lead to under estimation of their communicative competence and abilities; constructing power relations that establish the teacher as sole arbiter of 'truth' and limiting the flow of social interactions among students. By becoming explicit in our thinking about classroom participant structures, we can learn to use them fairly.
>
> (Reid, 1998, p. 392)

Rogoff *et al.* (1993) recognise a number of these issues in their study of guided participation. They view individual development as dependent on interactions with other people in which societal values, intellectual tools and cultural institutions function as mediating cultural artefacts.

> Although many researchers treat the zone of proximal development as interaction between children and their social partners, such analysis is incomplete unless it also considers the societal basis of the shared problem solving the nature of the problem solving – the nature of the problem the partners seek to solve, the values involved in determining the appropriate goals and means, the intellectual tools available (e.g. language and number systems, literacy, and mnemonic devices), and the institutional structures of the interactions (e.g. schooling and political and economic systems).
>
> (Rogoff *et al.*, 1993, p. 232)

This position raises the interesting question as to the design of pedagogic practices in the broadest sense. If it is to be acknowledged that macro institutional and cultural factors are at play in the formation of pedagogic identities and possibilities then how should we set about designing such contexts? At one level of analysis the answer may be couched in terms of the kinds of metacognitive and procedural tools that are sustained in the pedagogic context. This must surely be a partial answer. The complexity of insights that come from the three sources listed below alone suggest there is a requirement to consider the ways in which the concrete social organisation of activity exerts a formative effect on psychological functioning.

- the third generation activity theory with its emphasis on complex multiple activity systems e.g. Engeström (1999);
- the content based curriculum initiatives with their analysis of Vygotsky's view of conceptual development, e.g. Davydov (1995);
- Vygotsky's opposition to dualisms such as cognitive/affective functioning (see Chapter 2).

Ratner suggests that a major limitation to be found in the work of Vygotsky and Luria is that when they did address cultural issues, they only discussed the importance that symbolic concepts (such as language) had for organising psychological functions.

> For example, in his 'Experimental Study of Concept Formation', Vygotsky stated that social life is important for the development of conceptual thinking in adolescence. However, instead of analyzing the social demands and activities that occur during adolescence, he postulated that a new abstract use of words during adolescence generates concept formation (Vygotsky, 1987, pp. 131, 160). Vygotsky never indicated the social basis for this new use of words. His social analysis thus reduced to a semiotic analysis that overlooked the real world of social praxis.
>
> (Ratner, 1997, p. 103)

I am making a plea for the expanded model of pedagogy I discussed in Chapter 1. This is not to deride the interventions I have discussed in this chapter. Each has made a significant contribution. My concern is that, following Cole's (1996) metaphor of context as that which weaves together, we do not omit crucial aspects of context when we come to design and analyse pedagogic practice. He refers to an Oxford English Dictionary definition of context as 'the connected whole that gives coherence to its parts' (Cole, 1996, p. 135). My argument is that in order to fully understand the connected whole of a pedagogic practice we must not neglect some of its, albeit more elusive, parts. This is the project that Ivic announced as follows:

> The critical analysis of institutions, including schools, and of social and cultural agents could clarify the conditions in which sociocultural tools and instruments become the formative factors of development.
>
> (Ivic, 1989, p. 433)

Chapter 5

The institutional level of regulation and analysis

In this final chapter I will discuss ways in which the broad definition of pedagogy outlined in Chapter 1 may be brought to life within the social, cultural-historical approach. In Chapters 2 and 3 I discussed a number of the possible interpretations and extensions of Vygotsky's theoretical legacy. In Chapter 4 I provided a necessarily constrained overview of some of the interventions that have been pursued under the guidance of some of the theories discussed in Chapter 2 and 3. Throughout these four chapters I have suggested that the development of this body of work has yet to explore fully aspects of broadly defined socio-institutional effects and the production of specific forms of cultural artefact or psychological tool in specific contexts. Additionally there has been relatively little investigation of the mediational properties of non-linguistic cultural artefacts such as visual images. One way of describing the problem is that post-Vygotskian theory lacks a sociology of pedagogy.

In this chapter I will discuss research, carried out in collaboration with others, which pursues these and other themes through empirical study. In one sense this is an attempt to progress the debate concerning means of mediation. In the study of cultural transmission and appropriation, how should we construct an operational definition of culture commensurate with a broadly based definition of pedagogy?

Van der Veer (1996) argued that Humboldt with reference to linguistic mediation and Marx with reference to tool–use and social and cultural progress influenced Vygotsky's concept of culture. He suggested that the limitations in this aspect of Vygotsky's work are with respect to non-linguistically mediated aspects of culture and the difficulty in explaining innovation by individuals. Ratner (1997) makes a plea for a definition of culture which goes beyond shared semiotic or symbolic processes and emphasises the concrete societal nature of cultural artefacts.

> Culture includes social concepts but also concrete social institutions that are arranged in a division of labour and governed by definite principles of behaviour, forms of control and power, allocation of opportunities, and rewards and punishments.
>
> (Ratner, 1997, p. 116)

Ratner discusses the ways in which activity may become institutionalised and in so doing structures and organises certain possibilities for the characteristics of psychological phenomena. He wishes to acknowledge the formative effects of institutional factors and at the same time account for the ways in which they themselves are shaped and developed. His approach to cultural psychology takes an explicitly broad view of the contexts in which cognition develops. Here Ratner both emphasises Vygotsky's assertion that humans control themselves from the outside and that cognitive and affective development and functioning should not be construed in terms of dualisms.

> Acknowledging that people construct their psychology by constructing their social activity grants them the power to alter their psychology by transforming their social activity. The intellectualist view of cultural psychology leads to championing psychological change apart from socioeconomic-political change. In this view, psychological change can be accomplished by simply changing one's concepts or outlook. There is no need to alter social institutions or conditions, since these are unrelated to cultural psychological phenomena. . . . Social activity is in psychological phenomena and psychological phenomena are in practical social activity. Culture is institutionalized practical behaviour, but it is also concepts and values, psychological phenomena, and human purpose. Similarly, psychological phenomena comprise a distinctive realm of diverse modalities (feelings, perceptions, thoughts, recollections, needs), yet they are also conceptual and are shaped by and promote practical social activity. Activity and psychological phenomena are different forms of a common medium; they are not separate entities. Their unity is what accounts for their ability to affect each other.
>
> (Ratner, 1997, p. 117)

Differences in definitions of culture raise issues which are isomorphic to those raised when definitions of pedagogy are considered. The broader or perhaps 'more sociological' the definition the greater the range of factors that must be considered as formative at the psychological level of analysis. Within the post-Vygotskian theoretical framework there is a requirement for a structural description of social settings which provides principles for distinguishing between social practices. Descriptions of this sort would be an important part of the apparatus required to carry out empirical investigation and analysis of the psychological consequences for individuals of different forms of social organisation. However, description itself would not be enough. Vygotsky's writing on the way in which psychological tools and signs act in the mediation of social factors does not engage with a theoretical account of the appropriation and/or and production of psychological tools within specific forms of activity within or across institutions. It is clear from reviews by Atkinson (1985), Moore (1984), Diaz (1984), Tyler (1983) and the work of Bernstein himself that he directly addresses the issues of concern in this chapter.

Essentially and briefly I have used Durkheim and Marx at the macro level and Mead at the micro level, to realize a sociolinguistic thesis which could meet with a range of work in anthropology, linguistics, sociology and psychology.

(Bernstein, 1972, p. 160)

Bernstein's thinking was influenced profoundly by his acquaintance with the various philosophical and anthropological authors on language and symbolism – including Cassirer and Whorf. To this was added the work of the Russian psychologists Vygotsky and Luria.

(Atkinson, 1985, p. 14)

However, as Atkinson (1985) notes, Bernstein's approach epitomises an essentially macrosociological point of view.

It is undoubtedly true that in Bernstein's general approach there is little or no concern for the perspectives, strategy and actions of individual social actors in actual social settings.

(Atkinson, 1985, p. 32)

On the one hand, Durkheim's notion of collective representation allowed for the social interpretation of human cognition; on the other it failed to resolve the issue as to how the collective representation is interpreted by the individual. This is the domain so appropriately filled by the later writings of Vygotsky. The fact that Bernstein has utilised Mead and Vygotsky in the formulation of his model allows for the exploration of interpersonal relations at the face-to-face level in the classroom. Many of the symbolic interactionist and Vygotskian insights noted above can be subsumed into his model which affords the wider social dimension a central place in a general thesis. The importance of such a theoretical move has been acknowledged for some time.

The failure to make the connection between Meadian social psychology and the sociology of knowledge on the part of the symbolic interactionists is of course related to the limited diffusion of the sociology of knowledge in America, but its more important theoretical foundation is to be sought in the fact that both Mead himself and his later followers did not develop an adequate concept of social structure. Precisely for this reason, we think, is the integration of the Meadian and Durkheimian approaches so very important.

(Shibutani, 1962)

Hundeide (1985) has shown, in a study of the tacit background of children's judgements, how participants in an activity, in part, create the setting. These 'taken for granted background expectancies' reflect in part the sociocultural experience that the individual brings to the situation.

> One needs a framework that takes into account the historical and cultural basis of individual minds: the collective institutionalized knowledge and routines, categorization of reality with its typifications, world view, normative expectations as to how people, situations, and the world are and should be, and so forth. All this is tacit knowledge that has its origin beyond the individual, and it is this sociocultural basis that forms the interpretive background of our individual minds.
>
> (Hundeide, 1985, p. 311)

In the absence of an appropriate theoretical framework wider social institutional factors will have been reduced to lower levels of explanation. In the same way psychological studies of learning which ignore contextual constraints will confound and confuse the interpretation of results. Vygotsky's approach lacks that which Bernstein explicitly has set out to provide – a theoretical framework for the description and analysis of the changing forms of cultural transmissions:

> I wanted to develop a different approach which placed at the centre of the analysis the principles of transmission and their embodiment in structures of social relationships.
>
> (Bernstein, 1977, p. 3)

Bernstein seeks to link semiotic tools with the structure of material activity. Crucially he draws attention to the processes which regulate the structure of the tool rather than just its function.

> Once attention is given to the regulation of the structure of pedagogic discourse, the social relations of its production and the various modes of its recontextualising as a practice, then perhaps we may be a little nearer to understanding the Vygotskian tool as a social and historical construction.
>
> (Bernstein, 1993)

He also argues that much of the work that has followed in the wake of Vygotsky 'does not include in its description how the discourse itself is constituted and recontextualised'.

> The socio-historical level of the theory is, in fact, the history of the biases of the culture with respect to its production, reproduction, modes of acquisition and their social relations.
>
> (Bernstein, 1993, p. xviii)

As Ratner (1997) notes, Vygotsky did not consider the ways in which concrete social systems bear on psychological functions. He discussed the general importance of language and schooling for psychological functioning; however, he failed to examine the real social systems in which these activities occur and reflect. Vygotsky never indicated the social basis for this new use of words. The social analysis is thus reduced to a semiotic analysis which overlooks the real world of social praxis (Ratner, 1997).

> The feature that can be viewed as the proximal cause of the maturation of concepts, *is a specific way of using the word*, specifically the functional application of the sign as a means of forming concepts.
>
> (Vygotsky, 1987, p. 131)

Whilst it is quite possible to interpret 'a specific way of using the word' to be an exhortation to analyse the activities in which the word is used and meaning negotiated, this was not elaborated by Vygotsky himself. The analysis of the structure and function of semiotic psychological tools in specific activity contexts is not explored. In Engeström's (1996) work within Activity Theory the production of the outcome is discussed but not the production and structure of the tool itself.

Thus the following issues may be regarded as points for development in contemporary post-Vygotskian theory and research:

* insufficient empirical study of socio-institutional effects;
* tendency to under-theorise differences between schools in terms of institutional effects on the social formation of mind;
* lack of theory of structure of discourse as a cultural artefact;
* lack of theory of constitution and recontextualisation of the psychological tool/cultural artefact.

Bernstein's sociology of pedagogy

Bernstein's (1981) paper outlined a model for understanding the construction of pedagogic discourse. In this context pedagogic discourse is a source of psychological tools or cultural artefacts.

> The basic idea was to view this (pedagogic) discourse as arising out of the action of a group of specialised agents operating in specialised setting in terms of the interests, often competing interests, of this setting.
>
> (Bernstein, 1996, p. 116)

Bernstein's work on the school shows his continuous engagement with the interrelations between changes in organisational form, changes in modes of control and changes in principles of communication. Initially he focuses upon two levels: a structural level and an interactional level. The structural level is analysed in terms of the social division of labour it creates and the interactional level with the form of social relation it creates. The social division of labour is analysed in terms of strength of the boundary of its divisions, that is, with respect to the degree of specialisation. Thus, within a school the social division of labour is complex where there is an array of specialised subjects, teachers and pupils, and it is relatively simple where there is a reduction in the specialisation of teachers, pupils and subjects. Thus, the key concept at the structural level is the concept of boundary, and structures are distinguished in terms of their boundary arrangements and their power supports and legitimations (Bernstein, 1996).

The interactional level emerges as the regulation of the transmission/acquisition relation between teacher and taught: that is, the interactional level comes to refer to the pedagogic context and the social relations of the classroom or its equivalent. The interactional level then gives the principle of the learning context through which the social division of labour, in Bernstein's terms, speaks.

He distinguished three message systems in the school: curriculum, pedagogy (practice) and evaluation. Curriculum referred to what counted as legitimate knowledge and the latter was a function of the organisation of subjects (fields), modules or other basic units to be acquired; pedagogy (practice) referred to the local pedagogic context of teacher and taught and regulated what counted as a legitimated transmission of the knowledge; evaluation referred to what counted as a valid realisation of the knowledge on the part of the acquirer. Curriculum was analysed not in terms of contents but in terms of relation *between* its categories (subjects and units). Pedagogic practice again was not to be analysed in terms of its contents but in terms of the control over the selection, sequencing, pacing and criteria of communication in the transmitter/acquirer relation. It is apparent that the curriculum is regarded as an example of a social division of labour and pedagogic practice as its constituent social relations through which the specialisation of that social division (subjects, units of the curriculum) are transmitted and expected to be acquired.

Bernstein uses the concept of classification to determine the underlying principle of a social division of labour and the concept of framing to determine the principle of its social relations and in this way to integrate structural and interactional levels of analysis in such a way that, up to a point, both levels may vary independently of each other.

Classification

Classification is defined at the most general level as the relation between categories. The relation between categories is given by their degree of insulation. Thus, where there is strong insulation between categories, each category is sharply distinguished, explicitly bounded and having its own distinctive specialisation. When there is weak insulation then the categories are less specialised and therefore their distinctiveness is reduced. In the former case, Bernstein speaks of strong classification and in the latter case Bernstein speaks of weak classification.

Framing

The social relations generally, in the analyses, are those between parents/children, teachers/pupils, doctors/patients, social workers/clients, but the analysis can be extended to include the social relations of the work contexts of industry or commerce. Bernstein considers that from his point of view all these relations can be regarded as pedagogic.

> Framing refers to the control on communicative practices (selection, sequencing, pacing and criteria) in pedagogical relations, be they relations of parents and children or teacher/pupils. Where framing is strong the transmitter explicitly regulates the distinguishing features of the interactional and locational principle which constitute the communicative context. . . . Where framing is weak, the acquirer is accorded more control over the regulation. Framing regulates what counts as legitimate communication in the pedagogical relation and thus what counts as legitimate practices.
>
> (Bernstein, 1981, p. 345)

In that the model is concerned with principles of regulation of educational transmission at any specified level, it is possible to investigate experimentally the relation between principles of regulation and the practices of pupils. Relations of power create and maintain boundaries between categories and are described in terms of classification. Relations of control revealed in values of framing condition communicative practices. It becomes possible to see how a given distribution of power through its classificatory principle and principles of control through its framing are made substantive in agencies of cultural reproduction, e.g. families/schools. The form of the code (its modality) contains principles for distinguishing between contexts (recognition rules) *and* for the creation and production of specialised communication within contexts (realisation rules).

> Through defining educational codes in terms of the relationship between classification and framing, these two components are built into the analysis at *all levels*. It then becomes possible in one framework to derive a typology of educational codes, to show the inter-relationships between organizational and knowledge properties to move from macro- to micro-levels of analysis, to delate the patterns internal to educational institutions to the external social antecedents of such patterns, and to consider questions of maintenance and change.
>
> (Bernstein, 1977, p. 112)

The analysis of classification and framing can be applied to different levels of school organisation and various units within a level. This allows the analysis of power and control and the rules regulating what counts as legitimate pedagogic competence to proceed at a level of delicacy appropriate to a particular research question.

Bernstein (1996) refined the discussion of his distinction between instructional and regulative discourse. The former refers to the transmission of skills and their relation to each other, and the latter refers to the principles of social order, relation and identity. Whereas the principles and distinctive features of instructional discourse and its practice are relatively clear (the what and how of the specific skills/competences to be acquired and their relation to each other), the principles and distinctive features of the transmission of the regulative are less clear as this discourse is transmitted through various media and may indeed be characterised as a diffuse transmission. Regulative discourse communicates the school's (or any institution's) public moral practice, values, beliefs and attitudes, principles of conduct, character and manner. It also transmits features of the school's local history, local tradition and community relations. Pedagogic discourse is modelled as one discourse created by the embedding of instructional and regulative discourse. This model of pedagogic discourse provides a response to one of the many theoretical demands which have remained unfulfilled in the post-Vygotskian framework. The rejection of the cognitive/affective dualism which Vygotsky announced was not followed by a model within which a unitary conception of thinking and feeling could be discussed and implemented within empirical research.

The language that Bernstein has developed allows researchers to take measures of school modality. That is to describe and position the discursive, organisational and interactional practice of the institution. Research may then seek to investigate the connections between the rules the children use to make sense of their pedagogic world and the modality of that world. Bernstein provides an account of cultural transmission which is avowedly sociological in its conception. In turn the psychological account that has developed in the wake of Vygotsky's writing offers a model of aspects of the social formation of mind which is underdeveloped in Bernstein's work.

As I mentioned in Chapter 2, in his last journal paper, Bernstein (1999b) moved his analysis to the internal principles of the construction and social base of pedagogic discourses. Having provided a theory of the construction of pedagogic discourse he moved to an analysis of the discourses subject to pedagogic transformation. This move will be of particular significance when this body of theory and its language of description is brought to bear on the discussion of the relationship between everyday and scientific concepts as outlined in *Thinking and Speech*. The analysis outlined by Bernstein (1999b) allows for greater differentiation within and between the forms identified by Vygotsky. The analytical power of the distinctions made between vertical and horizontal discourses and hierarchical and horizontal knowledge structures provides research with an enhanced capacity to provide descriptions that capture the delicacy of the forms and their interrelation. This last paper sets an important agenda for work in the future.

In the next section of this chapter I will argue that an Activity Theory driven approach may be enhanced through the development of a more sophisticated account of 'tool'/cultural artefact within the general model developed by Engeström. In this case it is the model of pedagogic discourse as an embedded discourse which is of particular value.

An expansive learning approach to studying Emotional and Behavioural Difficulties (EBD) in mainstream schools

In much of our work on policy and provision for pupils described as having Emotional and Behavioural Difficulties (EBD) we have shown that patterns of staff relation and forms of pedagogic discourse in schools have a significant effect on the possibilities for widening participation in mainstream schooling (Daniels, Cole et al., 2000; Cole et al., 1999). We argue that collaborative patterns of staff working and the retention of a discourse of values in education within a school are key indicators of what we define as good practice.

In Chapter 3 I discussed the development of Engeström's approach to activity theory and his theory of expansive learning (Engeström, 1984, Engeström et al., 1999). He sketches the stages of an expansive learning approach to research as follows:

- The first action is that of questioning, criticising, or rejecting some aspects of the accepted practice and existing wisdom. For the sake of simplicity, I call this action 'questioning'.
- The second action is that of analysing the situation. Analysis involves mental, discursive, or practical transformation of the situation in order to find out causes or explanatory mechanism. Analysis evokes 'why?' questions and explanatory principles. One type of analysis is historical-genetic; it seeks to explain the situation by tracing its origination and evolution. Another type of analysis is actual-empirical; it seeks to explain the situation by constructing a picture of its inner systemic relations.
- The third action is that of modelling the newly found explanatory relationship in some publicly observable and transmittable medium. This means constructing an explicit, simplified model of the new idea that explains and offers a solution to the problematic situation.
- The fourth action is that of examining the model, running, operating, and experimenting on it in order to fully grasp its dynamics, potentials, and limitations.
- The fifth action is that of implementing the model, concretising it by means of practical applications, enrichments, and conceptual extensions.

We have applied this model to the design of our own empirical work in the EBD field.

1. Questioning

There is international concern about the extent to which pupils are excluded from school. Between and within countries there is significant variation in the numbers of pupils whose behaviour is regarded as problematic, challenging and inappropriate. The variation suggests that either definitions are inadequate or that the EBD is, to some extent, a context specific phenomena, or both. The causes of EBD are now thought of as complex and systemic involving home, school and less frequently biological factors. This complexity gives rise to questions concerning the relationship between individuals, the ways that they think, feel and act, and the institutions in which they are placed.

There are social, cultural and historical issues in play here. Changes in schooling over the last decade have increased demands on schoolteachers particularly with respect to standards. There have been increased pressures to raise standards of attainments through teaching and assessing the English National Curriculum in locally managed schools, under a more stringent inspection system. There has also been growing concern about the extent to which the concept of emotional and behavioural difficulty has been realised in schools as a desire to control inappropriate behaviour without reference to the affect. The cognitive/affective dualism, which so concerned Vygotsky, is 'writ large' in aspects of the social administration of schooling. Additionally, interventions have tended to involve instrumental approaches to changing practice. The attempt to change practice in schools through the formulation and promulgation of specific protocols has tended to take place in the absence of discussion 'of values and type of society to which schools articulate/adhere' (Slee *et al.*, 1998).

Following Bernstein we could say that there has been a shift in the structure of pedagogic discourse which has involved the foregrounding of instructional discourse and the relative backgrounding of regulative discourse. Matters of order, identity and relation have been subjugated by concerns for curriculum content, sequence and pace assessment criteria and modes of assessment.

2. Analysing

In our work we sought to understand the nature of good practice in schools. In so doing we sought to understand the relationship between definitions, dis-courses, interventions and socio–institutional context. The relationship between instructional and regulative discourse within the pedagogic discourses of specific schools became a central concern. We focused upon the processes by which good practice had been achieved and sustained. Key players in the management and operation of behaviour and SEN policies in the LEAs and schools were interviewed, classroom observations were made and relevant documents were examined. Interviews were conducted with educational psychologists, advisers, behaviour support service personnel and educational welfare or social workers. We were concerned with current beliefs and practices as well as the ways in which they had evolved.

The framework for the collection of qualitative data during the detailed study of the ten schools in the final phase of the project evolved from visits made to twenty-seven schools in three administrative regions within England. These visits had in turn been planned in the light of the overview of relevant issues provided through an extensive literature review and focus groups using a nominal group technique.

3. Modelling

We were faced with a complex task. Our intention was to provide an up-to-date analysis of 'best' practice in mainstream schools. Our data suggested a relationship between the patterns of social relation within the school and the forms of pedagogic discourse that predominated. We were therefore concerned to model the social relations which gave rise to specific forms of discursive tool. Here we turned again to Engeström's work.

In order to try to discuss innovation and improvement of specific forms of multiprofessional activity, Engeström *et al.* (1997) develop a three-level notion of the developmental forms of epistemological subject-object-subject relations within a Vygotskian framework. They call these three levels 'co-ordination, co-operation and communication'. Within the general structure of co-ordination actors follow their scripted roles pursuing different goals (see Figure 5.1).

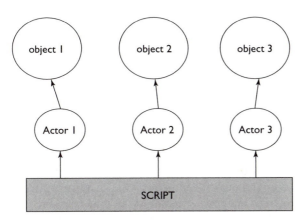

Figure 5.1 The general structure of co-ordination.

Within the general structure of co-operation actors focus on a shared problem. Within the confines of a script the actors attempt to both conceptualise and solve problems in ways which are negotiated and agreed (see Figure 5.2). The script itself is not questioned. That is, the tacitly assumed traditions and/or the given official rules of engagement with the problem are not challenged.

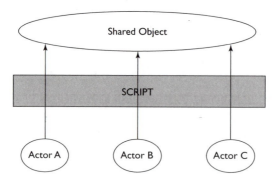

Figure 5.2 The general structure of co-operation.

Engeström *et al.* (1997, p. 373) discuss reflective communication 'in which the actors focus on reconceptualising their own organisation and interaction in relation to their shared objects and goals (see Figure 5.3). This is reflection on action. Both the object and the script are reconceptualised, as is the interaction between the participants.'

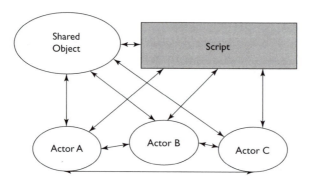

Figure 5.3 The general structure of communication.

Implicit in this general structure of communication is a version of Vygotsky's (1978) concept of the Zone of Proximal Development (ZPD). That is, the 'area that is beyond one's full comprehension and mastery, but that one is still able to fruitfully engage with, with the support of some tools, concepts and prompts from others' (Bazerman, 1997, p. 305). The description provided by Newman *et al.* (1989) of this form of activity in the classroom can be transposed to the actions of adults:

> The multiple points of view within a ZPD are not seen as a problem for analysis but rather the basis for a process of appropriation in which children's understandings can play a role in the functional system.
>
> (Newman *et al.*, 1989, p. 136)

4. Interrogating the model

The development and discussion of our data in schools and seminars gave rise to a focus on two related concerns. Firstly it seemed that a 'good' school would be a place where there was a collaborative culture. The 'community' would be regulated by collaborative 'rules' in such a school. Secondly, the institution would be one in which individuals could develop thoughts, values and aspirations together. In so doing they would revive and sustain the local regulative discourse of schooling. An explicit focus on regulative discourse was seen to be associated with sophisticated and effective approaches to pupils whose problems may be described as EBD.

5. Implementing the model

In order to implement the key aspects of our findings we sought a way of shifting the patterns of participation towards a 'communication' based model (Engeström *et al.*, 1997). We did so in the belief that this would give rise to a more explicit emphasis on the regulative discourse within the school.

The creation and development of collaborative problem-solving groups in schools in England (Creese *et al.*, 1997; Creese *et al.*, 2000) and Spain (Parrilla and Daniels, 2000) followed the argument that collaborative social environments enhance the cognitive potential of actors within institutions. In the context of the EBD work we were keen to facilitate the development of collaborative problem-solving groups as a means of shifting the structure of pedagogic discourse in schools.

The role of a collaborative professional culture in schools is an important but under-researched aspect of school effectiveness and improvement literature. Our model of Teacher Support Teams (TSTs) may be seen as a form of inter-vention which seeks to alter the sociocultural context of schooling through the development of a culture of collaborative peer problem solving. In this way TSTs aim to enhance the capacity of the school to respond to diverse student populations. It is thus an intervention which seeks to alter the context in order to enhance collective thinking. Teachers are, as Stringer (1998) suggests, 'seen as the target and agent of change'.

The ways in which schools are organised and constrained to organise them-selves are seen to have an effect on the possibilities for teacher peer collaboration and support. However, the theoretical tools of analysis of this kind of organisational effect are somewhat underdeveloped within the post-Vygotskian framework.

A TST is an organised system of peer support which consists of a small group of teachers who take referrals from individual teachers on a voluntary basis. The referring teacher brings concerns about classes, groups or individuals in order to discuss and problem solve with their peers. Follow-up meetings are held as necessary. The process is as confidential as the requesting teacher wants it to be. TSTs are novel in that they are an example of a school-based development designed to give support and assistance to individual teachers. In this way, TSTs address a significant but neglected area of school development which has the potential to enhance the working conditions of teachers. They involve a sharing of expertise between colleagues, rather than some teachers acting as experts to others.

TSTs seek to alter the communicative practices of teachers in schools. They engage with the tensions, dilemmas and even conflicts which teachers experience in the social worlds of the schools they inhabit. If the ZPD is redefined from a broader affective as well as cognitive perspective, as suggested by del Rio and Alvarez (1995), then a more robust and coherent concept emerges. It would be more robust in that it should seek to take account of both cognitive and affective domains. It would be more coherent in that it should handle these domains as highly interrelated and/or embedded matters.

From a Vygotskian perspective, these mediating communicative patterns in professional development constitute tools for action, thinking and feeling. As Bazerman notes:

> Though each participant in a discursive field need not think alike – indeed the discursive activities of disciplines largely rely on people not thinking precisely alike – each must draw on a common body of resources, cope with the same body of material and symbolic artifacts, master the same tools, and gain legitimacy for any new resources they want to bring into the field by addressing the same mechanisms of evaluation by which new concepts, tools, or phenomena gain standing in the discourse.
>
> (Bazerman, 1997, p. 305)

Meadows (1998) argued that 'collaboration with others . . . may make things achievable which were not and – indeed still are not – achievable by the individual acting alone. There can of course be many reasons for this social facilitation of development.' Our evaluation of TSTs reveals a range of outcomes associated with collaboration between teacher peers. As such it can be seen to provide support for some of the more recent developments in post-Vygotskian theory. Intervention in the cultural context of the institution which seeks to alter teachers' communicative practices can make a difference to the pedagogic practices in classrooms. Collaborative problem solving between teachers can provide an engine for development in schools.

The limits of teacher tolerance for pupil diversity are in part constructed by external demands placed on schools. Recent emphasis on attainment may have reduced teacher tolerance for low attainment on the part of pupils. This is acceptable to the extent that this lowering of tolerance or acceptance of failure is associated with active engagement designed to promote improved perfor-mance. It is clearly unacceptable if it leads to disengagement and rejection. Similarly the emphasis on attainment and instruction may also reduce tolerance, and engagement with and concern for emotional development and mental health in schooling. These accounts may be restated in terms of the relationship between instructional and regulative discourse discussed above. Our hypothesis is that introducing collaborative problem solving into schools through TST helps to transform patterns of social relation and lend to the development of pedagogic discourses and practices which place more emphasis on matters of value and moral regulation.

We have come to this hypothesis through a consideration of the relationships between the mediational means available to schools and the nature of the communities, rules and division of labour that exists in these schools. This was made possible through the perspective of Activity Theory. We feel that we have enhanced the analytical power of Activity Theory through an explicit reference to the structure of the semiotic means of mediation that is pedagogic discourse.

This example is, of course, very much at the exploratory stage. It is presented here because it provides an indication of the possibilities for enhancing the power of the Developmental Work Research approach. At another level it indicates that if the, almost traditional, divide between sociocultural and Activity Theory were to be resolved then the overall power of the theory would be significantly enhanced. As I outlined in Chapter 2, the lack of attention to the activity system setting in which dialogue occurs is as limiting as an underdeveloped analysis of processes of semiosis within activity systems. The present example is very crude. It merely invokes a simplified account of the structure of pedagogic structure in order to facilitate a fairly one-dimensional description of change and possibilities for change. It served to direct attention in the course of a fairly constrained research project. Bernstein and others provide approaches to modelling different discursive modalities. These descriptions could become analytical tools within an Activity Theory driven approach to institutional development.

Gender and resource allocation

Wells (1993, 1994a, b) has attempted to bring together theories of discourse with activity theory in the analysis of teaching and learning in the classroom. Voloshinov (1973, pp. 20–2). emphasised the importance of the relationship between utterance and context in the analysis of meaning; 'the sign may not be divorced from the concrete forms of social intercourse'. The concept of genre as developed in Australia (e.g. Christie, 1985, 1993) and North America, may be taken to refer to a set of formally definable text features that certain texts have in common across various contexts. Bazerman (1988, 1994) extends this notion of 'genre' beyond that of textual forms, to 'forms of life, ways of being, frames for social action' in his attempt to theorise environments for learning and teaching. Both Bazerman and Wells provide extensions to the concept of genre as developed in Christie's (1985, 1993) formulation of curriculum genres. These studies contribute to the development of a theory of learning and discourse within the activity of schooling yet still do not provide a verifiable model of socio-institutional effects.

Russell argues that Activity Theory analysis of genre systems may offer a theoretical bridge between the sociology of education and Vygotskian social psychology of classroom interaction, and contribute toward resolving the knotty problem of the relation of macro- and microstructure in literacy research based on various social theories of 'context' (Russell, 1997a, p. 1). Alternatively, it may be possible to use the concept of 'genre' as a means of differentiating between activities in analysis. It is this alternative that we pursued in the context of the studies that I will now outline.

In this section I will discuss a series of studies which, whilst not utilising a Bernsteinian framework for analysis, also seek to enhance the analytical power of the concept of 'psychological tool' or 'cultural artefact'. The major focus of this body of work was on the way in which gender is an influential factor within pedagogic practice. Initially our concern was with resource allocation for pupils with special educational needs (SEN) as a gendered and raced social process. This focus subsequently shifted to a more general interest in the institutional regulation of gender and learning (Daniels et al., 1998; Daniels et al., 1999).

The study of how and why pupils get allocated SEN provision requires that we look both at national, local and institutional (school) policies and provision, and at the social processes through which children come to be identified as having special needs, understand themselves to have 'special needs', and receive (or do not receive) available provision – as well as at how all such policies and processes are gendered. However, we are a long way from being able to provide such a full account, largely because explanations in the three areas involved – the nature of special educational provision, the conceptualisation of special educational needs, and analyses of gender inequalities – each have their specific foci and are the concern of different academic disciplines (and hence use different language and concepts/discourses); and because these different sorts of explanation have, up to now, been assiduously kept apart.

In many ways it would seem as if the practices of SEN had been insulated from the gaze and voice of equal opportunity initiatives. This may be because the socially driven account of disadvantage and failure which is located in the discourse of equal opportunity is 'switched off' when we turn to the discourse of SEN within which many of the preferred explanations of causation derive from models of individual deficiency.

Here then is a case for asking whether the notion of genre as advanced by Bazerman may be used as a tool to understand the consequences of the categorisation of pupils and the grouping of professionals and academics. Are these social groupings created by and do they create dominant ways of being – talking and acting?

> A genre is ordinarily best analyzed at the level of operation, a typified use of some tool(s), some mediational means, to carry out a typified, routine action, an action which in turn furthers the motive and acts upon the object of some collective (activity system).

> (Russell, 1997a, p. 6)

In the emprical work four schools of similar pupil population were identified on the basis of gender ratio, budget allowance for educational difficulty per head, and level of emphasis on Equal Opportunities policy and practice. It was our contention that the differences that these schools made in terms of their SEN practices could be related to the general meaning attached to SEN in management practices, and thence within teachers' practices.

All the schools recruited predominantly working class pupils despite the fact that some were in socially mixed areas. We grouped them crudely in two categories, 'moving' (or 'learning enriched') and 'stuck' (or 'learning impoverished') (Rosenholz, 1989) and linked this to how both 'types' predominantly conceive of their typical pupil as either a 'learner' or as a 'social casualty'. Rosenholz argues, that 'stuck' schools are characterised by a highly individualised culture with a lack of certainty about policy and roles, low morale and, generally, poor academic standards. Teachers in these stuck schools suggest that once they have acquired the skills and techniques necessary to be an effective teacher then life as a teacher becomes relatively unproblematic. Teachers in such schools rarely take any risks and develop quite inflexible patterns of working. In contrast, in 'moving' schools one is more likely to find a collaborative culture with respect to planning and the sharing of ideas and resources, and support for problem solving.

Resnick and LeGall (1996) suggest that school cultures may act to position learner and teacher beliefs. They believe that schools which are oriented to promoting pupil effort, with a continuous press for strategic learning behaviour, and which embody a belief in each child's ability are those which are more likely to be successful. They further argue that teachers in such schools are more likely to believe that they can successfully teach each child and also to view *themselves* as learners. That is that they treat teaching as a competency to be continuously increased and a child's failure to learn as a problem to be solved by teaching. These are the characteristics of the 'moving' school.

In the final sample of schools we studied in detail we found examples of both types of school. We found two schools which we felt were most appropriately categorised as 'stuck' and two schools which we felt could be described as 'moving'. The management systems appear to be associated with 'folk' psychology concepts of causality and belief about professional practice and development. It is, perhaps, in this sense that the term genre provides a more sophisticated analytical tool by virtue of the linkage with the notion of activity system.

> Genre is an analytical category useful for understanding both individual behaviour (psychology) and collective behaviour (society or culture). By operationalizing recurring actions into genres, individuals participating over time in an activity system come to recognize and perform actions in typical ways using typical tools, thus appropriating ('picking up' or learning) the tools (including discursive tools) and perhaps the object, motive, and subjectivity (identity) of the collective. Similarly, by operationalizing

> recurring actions into genres, collectives [re]create and temporarily stabilize
> their object, motive, tools (including discursive tools), and collective identity.
> (Russell, 1997a, p. 6)

The descriptions of the four study schools provide what may be seen as a first
step in the identification of the genres in place at specific sites.

Genre One – Moving schools/learning pupils

School A

This was a school with a gendered distribution of resources which favoured
girls. The headteacher specifically rejected the idea that a boy with behavioural
problems was necessarily a pupil with SEN. The school had developed positive
behaviour rules on the basis of lists constructed by each group for their
classroom. These were discussed and developed by staff and parents. After a full
period of consultation and adjustment these rules were displayed and monitored.
Bullying, name calling, social isolation, teasing, verbal abuse were taken seriously
as impeding learning. Interventions were designed to facilitate their learning.
The school has detailed planning procedures, curriculum review meetings and
training linked to identified targets. Consistency of values was seen as a priority
by the head.

In responding to behaviour through an effective whole-school policy, this
school avoided the need to divert SEN resources from supporting learning.
In addition, the school used objective tests as part of the process of identifying
pupils who might need additional support. This could be part of an effective
approach to ensuring that girls receive the support to which they are entitled.
In this school, SEN resources were targeted towards individuals, and were seen
as providing learning support for pupils who were currently underperforming.

School B

School B was attempting to develop a similar form of practice to that observed
in school A. The following story told to one of the team illustrates the extent to
which the school regards itself as having developed from a 'low base'.

School B 'Early Days'

The children running in and out of the staffroom and screaming things,
going to the head's office without knocking and barging through, no respect
for hardly any of the adults that were in here, and my friend came on a visit
and she walked through the playground and she asked somebody really
nicely 'Would you tell me where Miss X is?' and the boy replied 'How the
f★★★ should I know'!

This new school emerged from an unhappy merger between two other schools and was now 'under new management'. Although explanations of pupils' difficulties could have rested on social disadvantage the school was attempting to address a difficult situation. It had developed a focus on systems development and raising the standards and aspirations of the children. However, in this chaotic but 'moving' situation there was some confounding of the needs of the school with the needs of the pupils. Funding which could have been used to support individual pupils was diverted into improving the classroom practice of inexperienced teachers working in difficult situations.

Genre Two – Stuck schools: social casualties

School C

This is a school which the head conceives of as being 'a very tough inner city school'. Inspection of demographic data suggested little difference between the social and cultural backgrounds in the four schools.

The allocation of SEN resources reveals a global conceptualisation of need. Problems are defined with reference to social disadvantages. The uniform distribution of resources across classes is rationalised in terms of the global social disadvantages which all the pupils encounter. This is taken as an act in favour of equality of opportunity. This action is often referenced to race.

The school's account of a 'race' effect appears in two contradictory ways. Negatively in the difficult and disruptive behaviour of black boys. Positively with respect to black girls who are said to be doing well and are praised for acting as school playground and even classroom monitors:

> So you find you have to make a conscious effort to try to make sure the girls aren't swallowed up by the boys 'cause they're very dominating but right from the start it was a case of there are only eight girls . . . fortunately we've got . . . I could say half of them very strong girls so they're (able to look after themselves) . . . they've actually been used to help settle some of the more unsettled boys and they've been wonderful . . . I mean it's hard work getting him (Keith) to sit down and do anything and Naomi's brilliant . . . we're talking about strong girls like Natalie and Charmian who sit on people like Keith. . . .
>
> (Class teacher, African Caribbean woman)

The rationale of equal *lack* of opportunities leaves no space for distributing the resources to individual need. The construction of the situation as being primarily about toughness immediately conceded the ground to the boys.

School D

This is the second of the 'stuck' schools. Nurture and understanding is the first response to the children who present with difficult or 'challenging' behaviour. The teachers talk of getting behaviour right before learning can take place. Pupils with SENs were largely perceived as 'socially damaged', a view which inevitably led to SEN resources being substantially used to provide behaviour support, almost exclusively to boys.

These four schools exhibit a high degree of similarity in pupil populations and yet differ markedly in the gender ratios within SEN categories. School A kept a pedagogic focus throughout. It was organised to learn about itself. School B was starting to 'move', albeit slowly. It was starting to develop systems and practices of institutional learning and development. As a consequence, the perception of pupil difficulty was also in the process of change. Schools C and D were both 'stuck'. These schools all made differences. These differences may be seen as genres within the more general activity system of schooling. These genres take up different positions on both gender and race.

If these genres are regarded as qualitatively different tools within an activity theory framework then historical and empirical analysis of activities within the institutions should reveal different subject positions and outcomes. This points to another potential direction for development which may approach the analysis of socio-institutional effects within the post-Vygotskian field.

Gender and learning

Our first study gave us evidence that different forms of educational outcome in schools were associated with particular forms of social 'language' and of social practice which were informed by specific forms of pedagogic belief and practice. From this base we then moved to consider gendered differentials in the attainment of pupils in relation to particular forms of pedagogic belief (Hey *et al.*, 2000; Fielding *et al.*, 1999; Daniels *et al.*, 2000; Hey *et al.*, 1998; Daniels, 1998).

There has been a shift away from public concern about girls' achievement to boys' achievement at school in exams. The concern about 'boys' under-achievement' has been characterised in educational policy initiatives at national, local and school levels, most significantly in the imposition of a national literacy strategy (QCA, 1998; Barrs and Pidgeon, 1998). However, overall improvements in achievement are often ignored and gender differences are ascribed to the deleterious effects of 'the feminisation of teaching' (Epstein *et al.*, 1998). The concern for boys' underachievement has been problematised by Murphy and Elwood (1998) who draw on Hildebrand (1996) to argue that improvement in female achievement is *not shared* by girls from low socio-economic backgrounds and may not be apparent in some subjects.

A preliminary hypothesis which guides our work is that boys experience a contradiction between cultural messages and practices associated with hegemonic masculinity and those teaching practices conducive to optimal learning within primary schooling. A masculine orientation to learning may be invested in autonomy (authority, aggression and technical competence), whereas the discourses and practices of learning within primary schooling are centred around group and team work. Such collaborative practices presume co-dependency. In order to shed light on these interactive practices we argued that it is essential to re-engage with girls' experience of learning in order to cast more light on why boys appear to be adopting less effective strategies.

Specifically we suggest that males are encultured into a view that they should learn alone or under the guidance of the teacher. This is in contrast to females who we suggest are more likely to seek and offer help to each other in learning. We argue that this aspect of emergent masculinity in schools gives rise to higher level of bidding for teacher attention from males. Given the limited amount of teacher time available for individual support, males must either become self-sufficient learners or seek other means of bidding for attention which are often disruptive. This is unlike girls who are more likely to engage with peers in dialogue concerned with learning. Whilst we accept that much of this dialogue may not be that between a learner and a 'more capable peer' we suggest that given the economics of classroom time, girls are more likely to be in receipt of appropriate 'scaffolds' for their learning than boys. We sought to investigate the beliefs that teachers and learners hold about classroom dialogue and about learning. We were concerned to establish whether such beliefs are gendered and raced and whether such beliefs condition classroom practice.

Our theoretical approach is concerned with the discursive construction of masculinities (Warren, 1997; Yates 1997). Warren (1997) suggests that male identities/identifications are neither normative nor biologically nor socially reproduced. He and others have argued that they are best understood as positionings, afforded, or made available and subsequently taken up within specific discourses. Forms of schooling have been found to embed patterns of talk that are associated with factors of class and achievement. In a study of schools differing on measures of effectiveness and socio-economic status (SES), Duffield (1998) found longer and more frequent writing and sustained reading in English classes in low SES schools with far less time spent on pupil collaborative/discussion tasks. All the above suggests a potentially powerful linkage between questions of difference, the quality of the pedagogic discourse and practice, the type of emergent masculinities and femininities, and impacts on achievement.

Our original suggestion was that boys *could* be encultured to read social practices, including learning, as intrinsically individualistic. There is thus a high likelihood that because they understand/experience learning as solitary working they live it competitively. Help can only be legitimately sought from the 'non-competitor', i.e. the teacher. This approach almost *requires* boys to equate success with self-sufficiency. Those boys who cannot be (seen as) autonomous learners are particularly 'at risk' of being seen as disruptive given the multiple demands on teacher time. This contrasts with girls who, under this model, were more likely, because of their general collaborative orientation to the social and schooling, to be in communicative and social dialogue with each other.

Our interest in the different languages and practices of classroom learning focused critical attention upon the salience of the above in constituting and *mediating* the different constructions of masculinity and femininity in classrooms. We approached this via the central idea that boys are subject to two irreconcilable messages, one about being a powerful boy and one about what it means to be an effective learner. In the first, they are confronted by the cultural messages and practices of hegemonic masculinity (Connell, 1995) and the second, the practices of effective learning in the school. This contradiction required us to prioritise the role of discourse and language in the production, construction and negotiation of pedagogic practices and scrutinise how such discourses provide scope for individual subjectivities and interpersonal identifications (Hey, 1997).

Here we sought to *articulate* (Hall, 1996) post-Vygotskian insights about the sociocultural nature of learning with the feminist poststructuralist emphasis upon the density, variability, and multiplicity of how we come to be 'who we are, where we are, when we are'. Our theoretical foci on prevailing or hegemonic discourses and pedagogy as *de-limiters* of possible positions (re)establishes a framework for examining the ways in which children come to 'correctly position' themselves as particular sorts of learners in specific pedagogic and geographical locations.

This was a two-phase, split site, multidisciplinary (feminist theory, psychology, sociology, socio-linguistics, cultural geography) project. Our methodological approach was formulated jointly so that we could combine appropriate elements from our contrasting conceptual languages. We selected a sample of twelve schools which varied in terms of gender differences in attainment and overall attainment in the school. Data were collected at the levels of the school organisation, theories of instruction and pedagogic belief on the part of teachers and learners as well as direct ethnographic study of learning and communicative practice.

This approach was informed by principles derived from the ethnography of communication. We were interested in:

- how teachers and pupils instigate, maintain and transform various configurations of collaborative and competitive discourses through whole class and formal learning group activities;
- ways of speaking that teachers and pupils develop within the culture of their class and school, and how these discourses become shared;
- dimensions of contrast within classrooms and across schools;
- how learning is bound up in the sociocultural ethos created by teacher pedagogy and whole school philosophy.

We enabled the teacher and children to familiarise themselves with the interviewers, before interviews and activities. Researchers drew classroom maps, collected school documentation, took photos of the children and recorded who worked with whom, where and why. Observations were written up into analytic vignettes which are interpretative accounts of participant observation devised in order to understand the immediate and local meanings of actions defined from the actors' point of view (Erickson, 1990).

Through pupil interviews and observations we were able to show how children's talk discursively mediated and constituted complex inter-subjective social and pedagogic identifications. Two main strands were maintained:

- what children said about learning;
- how children verbally and non-verbally engaged in, were positioned in and developed and displayed friendship and learning groups.

We became interested not only in what the different all-boy and all-girl friendship groups *say* about gendered learning but also how they *perform their masculinities and femininities* in answering the question. We also observed children as they engaged in particular tasks. The aims of the tasks were to: provide a reading activity which would be demanding for most pupils; provide opportunities for pupils to help one another; provide an opportunity for collaborative work and discussion; and gather pupils' views about effective learning.

The data suggested strongly that a pedagogic focus on learning (as distinct from learners) in an environment where collaboration is supported and fostered by both the school and teacher, is associated with low levels of gender difference in attainment. The data showed also that class based differences are central factors in the discussion of gendered patterns of attainment. This confirmed the observations noted by Murphy and Elwood (1998) at the level of pupils and Duffield (1998) at the level of pedagogies. In order to advance these particular boys' educational achievement there is a need to do several things at once based on a complex awareness of differences *between* genders and differences *within* genders.

We identified boys who have been persuaded to move their position away from conceiving of formal education in win/'fail' dualities. In doing so they have acquired new positions in pedagogic practice and thus new ways of expressing their emergent masculinities. In short they have learnt to enjoy and benefit from collaboration. Given boys' general predisposition towards competition, teachers need to offer explicit teaching on how to collaborate through active interventions (e.g. Mercer *et al.*, 1999). This cannot be done as a mere rhetorical or technical trick. Collaboration and co-operation has to be embedded at the very heart of the school's philosophy and practices. It has to be located in how difference is addressed. By taking a collaborative learning approach boys are placed in learning structures that demand they share, listen and negotiate. These practices appear to produce a masculine learning identity that seems to be more relational, less boundaried, more collegial and able to seek and offer help. These are behaviours associated with more effective learning strategies.

An awareness of differences *within* masculinities needs to be considered at the same time as an awareness of general differences *between* genders is considered.

With these findings in mind I now wish to return to two of the definitions of pedagogy that were discussed in Chapter 1.

> Pedagogy is a practice of the social administration of the social individual. Since at least the 19th century pedagogical discourses about teaching, children, and learning in schools connected the scope and aspirations of public powers with the personal and subjective capabilities of individuals. This administration of the child embodies certain norms about their capabilities from which the child can become self-governing and self reliant.
>
> (Popkewitz, 1998, p. 536)

> Pedagogy is a sustained process whereby somebody(s) acquires new forms or develops existing forms of conduct, knowledge, practice and criteria, from somebody(s) or something deemed to be an appropriate provider and evaluator. Appropriate either from the point of view of the acquirer or by some other body(s) or both.
>
> (Bernstein, 1999a, p. 259)

The findings from the gender studies suggest the need for detailed study of the institutional regulation of the possibilities for development and functioning. Studies such as these hint at the subtlety and complexity of such regulation. When Michael Cole (1996) speaks of context as 'that which weaves together' he provides a metaphor for the development of research and understanding of a broadly construed notion of pedagogy. The 'warp' and 'weft' of such a process of weaving are, as yet, somewhat crude. I have used a brief description from our work on gender as an illustration of the need for detailed ethnographic study which will enable us to 'see' some of the ways in which institutional effects contribute to the 'social administration of the social individual'. I would suggest that there is much to be done in 'learning the landscape' (Greeno, 1991) of socio-institutional effects from a post-Vygotskian perspective. From an activity theory point of view this becomes the development of a more sophisticated model of discourse and discursive practice. From a sociocultural perspective this becomes a matter of locating such models within an account of activity systems that reveals how such discourses are produced and changed.

Subject specific communicative competences

In this section I return to Bernstein's work in order to illustrate how his model may be used to relate the production of specific forms of pedagogic discourse to communicative competences acquired by pupils (Daniels, 1995). In Chapter six of *Thinking and Speech* Vygotsky claims a particular function of speech in instruction within schooling.

The instruction of the child in systems of scientific knowledge in school involves a unique form of communication in which the word assumes a function which is quite different from that characteristic of other forms of communication . . .

1) The child learns word meanings in certain forms of school instruction not as a means of communication but as part of a system of knowledge.
2) This learning occurs not through direct experience with things or phenomena but through other words.

(Vygotsky, 1987, p. 27)

Participation in specific forms of social practice is linked with the development of word meaning. In order to understand the development of word meaning the characteristics of particular communications practices must be understood. As Minick (1990) shows, Vygotsky maintained that various activities such as science, schooling, art, and reading stimulate unique kinds of thinking. Activities do not express pre-formed, natural cognitive, emotional, or personality characteristics of the individual. On the contrary, artistic, literary, scientific and educational activities generate psychological functions. The concrete social relations and cultural technologies that are germane to the activities organise the individual's psychological processes (Minick, 1990, p. 167).

Vygotsky argues that the forms of instruction in scientific concepts of formal schooling (i.e. mathematics, the natural sciences) involve the child in new ways of using words in communication. Vygotsky saw the psychological characteristics of the scientific concept as inseparable from the unique use of words in the social interaction that occurs between teachers and pupils in formal school instruction (Minick, 1985, p. 107). If socio-institutional effects of schooling are to be considered within a Vygotskian framework then one approach is to compare the effects of different forms of organisation of subjects of instruction. This calls for a description and analysis of structures and of effects. Bernstein provides the structural level of analysis and Vygotsky furnishes the theoretical framework which can account for the position of the individual.

The study I wish to discuss focused on the relation between school and classroom organisation and pupils' ability to realise criteria of communicative competence generated by specific discourses in schools displaying variation in organisational form. It was shown that pupils' discriminations and realisations of such texts were related to the classification and framing values of the school's organisation and pedagogic practice. The specialised discourses of subjects with their own unique generating and evaluating procedures were examined. The relation between categories of specialised discourses was considered across schools. The schools studied were drawn from the special school sector which exhibits a high degree of between-school variation.

The empirical focus of the study was on the extent to which boundaries between subject categories are distinguishable by children and the extent to which they produce speech which constitutes a realisation of these boundaries. The focus was thus on a form of discrimination which is not formally or informally taught. Thus, concern was with a form of textual production which must be tacitly inferred. There are parallels here with Mercer's (2000) work on classroom talk. He was concerned to make explicit that which was tacit.

In order to create a description of the schools which carried with it predictions for speech usage, the boundaries between subjects, distinctions between teachers, and schools as organisations were considered. A general model of description was developed under the headings: 1. Theory of Instruction, 2. School Organisation, 3. Classroom Practice, and 4. External School Relations. From this general model attributes relevant to the research were selected. The point of departure was the theory of instruction. As Bernstein (1985) states:

> The theory of instruction is a crucial recontextualized discourse as it regulates the orderings of pedagogic practice, constructs the model of the pedagogic subject (the acquirer), the model of the transmitter, the model of the pedagogic context *and* the model of communicative pedagogic competence.
>
> (Bernstein, 1985, p. 14)

It was argued that the organisation of the staff, pupils and use of specialised discourses should be in direct relation to the theory of instruction. The school will be organised so as to allow the required theory to be put into practice. Each level of school organisation will have its own division of labour (classification) and its own social relation (framing). Where the theory of instruction gives rise to a strong classification and strong framing of the pedagogic practice it is expected that there will be a separation of discourses (school subjects), an emphasis upon acquisition of specialised skills, the teacher will be dominant in the formulation of intended learning and the pupils are constrained by the teacher's practice. The relatively strong control on the pupils' learning, itself, acts as a means of maintaining order in the context in which the learning takes place. The form of the instructional discourse contains regulative functions. With strong classification and framing the social relations between teachers and pupils will be more asymmetrical, that is, more clearly hierarchical. In this instance the regulative discourse and its practice is more explicit and distinguishable from the instructional discourse. Where the theory of instruction gives rise to a weak classification and weak framing of the practice then children will be encouraged to be active in the classroom, to undertake enquiries and perhaps to work in groups at their own pace. Here the relations between teacher and pupils will have the appearance of being more symmetrical. In these circumstances it is difficult to separate instructional discourse from regulative discourse as these are mutually embedded.

Allowance was made for the existence of a distinction between the official theory of instruction of a school and the theory of instruction of a particular classroom. Local variation is more likely to develop when there is a low degree of central control over pedagogic practice in the school. Whilst there was variation between teachers' practice in the schools with weaker values of framing regulating teacher practice, the actual classes studied were taught by teachers who did adhere to the overall official school practice.

Four special schools catering for pupils designated as having moderate learning difficulties, with adjoining catchment areas in one Local Education Authority were studied. Each school was situated in a residential area of a town and drew 120 pupils in the age range 4–16 from a mixed urban and rural catchment area.

The schools were referred to as TC, A, WH, and CH. The coding of each school in terms of specific classification (strength of category relation) and framing (social relation) values was based upon observation and interview data, together with the agreed statements from which each school's theory of instruction could be reliably inferred. It cannot be over-emphasised that the assigning a value to a function was in the nature of a hypothesis. Codings and descriptions were discussed and ratified with members of staff in the schools.

In comparison with school TC, in school A there was a strengthening of values of classification of teachers and subjects at junior level with stronger framing governing the socialisation of the pupils within the practice of the classroom. In school WH there was evidence of very strong classification and strong framing of teachers and subjects. The ideology of the school appears, when viewed from the perspective of the external values of framing, to be more integrationist than TC or A apart from with respect to mainstream school. In school CH there was evidence of very strong framing and strong classification over subjects.

In terms of values of classification and framing of teachers and subjects there was a cline of schools from TC (weaker) to WH (stronger). It was theoretically expected that the move from the values of classification and framing of the school and classroom to the pupils' practice is mediated through recognition and realisation rules of the instructional practice. These rules are hypothesised functions of the values of classification and framing. Concretely, it was expected that children would produce different texts under different conditions of classification and framing.

The curriculum subject contexts chosen for study were those of art and mathematical/scientific studies. The selection was made because these contexts allow the maximum observable differences in language use. Ten boys from the 10–11 age group in the four schools were identified. No significance between school differences were found for WISC(R) full scores, social class with reference to the Registrar General's scale, or expressive language ability.

The following procedure was used in carrying out this study. Ten picture stimuli were presented to the children in each of two instructional contexts. The order of presentation and instructional context of presentation were randomised for each task and each child. Each stimulus was presented to each child in each curriculum context with the following question form:

We are in a (Maths/Art) lesson. Your teacher is teaching you about (Maths/ Art). What would your teacher like to hear you say about this picture in this lesson?

The children's responses were recorded and subsequently transcribed. Two observers transcribed a selected sample of taped material in order to check the reliability of the transcription. For each child the pairs of statements (one from an artistic and one from a mathematical context) were pasted onto a single sheet of card. The relative order of the members of pairs for each of the ten pairs for each child was randomised. Two teacher observers were asked independently to compare the statements in each pair. One teacher was from CH, the other from TC. As there were 800 paired statements to be evaluated, the process was staged over a period of two months; the order of presentation was randomised across children and schools for each teacher. For each statement pair each teacher was asked:

1. Can you tell the difference between these two statements?
2. If you can, which one do you think was made in which context?

There were significant differences between (1) TC and CH and (2) TC and WH. The position of schools relative to one another with respect to children's ability to produce distinguishable text reflects the relative positions with respect to classification and framing.

Where the values of classification and framing of the culture of subjects were strong, the children realised the criteria of communicative competence held by their teachers with respect to discrimination between subjects to a greater extent than when, in a school such as TC, values of classification and framing were weak. The individual measures of expressive language ability would suggest that the school differences revealed in the study are not attributable to individual differences. A high level of agreement of teacher evaluation is suggestive of a common basis of understanding as to the language of school subjects: the implication being that it is neither the ability of the pupils nor teacher capacity/understanding that conditions the variations in school responses; rather the responses are modulated by the schools themselves.

The study confirmed a relation between organisational form and the possession of realisation rules. This conclusion is given added strength by the observation of a school transfer. Here a child appeared to have acquired realisation rules on transfer. This boy who transferred from a regime of weak values of classification and framing to a regime of strong values showed a marked and rapid increase in ability to discriminate between discourses. The stronger the value of classification and framing in the school the greater the likelihood that any one child will be able to realise the communicative competence held for specific subjects.

The study then moved to a focus on recognition rules. Rather than using teachers as the sources of competent distinguishing ability between texts, children were also asked to distinguish between utterances of other children. If children are judged as being able to realise appropriate texts, do these children recognise the appropriate texts of others? These competences have been learned and thus their nature must have been sensed in some way. A research question closely allied to this is whether children who do not produce many statements that are judged to be distinctive to specific discourses can on the other hand correctly distinguish between other children's statements. If this were found to be the case an implicit developmental sequence would be revealed.

On the basis of the data generated by this investigation, it would appear to be reasonable to assume that almost all the children in these schools are able to recognise different discourses produced by other children, but not all children produce speech in particular contexts that may be seen to be belonging to specialised discourses. This is seen to be a school effect. The basic hypothesis which related boundary features of the school to pupils' ability to recognise differences between subjects and realise these differences in subject specific talk acceptable to teachers was supported by the data.

It is important to reflect on the fact that the rules of speech in pedagogic contexts are rarely explicitly taught and that it was some of these that were the rules of interest in this study. For example, pupils are rarely formally taught how to *recognise* and *realise* (produce) subject specific speech, e.g. to recognise and/or to make a statement which counts as an artistic statement or a scientific statement. It is even rarer for them to be given explicit lessons in their difference. Children have to realise different communicative competences in the different schools, although they may enter school with shared competences and recognition rules of subject specific discourses. This finding echoes that of Foley (1991).

> What clearly showed up was that the restriction in teaching of a limited number of writing type activities (genres) was denying the child the opportunity of educational success. Whereas the introduction of a genre-based approach to the development of writing which gives exposure to a wide range of genres gives access to writing as a tool for entry into the culture.
>
> (Foley, 1991)

The major strength of the investigation was that it provided a body of evidence that strongly suggests a relation between the macro structure of school organisation and the micro practices of individual pupils. In terms of the original Vygotskian thesis there is also the more general question as to whether specialised speech within a curriculum subject constitutes a specialised psychological tool. Foley (1991) is clear in his answer to this question:

> . . . is to see technicality and abstraction as tools (in the Vygotskian sense) with which to explore the subject areas of the curriculum. The student,

therefore has to learn to marshal the language of technicality and abstraction in ways appropriate to each discipline. The special registers of the subject areas of the school curriculum should reflect how those registers are used in real life as these have evolved as ways of getting on with different kinds of work in the world. Knowledge of specialised registers is a powerful means of access into society and therefore needs to be taught as this gives the student conscious control, at least to some degree, of these technologies.

(Foley, 1991, p. 32)

The suggestion that different types of schooling give rise to different types of effect carries with it questions of structural fitness for purpose. The analytic tools of some forms of social and educational psychology are blunted by their inability to investigate socio-institutional effects. Similarly the gaze of sociologically inspired policy studies is averted from effects on individuals. The development of a socially extended post-Vygotskian model offers the possibility of understanding the consequences of specific policy developments at the level of individual effects. The use of units of analysis which are conceptualised in terms of the use of psychological tools in contexts raises questions of differences between contexts. Differences in the structure of pedagogic practices constitute differences in contexts which are of semiotic significance. Bernstein both theorises the semiotics of the transmission and provides a language with which differences in structure can be brought to the focus of empirical studies of individual acquisition. A development of Bernstein's thesis offers the potential of an appropriate form of sociological theory to the post-Vygotskian enterprise.

Beyond speech?

In this section I will discuss a study which considered the role of non-linguistic artefacts as means of mediation in two of the schools from the previous study (Daniels, 1989). As I have argued in Chapters 1 and 2, the emphasis on speech has predominated in sociocultural studies of learning.

In different schools (or cultures) actions and objects signify different meanings. Indeed at a very general level it is possible to conceive of cultures or schools as worlds of signs and signs about signs (Hawkes, 1977). In a sense adapting to cultural change is a process of adapting to changing systems of signification. For a child, particularly a child who finds learning difficult, moving from home to school is itself an act of cultural change and, for some, entails culture shock. That which is taken to signify competence in one culture may signify incompetence in another or irrelevance in a third. How then does a school transmit to children the criteria that are taken to signify appropriate learning? What are the cues offered to children in their attempts to read the signs of schooling? It is argued here that art displays are part of the system of signs that constitute the culture of schools, that through these acts of publicity the principles which regulate the curriculum are realised. Cole (1987) draws attention to the importance that was placed on the 'shaping' effects of visual images by Vygotsky's immediate colleagues and peers.

> Luria's project was his hope that by uncovering the specific dynamics of thought in pre-literate societies, he could collaborate in a program of film-mediated education that would bring Soviet peasants a richer understanding of their historical circumstances, the better to guide their own destinies. Sergei Eisenstein had been experimenting with the way in which visual images could be artfully combined to evoke emergent generalizations in the viewers of his films, even though they could not read and the films were silent. Luria hoped that his work would aid his effort by revealing the cognitive dynamics of pre-industrial peoples as a basis for arranging the sequence of film images.
>
> (Cole, 1987, p. xii)

In many schools to have a 'nice bright classroom with lots of good display work' is one of the commonly held indicators of good teaching practice. Not only is display work important to parents but also to children. Children like having their work displayed on the wall. This very public way in which a teacher shows approval of a child's activity is highly valued. By putting works of art on the wall the teacher is telling the child that he/she approves of it and at the same time is offering a model of good practice to the rest of the class. This, of course, is one of the reasons why children feel so proud when their work is displayed, their friends are being offered their work as a model. The way in which work is selected for display and indeed the way in which the display is arranged is effectively an act of publicity of the teacher's desired model of good practice. Such publishing activities have focused the attention of theorists in the fields of Art and Education.

> Publicity is the culture of the consumer society. It propagates through images that society's belief in itself.
>
> (Berger, 1972, p. 139)

Two of the schools from the previous study (of subject specific speech) were used in this investigation: CH and TC. The procedure used was that each headteacher and classroom teacher was interviewed, in an informal setting. Every classroom was observed on three occasions, each lasting half a day. These observations were conducted on a Monday, Wednesday, and a Friday morning. The information gathered in this way was collated and draft descriptions were written. These were then shown to the classroom teachers and headteachers. The descriptions were amended if any party considered them to be inaccurate. There were no conflicting views.

These two schools were structured in very different ways: one in which there are a variety of highly structured subjects where the child has little choice over what it will learn, the other where a broad, integrated thematic approach is taken within which children and teachers are relatively autonomous in their actions. These two approaches approximate to the 'collection' and 'integrated' types identified by Bernstein (1977): one in which things must be put together and the other where things are kept apart.

When illustrating the differing nature of the criteria that the child is supposed to acquire in different teaching situations, reference is made to the teaching of art. In what is termed the visible pedagogy that is associated with the collection type of curriculum with its strong classification and framing the following example is given:

> What are the children doing? They are making facsimiles of the outside. They are learning a reproductive aesthetic code. They may be drawing or painting figures, houses, etc. The teacher looks at the product of one child and says, 'That's a very good house, but where is the chimney?', or 'There are no window in your house', or 'That man has got only three fingers', etc. Here the child is made aware of what is missing in the production and what is missing is made explicit and specific, and subject to finely graded assessment.
>
> (Bernstein, 1977, p. 119)

Whereas with the invisible pedagogy in the integrated type curriculum realised through weak classification and framing:

> The children have a large sheet of paper, and not a small box of paints but an assembly of media whereby their unique visual imagination may be momentarily revealed. This is allegedly not a reproductive aesthetic code, but a productive aesthetic code. The teacher here is less likely to say, 'What's that?', is less likely explicitly to create in the child a consciousness of what is missing in the product: the teacher is more likely to do this indirectly, in a context of general, diffuse support. Where the transmission realises implicit criteria, it is as if the acquirer is the source of the criteria.
>
> (Bernstein, 1977, p. 119)

These statements come very close to describing the practices of the two schools used in this study. Clearly these schools should not be taken as examples of pure types, rather as complex systems which embody significant differences. These differences are revealed in the notes taken in art lessons in the schools.

In an art lesson observed in CH the teacher read a story called 'Where the Wild Things Live'. She then told the children that they were going to 'make pictures of the wild things'. The teacher had prepared a number of different pieces of sugar paper and proceeded to assign children to these pieces of paper. Each piece of sugar paper had an outline of a 'Wild Thing' on it and most of them had sections/areas of the paper marked off. Each section contained a code number and thus could be translated by a key at the bottom of the piece of paper. The children followed the key which dictated the material to be used to 'fill in' the sections/areas marked on the paper. The 'Wild Things' were thus constructed. The department head said of art lessons, 'We are interested in the results of art, of good productions rather than "experiencing" the materials.'

In an art lesson observed in TC the children were given different grades of paper, powder paint and a piece of foam rubber or sponge. The teacher then told the children to wet the paper and flick paint at it with the sponge. The children were encouraged to use different kinds of paper with different degrees of dampness. They were told to experiment with ways of applying the powder paint. Similiar differences in pedagogic practice were noted on every observation day.

Gearhart and Newman argued that, for the nursery school children they studied, learning the social organisation of a classroom and learning its curriculum could not be distinguished.

> What children know about drawing is intimately tied to what they . . . understand of drawing activities undertaken in a particular social . . . context.
>
> (Gearhart and Newman, 1980, p. 183)

They discussed the importance of the way the teacher spoke to the children about their drawings and also drew attention to the particular form of pedagogy in the classroom.

> Drawing was also being learned from the teacher's efforts to teach the organizational independence of individual production tasks. Reflexively, this individual task organization was being learned from the teacher's efforts to teach independently planful drawing.
>
> (Gearhart and Newman, 1980, p. 183)

Whilst Gearhart and Newman's study is of interest, it failed to undertake the comparative work needed to show how ways of learning to draw differ under different forms of classroom social organisation. Also, following as it does an explicitly Vygotskian experimental approach, it lacks the potential for describing and analysing the social organisation of classrooms in structural terms (Wertsch, 1985). In its failure to do this it confines interpretation to a very local domain. Through focusing on wall display rather than pupil–teacher and teacher–pupil verbal communications, a wider perspective on semiotic mediation was being drawn.

It is important to note that the photographs that are to be discussed here were representative of each school's display work. All the work displayed at one time in both schools was recorded and selected examples are presented. The selection was made by the teachers of the classes of 9–12 year old children in each school.

That is the (two) teachers in each school were shown the entire sample of photographs for their school and asked to select the three that best represented the school's display work. Emphasis was laid on the display rather than the individual pictures. Equally important is the fact that all the teachers responsible for this display work viewed their efforts as the result of a 'common sense' approach to the task. They did not regard themselves as having been instructed or coerced to work in this way, nor did they regard their work as potentially different in form from display work in any other school. These photographs are those displayed in Figures 5.4–5.9.

What then is revealed by an inspection of a sample of the display work in these schools? The control over what is expected is clearly high in displays A, B and C. In A the faces all have the same structure – they are all the same shape! In B the faces of the flowers are structurally similar. The faces were all yellow, all on the same plates, all with red lips and all had eyebrows. The levels of similarity in C are so marked that they require no comment.

On the other hand, the control over what is taught/expected is of a very different nature in D, E and F. In D there is an integrating theme of transport and yet children have produced different illustrations relating to the central theme. These are drawn, crayoned or painted using a variety of techniques. In E and F there are no underlying themes and the work is very varied in terms of the techniques used and the content portrayed. It seems there are at least two principles at this level of control which distinguish the schools. In one school there is a high degree of control over what is to be portrayed and also over the techniques and materials to be used. In the other school, the level of control over these factors is much lower.

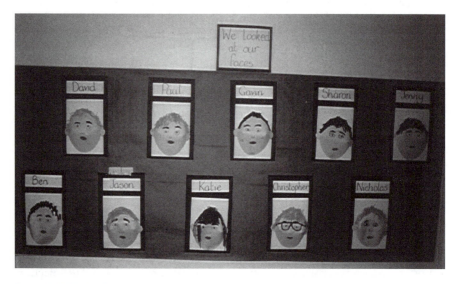

Figure 5.4 Display A.

Figure 5.5 Display B.

Figure 5.6 Display C.

It is perhaps worth considering the relation of the conceptual foci of two of these displays. The concept underlying display C is that of letter recognition and this is explicitly noted in the labelling. The implicit concept underlying D is of a different order – transport. It may be that this reveals different theories of curriculum sequencing. On the one hand, a 'top down' strategy is revealed in

Figure 5.7 Display D.

Figure 5.8 Display E.

Figure 5.9 Display F.

the integrated approach of the theme transport, and on the other hand a 'bottom up' strategy, that of a phonic approach to the teaching of reading, is implied.

This is reminiscent of a familiar debate. Displays A, B and C appear to be in accord with the strategic principle advocated by Gagne (1988) who argued that children cannot understand complex ideas before they have mastered the notions which are more conceptually primitive. Whereas displays D, E and F appear to reveal the strategy accorded to Bruner (1986) who argued that children will not understand and remember 'simple' ideas until they recognise the framework into which they fit.

Each school appears to some extent to have a characteristic style of structuring the displays. Whereas in A and C the pictures are arranged in straight lines with regular spacings between pictures, in D, E and F the pictures are closely grouped in irregular patterns. It is perhaps not entirely coincidental that in picture D the work displayed was produced by children in the age range 5–14 whereas each display in the other school was produced by one age group only. These two factors perhaps reveal underlying levels of classification. On the one hand, ages and individuals are grouped and on the other separated by clearly marked boundaries. It is in this way possible to argue that the principles on which the curriculum is organised are realised in the way work is displayed. Yet this analysis is from the point of view of a detached adult; the question remains as to what the children perceive in these situations.

The children in the two schools were interviewed using a technique derived from personal construct analysis (Bannister and Fransella, 1984). The original theoretical background of the development of this technique is couched in terms of the *individual* making sense of the world.

> Kelly emphasises the way people interact with their world and actively process rather than passively store their experiences. He describes people as developing sets of hypotheses or construct systems in which their present abstractions are tentatively placed on past experiences and then are later projected upon future events in order to cope with those events.
>
> (Diamond, 1985, p. 15)

There are links here with Woods' (1983) notion of 'perspective' – 'the frameworks through which people make sense of the world'. The model of the individual as personal scientist, constructing and testing hypotheses about the world lacks any reference to the social structure. What Kelly does provide is a non-directive approach to interviewing which may be subsumed within a model which articulates a process of social/cultural transmission.

Constructs may be seen as the bipolar dimensions with which the individual interprets the social world. Within the model adopted here their origins are the mediated effects of the social and cultural context. Three groups of three children ranging in age from 9 to 12 years in each of the two schools were interviewed. Each group was told that the photographs were from two schools and then asked to group them. This they all did correctly, that is they grouped the photographs on the basis of the school of origin. The groups were then shown photographs in groups of three and asked to say what was the same about the two photographs from one school and different about the photograph from the other school. It should be emphasised that this corruption of the personal construct technique will only provide general indicators of group perceptions. The constructs were grouped together on the basis of their similarity irrespective of the actual combination of eliciting elements (photographs).

The analysis revealed a school effect in terms of attributes perceived by the children. Children from both schools noted differences in variation in content, technique and medium. Children from school CH seemed to be more sensitive to variation in degree of attention paid to labelling work produced by individual children and entitling of group themes. Children from school TC seemed to be aware of the spatial arrangement of the display and the pedagogy employed in the classroom.

In school CH subjects are clearly marked, the criteria of evaluation are explicit and these are transmitted within a highly structured scheme. All the children recognise these points. However, children in school CH do appeared to pay particular attention to the labelling of their work, the purpose of that work. That is, they were concerned with their identity in relation to pre-ordained goals and see the products of schooling as being of paramount importance. The displays relay to these children the general principles of strong classification and framing of their school and reveal a focus on individual identity through performance.

Whereas in school TC with its integrated day approach and the pedagogy designed to facilitate the acquisition of understanding, the children also recognise the same general points. However, they pay particular attention to the pedagogy employed and relationships between children's work.

When asked which school they would choose to attend they were more concerned with the underlying social principles of the school, i.e. children from TC referred to the ability of children to think for themselves and of the danger of being spoilt and/or naughty. Thus emphasis here was on self and/or moral regulation. On the other hand, the children from CH chose their school on the basis of the performances produced in the schools, i.e. 'lovely pictures', 'do more older things' and 'more interesting 'cos all about travelling places'. One school concentrates on the outcomes of schooling in terms of required performances and the other on the contexts in which children will develop. It appears that the children schooled to perform attend to performances, and children schooled through immersion in contexts attend to the social and moral nature of those contexts and their consequences.

It appeared that the wall displays examined here acted as relays of the fundamental regulatory principles that govern the schools at least as viewed by adults. More surprising is the implication that children are sensitive to the messages relayed by these displays. The fact that these children were described as having moderate learning difficulties further implies that either this transmission process is very strong or operates through an unimpaired channel.

In summary, all the children appear to be able to read many of the signs from these displays. Children in a structured school were concerned with individual identity in relation to performance, whereas in the other school the children emphasised principles of social relation. The school environments were specified in terms of what is ultimately their social nature. It has been demonstrated that the principles that regulate these environments are relayed through the wall displays in these schools. The different aesthetic principles of the schools in question are contained within very different institutions. The arrangements through the production, selection and combination of children's painting were shown to act as a relay of the deep structure of the pedagogic practice of particular schools. As far as the teachers were concerned, they were simply mounting wall displays rather than using wall displays explicitly as relays of the focus of their practice. Whilst they were keen to create a good impression through their wall display work they were not aware of their expression of the underlying principles of school practice.

Following the directions given by Vygotskian psychology it would seem profitable to investigate the meaning of wall displays for children as a step in the process of understanding what counts as important in a particular school (Wertsch, 1985a, b). In the investigation of wall display it is important to remember that the children also produced the pictures and thus were socialised by that activity. The products of these socialising activities are then selected, combined and organised by the teacher in a way which celebrates and announces the expected competences required of a particular school and/or classroom. Rather than reading backwards from statistics describing the outputs of schooling it would seem worthwhile to consider what is relayed to children by particular activities. From this perspective schools may be considered as generators of a specialised semiotic. The meaning of these signs for the participants in the practice of schooling then becomes the object of study. The study of wall displays indicated that children from different schools 'saw' different meanings in the same displays. They were oriented towards different sets of recognition and realisation rules.

When the children were asked to differentiate between selected children's paintings, the children in CH referred to the importance of the individual producer of the painting in constructs 1 and 2. Children in TC did not echo these remarks about the labelling of individual children's work, and of the overall class task. Further, regarding preferences in terms of class placement, the children in CH talked about the school where the best pictures were produced. On the other hand, in TC the children talked about whether the children in the class could choose what they wanted to do, and paint in the way they wanted to paint rather than the way the teacher wanted. 'This school teaches you how to choose.' These children distinguished between classrooms on the basis of pedagogic relations within classrooms. Contrasts were drawn between classrooms where 'you paint what you see' and 'you paint what the teacher sees'. That is, between classrooms with strong and weak values of framing. Whereas children in CH talked about the individual producer of the painting, children in TC talked about the social relations of production of the pictures. The children were presented with the same stimuli but they realised different meanings. It would appear to be inadequate to talk about quality of wall display independent of a type of pedagogic practice. A complete analysis would also refer to the information that a display relays to children about the practice of the schooling of which they are the subjects.

This study used measures of school modality as described in the study of subject specific speech. Although somewhat crude these were measures of the discursive, organisational and interactional practice. Measures were then taken of the pupils' recognition and realisation rules with respect to visual relay of aspects of their pedagogic practice. A relationship was revealed. The relationship was tentative but exciting. A connection was made between the rules the children used to make sense of their pedagogic world and the modality of that world. This suggests that the study of non-linguistic means of mediation may form an important part of the more general move to understand institutional regulation within a post-Vygotskian framework.

On entering schools children have very quickly to learn 'what goes here'. If they fail to do this, for whatever reason, they can become marginalised in a variety of ways. We need to understand the infinitely subtle mechanisms by which schools send messages to children. The issues explored here may be of particular relevance to children in special schools but the underlying principles are of importance in all forms of pedagogic practice.

Difference and acceptability in institutions

In this section I wish to discuss a study which was concerned with the formative effects of specific pedagogic modalities set within different national cultures (Daniels *et al.*, 1996). The research used the same approach to the descriptions of schools as in the studies of speech and wall display in an analysis of personal perceptions of pupil behaviour. The international comparison between Denmark and the UK extends the power of this analysis. Denmark provides an ideal site for this comparison with the UK because it retains certain similarities in terms of the structure of its system of schooling yet reveals profound differences in its orientation to social policy and welfare. Thus, general ideological and cultural differences form a background to comparisons between schools.

Interviews of teachers and pupils to elicit perceptions of deviance were again conducted using a version of personal construct interview technique. Categories of constructs induced through these procedures were then analysed in terms of pedagogic context of elicitation and also gender of subject. Features of the coding of the institution were then related to features of the categories of the interview data.

Two schools were identified in each of the two countries: England and Denmark. One of each of the two schools in each country was selected as a model which clustered around descriptions of strong classification and framing and one of each of the two schools in each country was selected to cluster around weak values of classification and framing.

Classes of 13 to 14 year olds were identified within each school. The identification of pupils as elements for the personal construct interviews involved selecting two or three different teachers of the same class in each school. Teachers were asked to identify the four pupils (two females and two males) in the class whose behaviour was the most acceptable to them; they were then asked to identify the four pupils (two females and two males) in the class whose behaviour was least acceptable to them. There was a high level of agreement between the teachers in their identification of the eight pupils in each class. The eight pupils were then asked to carry out the same exercise, identifying pupils who were most acceptable and least acceptable, and also how they thought their teachers would judge these pupils. The eight pupils identified the greatest number of times by teachers and pupils were selected to act as elements for the personal construct interviews. This exercise showed a high level of agreement between teachers and pupils.

Triads of elements (children) that revealed contrasts between 'acceptable' and 'unacceptable' pupils were constructed for each class. The standard question used to elicit data from the triad presentation was: 'What do you think is the same about these two and different about this one?' The personal construct interviews were conducted using two prompts for each subject with each triad. One was referenced to the subjects' own perceptions of similarities and differences between elements in the triad; the other was referenced to pupils' views in the case of teacher subjects and teachers' views in the case of pupil subjects. (cf. 'What do you think that your teacher would think was the same about these two and different about this one?' and 'What do you think that your pupils would think was the same about these two and different about this one?'). In this way the perceptions of actors of the processes of transmission were open to scrutiny.

Equal numbers of male and female pupils were interviewed. Those selected represented a stratified sample from each class in terms of stated acceptability. Additional interviews were conducted with any pupils whose acceptability ranking was seen to differ markedly between pupils and teachers. One member of the research team who is bilingual in English and Danish translated interview data. The emergent system of constructs for each school was juxtaposed with the descriptions of the school derived from the general model derived from the classification and framing measures taken of the schools. The patterns of categorisation were analysed by type of school within and between countries as well as within countries.

In order to ground the classification and framing data in observations of each school each member of the team visited each of the four schools and coded the data within their national groups for subsequent cross-national discussion and verification. The two English schools will be referred to as school EA and school EB whilst the two Danish schools will be referred to as school DA and school DB.

Schools DA and EA appeared to adopt a position in which instructional matters are deeply embedded in regulative practice; the priorities of these schools seem to be highly associated with goals of social and personal development. In contrast, schools DB and EB appear to regard instructional matters as the overriding concern of schooling; for them regulation is a consequence of instruction. Thus, we had identified two pairs of schools which appear to conform to broadly defined types, one type in which instruction predominates and one type in which matters of social order and identity are paramount.

There was a strong trend in the data which was suggestive of a school organisational effect. This was revealed in the distribution across the schools of the constructs generally referring to the categories of school work, social behaviour and personality. Schools which appear to be structured through strong classification and framing are those in which teachers and pupils make more reference to school work in their constructs of deviance than teachers and pupils in schools structured through weak classification and framing. Constructs relating to social behaviour appear to be used more in conditions where weak values of classification and framing obtain. Similarly, constructs referring to matters of personality seem to be associated more with weak rather than strong values of classification and framing.

These data are suggestive of a relay of the structure of the pedagogic practices in the schools. Following the distinction between instructional and regulative discourse these data may be read as the effects of differing degrees of embedding on one discourse in the other. In the sites regulated through weak values of classification and framing (EA and DA) the regulative discourse would predominate. The relative emphasis (70 per cent) placed on personality and social behaviour in the constructs in schools EA and DA would appear to be a relay of this relation. Conversely, the relative emphasis (again 70 per cent) on school work in the constructs from sites of strong classification and framing, where instructional discourse predominates, was also suggestive of a transmission effect. The institutional effect was more evident than the national effect of the constructs. There was a strong association between the pedagogic modalities operating within the schools and the ways in which teachers and pupils construed pupil acceptability. There was no such association with national location. The institutional level of regulation appeared to exert a more powerful effect than the national level.

Although tentative, the data provide some grounds for increased acceptance of an extended Vygotskian model of analysis. Following the summary of the post-Vygotskian research agenda developed by Minick et al. (1993), this study may be seen to support suggestions that:

- Bernstein's model provides a way of understanding school structure in such a way that the 'culturally specific nature of schools' may be given close attention.
- Perceptions of social behaviour may be linked to schools viewed as structured agencies of cultural transmission and that these may 'mediate specific forms of social and psychological life in distinct ways'.
- Modes of thinking evolve as integral systems of motives, goals, values, and beliefs that are closely tied to concrete forms of social practice.

Thus, the data along with further development and research may yield an important framework for developing a greater understanding of school 'cultures' and some of the factors in the way in which a school is organised which affect pupil construction of reality.

Conclusion

In this chapter I have discussed examples from some of the research which my colleagues and I have undertaken. I did this solely to illustrate directions that research might take. In Chapters 1 to 4 I attempted to outline the strengths of the various accounts of mediated social, cultural, historical formation of mind which have been developed on the basis of Vygotsky's early twentieth-century contribution to social theory. Throughout this discussion I have also sought to indicate possible areas for future development within this field, my central claim being that there is a need to incorporate the institutional level of regulation and analysis into the post-Vygotskian account of mediation. I have argued that the advances that have been made within recent developments in activity theory may be supplemented through a more detailed discussion of the modalities and structure of, one of the central means of mediation within schooling, pedagogic discourse. Following the suggestion that specific forms of discourse may be associated with specific forms of activity I have argued that there is a need to develop an analysis of the production of pedagogic discourse within specific social institutions. Bernstein's work allows a connection to be made between the rules that children use to make sense of their pedagogic world and the modality of that world. This is done through taking measures of school modality. Depending on the research question, relevant aspects of discursive, organisational and interactional practice are measured. The connection between these measures and measures of pupils' recognition and realisation rules may then be analysed.

I have also suggested that the analysis of pedagogic relays involved in the processes of social, cultural, historical formation within schools should not be constrained to the study of speech. The study of wall display suggests that a more broadly based form of semiotic analysis may be beneficial as we seek to understand processes of mediation in schooling.

Vygotsky's rejection of dualisms is not revealed in a research tradition within which cognitive development has tended to predominate. In the study of schooling for pupils described as having EBD, the use of Bernstein's formulation of pedagogic discourse as an embedded discourse comprising instructional and regulative components suggests one way in which the cognitive/affective dualism may be handled as an entwined duality (Valsiner, 1998). The importance of this suggestion concerning the structure of pedagogic discourse is that the model also allows for the analysis of the production of such embedded discourses in activities structured through specifiable relations of power and control within institutions. The utility of this model within sociocultural and activity theory research awaits a full consideration. The study of the institutional regulation of subject specific speech hints at its potential. The international comparative study of the institutional shaping of constructs of deviance adds to this suggestion. The studies of the institutional regulation of emergent masculinities[1] and femininities suggest that the complexities of the processes of identity formation require very delicate models of the discourses of pedagogic practice if they are to be made available to scrutiny and thus change. These studies suggest that such processes are of relevance in the study of learning. The study of resource allocation also suggests that the tacit assumptions of pedagogic practice both exert significant influence and are beyond the gaze of many approaches to pedagogic research and development.

Bernstein's approach to the sociology of pedagogy provides one way of extending the power of sociocultural and activity theory research.

I opened this book with a discussion of the ways in which we might define pedagogy and an outline of the place of the concept of mediation within Vygotskian theory.

Throughout the book I have attempted to illustrate the power and potential of sociocultural and activity theory for the development of pedagogic theory and research. I would wish to stress at the close that I regard both traditions as necessary components of future developments. I have also sought to hint at ways in which these traditions may be enhanced through the incorporation of a sociology of pedagogy which would enhance the analytical power of the overall approach.

I have shown how important the analysis of curriculum content is within some branches of the theory. Vygotsky's discussion of concept formation in terms of the interplay between scientific and everyday concepts directs attention to the need to select content and structure activity with developmental priorities in mind. My suggestion is that Bernstein's extension of the scientific/everyday distinction to include models of vertical and horizontal discourse may provide an important way forward in developing a more sophisticated analysis. Bernstein's contribution to the sociology of pedagogy allows us to explore the implications of a generative model of pedagogic possibilities which connects a macro level of institutional analysis with the micro level of interpersonal analysis.

A model of pedagogy which reduces analysis to pupil–teacher interaction alone results in a very partial view of processes of social formation in schooling. Schools are organised institutions within which specific forms of pedagogic practice arise. They are institutions which give rise to the production of specific cultural artefacts such as curriculum formations and their associated modalities of pedagogic practice and discourse which mediate the teaching and learning process.

Schooling may be understood as an elaborate form of sociocultural activity. This understanding invokes a broadly based conception of pedagogy. Vygotsky's work provides a framework within which support for pupil learning and the positioning of pupils within specific discourse structures may be explored. It may also be used to consider the developmental implications of different aspects of knowledge and knowledge producing activities. Social relations which serve to mediate processes of individual transformation and change are pedagogic relations. As yet we know too little about the nature and extent of those social, cultural and historical factors which shape human development.

The implications of Vygotsky's contribution have yet to be fully explored and exploited within education. His work constitutes a cultural resource which itself must be developed and enhanced through theoretical speculation and empirical enquiry.

Notes

1 It was with some amusement that I discovered that my spell check does not have a check for masculinity whilst it does for femininity. It would appear that masculinity remains a singularity in some circles!

Bibliography

Akhutina, T.V. (1975) 'The role of inner speech in the construction of an utterance', *Soviet Psychology* XVI, 3: 3–30.

Anderson, J.R. (1980) *Cognitive Psychology and its Implications*, San Francisco: Freeman.

Asmolov, A.G. (1982) 'Basic principles of a psychological analysis in the theory of activity', *Soviet Psychology*, Winter 86/7, XXV, 2, Pedagogika Publishers.

Asmolov, A. (1998) *Vygotsky Today: On the Verge of Non Classical Psychology*, New York: Nova Science Publishers.

Atkinson, P. (1985) *Structure and Reproduction: An Introduction to the Sociology of Basil Bernstein*, London: Methuen.

Baillargeon, R. (1987) 'Object permanence in 3½ and 4½ month-old infants', *Developmental Psychology* 23: 655–64.

Bakhtin, M.M. (1981) *The Dialogic Imagination: Four Essays*, M. Holquist (ed.); translated by C. Emerson and M. Holquist, Austin: University of Texas Press.

Bakhtin, M.M. (1986) *Speech Genres and Other Late Essays*, C. Emerson and M. Holquist (eds), Austin: University of Texas Press.

Bakhtin, M.M. (1990) *Art and Answerability: Early Philosophical Essays*, M. Holquist and V. Liapunov (eds), trans. and notes V. Liapunov, Austin, Texas: University of Texas Press.

Bakhurst D. (1995) 'Lessons from Ilyenkov', *The Communication Review* 1, 2: 155–78.

Bakhurst, D. (1996) 'Social memory in Soviet thought', in H. Daniels (ed.) *An Introduction to Vygotsky*, 196–218, London: Routledge.

Bakhurst, D. and Sypnowich, C. (1995) Introduction in *The Social Self. Inquiries in Social Construction*, London: Sage.

Bannister, D. and Fransella, F. (1984) *Inquiring Man* (3rd edn) Harmondsworth: Penguin.

Barker, R.G. and Wright, H.F (1968) *Ecological Psychology*, Stanford: Stanford University Press.

Barrs, M. and Pidgeon, S. (1998) *Boys and Reading*, London: CLPE.

Bazerman, C. (1988) *Shaping Written Knowledge: The Genre and Activity of the Experimental Article in Science*, Madison: University of Wisconsin Press.

Bazerman, C. (1994) 'Systems of genres and the enactment of social intentions', in A. Freedman and P. Medway (eds) *Genre and the New Rhetoric*, 79–101, London: Taylor & Francis.

Bazerman, C. (1997) 'Discursively structured activities', *Mind, Culture and Activity* 4, 4: 296–308.

Belmont, J. (1989) 'Cognitive strategies and strategic learning. The socio-instructional approach', *American Psychologist* 44, 2: 142–8.

Bentley, T. (1998) *Learning Beyond the Classroom: Education for a Changing World*, London: Demos & Routledge.

Bereiter, C. (1985) 'Toward a solution to the learning paradox', *Review of Educational Research*, 55, 201–26, in M. Cole (ed.) *Cultural Psychology: A Once and Future Discipline*, Cambridge, MA: Harvard University Press.

Bereiter, C. (1997) 'Situated cognition and how to overcome it', in J.A. Whitson, D. Kirshner (eds) *Situated Cognition. Social, Semiotic, and Psychological Perspective*, Mahway, NJ: Lawrence Erlbaum.

Berger, J. (1972) *Ways of Seeing* London, BBC Publications/Penguin.

Bernstein, B. (1972) 'Social class, language and socialization', in P.P. Giglioli (ed.) *Language and Social Context*, Harmondsworth: Penguin.

Bernstein, B. (1977) *Class Codes and Control*, Vol. 3, *Towards A Theory of Educational Transmissions*, 2nd revised edn, London: Routledge & Kegan Paul.

Bernstein, B. (1981) 'Codes, modalities and the process of cultural reproduction: a model', *Language in Society*, 10: 327–63.

Bernstein, B. (1985) 'On pedagogic discourse', in J. Richardson (ed.) *Handbook of Theory and Research in the Sociology of Education*, Westport, CT: Greenwood Press.

Bernstein, B. (1993) Foreword in H. Daniels (ed.) (1993) *Charting the Agenda: Educational Activity After Vygotsky*, London: Routledge.

Bernstein, B. (1996) *Pedagogy, Symbolic Control and Identity: Theory, Research and Critique*, London: Taylor & Francis.

Bernstein, B. (1999a) 'Official knowledge and pedagogic identities', in F. Christie (ed.) *Pedagogy and the Shaping of Consciousness: Linguistic and Social Processes*, London: Cassell.

Bernstein, B. (1999b) 'Vertical and horizontal discourse: an essay', *British Journal of Sociology of Education*, 20, 2: 157–73.

Best, F. (1988) 'The metamorphoses of the term "pedagogy"', *Prospects*, XVIII, 2: 157–66.

Bidell, T.R. (1992) 'Beyond interactionism in contextualist models of development', *Human Development*, 35: 306–15.

Bliss, J., Askew, M. and Macrae, S. (1996) 'Effective teaching and learning: scaffolding revisited', *Oxford Review of Education*, 22: 1: 37–61.

Bourdieu, P. (1977) *Outline of a Theory of Practice*, Cambridge: Cambridge University Press.

Bower, T.G.R. (1974) *Development in Infancy*, San Francisco: Freeman.

Bozhovich (1977) 'The concept of the cultural historical development of the mind and its prospects', *Soviet Psychology*, 26,12: 5–22

Brice-Heath, S. (1983) *Ways with Words*, Cambridge: Cambridge University Press.

Brown, A.L. and Campione, J.C. (1990) 'Communities of learning and thinking, or a context by any other name', in D. Kuhn (ed.) *Developmental Perspectives on Teaching and Learning Thinking Skills, 21. Contributions in Human Development*, Basel: Karger.

Brown, A.L. and Campione, J.C. (1994) 'Guided discovery in a community of learners', in K. McGilly (ed.) *Integrating Cognitive Theory and Classroom Practice: Classroom Lessons, 229–72*, Cambridge, MA: MIT Press/Bradford Books.

Brown, A.L. and Palincsar, A.S. (1989) 'Guided co-operative learning and individual knowledge acquisition', in L.B. Resnick (ed.) *Knowing, Learning, and Instruction: Essays in Honor of Robert Glaser*, 393–451, Hillsdale, NJ: Lawrence Erlbaum.

Brown, A.L., Metz, K.E., and Campione, J.C. (1996) 'Social interaction and individual understanding in a community of learners: the influence of Piaget and Vygotsky', in A. Tryphon and J. Voneche (eds) *Piaget-Vygotsky: The Social Genesis of Thought*, Hove: Psychology Press.

Brown, J.S., Collins, A. and Duguid, S. (1989) 'Situated cognition and the culture of learning', *Educational Researcher*, 18,1: 32–42.

Bruner, J.S. (1975) 'From communication to language: a psychological perspective', *Cognition*, 3: 255–87.

Bruner, J. (1986) *Actual Minds, Possible Worlds*, Cambridge, MA: Harvard University Press.

Bruner, J. (1987) 'Prologue to the English edition', in L.S. Vygotsky, *Collected Works* 1: 1–16, R. Rieber and A. Carton (eds); N. Minick (trans.), New York:Plenum.

Bruner J.S. (1990) *Acts of Meaning*, Cambridge, MA: Harvard University Press.

Bruner, J.S. (1996) *The Culture of Education*. Cambridge, MA: Harvard University Press.

Bruner, J. (1997) 'Celebrating divergence: Piaget and Vygotsky', *Human Development*, 40: 63–73.

Bruner, J.S., Caudill, E. and Ninio, A. (1997) 'Language and experience' in R.S. Peters (ed.) *John Dewey Reconsidered* (The John Dewey Lectures, University of London, 1975), London: Routledge & Kegan Paul.

Burkitt, I. (1998) 'The death and rebirth of the author: the Bakhtin circle and Bourdieu on individuality, language and revolution', in M.M. Bell and M. Gardiner (eds) *Bakhtin and the Human Sciences*, London: Sage.

Campione, J.C. (1996) 'Assisted assessment: a taxonomy of approaches and an outline of strengths and weaknesses', in H. Daniels (ed.) *An Introduction to Vygotsky*, London: Routledge.

Cazden, C.B. (1979) 'Peekaboo as an instructional model: discourse development at home and at school', in *Papers and Reports on Child Language Development*, 17. Palo Alto, CA: Stanford University, Department of Linguistics.

Cazden, C.B. (1993) 'Vygotsky, Hymes and Bakhtin: from word to utterance and voice', in E.A. Forman, N. Minick and C.A. Stone (eds) *Contexts for Learning: Sociocultural Dynamics in Children's Development*, Oxford: Oxford University Press.

Cheyne, J.A. and Tarulli, D. (1999) 'Dialogue, difference, and the "Third Voice", in the Zone of Proximal Development', *Theory and Psychology* 9, 5–28.

Chi, M.T.H. and Bassok, M. (1989) 'Learning from examples via self-explanations', in L.B. Resnick (ed.) *Knowing, Learning, and Instruction: Essays in Honor of Robert Glaser*, 251–82, Hillsdale, NJ: Lawrence Erlbaum.

Christie, F. (1985) *Language Education*, Geelong, Australia: Deakin University Press.

Christie, F. (1993) 'Curriculum genres: planning for effective teaching' in B. Cope and M. Kalantzis (eds) *The Powers of Literacy: A Genre Approach to Teaching Writing*, 154–78, London: Falmer Press.

Clark, A. (1996) *Being There: Putting Brain, Body and World Together Again*, Cambridge, MA: MIT Press.

Clark, A. (1998) 'Magic words: how language augments human computation', in P. Carruthers and J. Boucher (eds) *Language and Thought: Interdisciplinary Themes*, Cambridge: Cambridge University Press. Reprinted in J. Toribio and A. Clark (eds) *Artificial Intelligence and Cognitive Science* 4, Language and Meaning, New York: Garland Press.

Cobb, P., Perlwitz, M. and Underwood, D. (1996) 'Constructivism and activity theory', in H. Mansfield, N.A. Pateman and N. Bednarz (eds) *Mathematics for Tomorrow's Young Children*, 10–58. Dordrecht: Kluwer.

Cole, M. (1985) 'The zone of proximal development: where culture and cognition create each other', in J.V. Wertsch (ed.) *Culture, Communication and Cognition: Vygotskian Perspectives*, Cambridge: Cambridge University Press.

Cole, M. (1987) *The Theory of A. R. Luria. Functions of Spoken Language in the Development of Higher Mental Processes*, Hillsdale, NJ: Lawrence Erlbaum.

Cole, M. (1991) 'On putting Humpty Dumpty together again: a discussion of the papers on the socialization of children's cognition and emotion', *Merrill-Palmer Quarterly*, 37, 1: 199–207.

Cole, M. (1994) 'A conception of culture for a communication theory of mind', in D. Vocate (ed.) *Intrapersonal Communication: Different Voices, Different Minds*, Hillsdale, NJ: Lawrence Erlbaum.

Cole, M. (1996) *Cultural Psychology: A Once and Future Discipline*, Cambridge, MA: Harvard University Press.

Cole, M. (1997) *Using New Information Technologies in the Creation of Sustainable After School Literacy Activities: From Intervention to Maximising the Potential*. Third year report: July 1996 – July 1997, submitted to Andrew W. Mellon Foundation. San Diego: LCHC.

Cole, M., and Engeström, Y. (1993) 'A cultural-historical approach to distributed cognition', in G. Salomon (ed.) *Distributed Cognitions: Psychological and Educational Considerations*, New York: Cambridge University Press.

Cole, M. and Griffin, P. (1983) 'A socio-historical approach to re-mediation', *Quarterly Newsletter of the Laboratory of Comparative Human Cognition* 5, 4: 69–74.

Cole, M., Engeström, Y. and Vasquez, O. (eds) (1997) *Mind, Culture and Activity: Seminal papers from the Laboratory of Comparative Human Cognition*, Cambridge: Cambridge University Press.

Cole, T., Visser, J. and Daniels, H. (1999) 'A model explaining effective EBD practice in mainstream schools', in *Emotional and Behavioural Difficulties* 4, 1: 12–18.

Collins, A. (1991) 'Cognitive apprenticeship and instructional technology', in L. Idol and B.F. Jones (eds) *Educational Values and Cognitive Instruction: Implications for Reform*, Hillsdale, NJ: Lawrence Erlbaum.

Collins, A., Brown J.S. and Newman, S.E. (1989) 'Cognitive apprenticeship: teaching the crafts of reading, writing and mathematics', in L.B. Resnick (ed.) *Knowing, Learning and Instruction: Essays in Honor of Robert Glaser*, 453–94. Hillsdale, NJ: Lawrence Erlbaum.

Connell, R. (1995) *Masculinities*, Cambridge: Polity Press.

Cox, B.D. (1997) 'Mathematics instruction and metamemory: examples of too much and too little social intervention in the process of invention', in B.D. Cox and C. Lightfoot (eds) *Sociogenetic Perspectives on Internalisation*, Hillsdale, NJ: Lawrence Erlbaum.

Creese, A., Daniels, H. and Norwich, B. (1997) *Teacher Support Teams in Primary and Secondary Schools*, London: David Fulton.

Creese, A., Norwich, B. and Daniels, H. (2000) 'Evaluating teacher support teams in secondary schools: supporting teachers for SEN and other needs', *Research Papers in Education* 15, 3: 307–24.

Damasio, A.R. (1994) *Descartes' Error: Emotion, Reason and the Human Brain*, New York: G.P. Putnam's Sons.

Damasio, A.R. (1999) *The Feeling of What Happens: Body and Emotion in the Making of Consciousness*, London: Harcourt Brace.

D'Andrade, R. (1990) 'Some propositions about the relations between culture and human cognition', in R. Shweder and R. LeVine (eds) *Cultural Psychology: Essays in Comparative Human Development*, Cambridge: Cambridge University Press.

Daniels, H. (1989) 'Visual displays as tacit relays of the structure of pedagogic practice', in *British Journal of Sociology of Education* 10, 2: 123–40.

Daniels, H. (ed.) (1993) *Charting the Agenda: Educational Activity after Vygotsky*, London: Routledge.

Daniels, H. (1995) 'Pedagogic practices, tacit knowledge and discursive discrimination: Bernstein and post-Vygotskian research', in *British Journal of Sociology of Education* 16, 4: 517–32.

Daniels, H. (1996). 'Introduction: psychology in a social world', in H. Daniels (ed.) *An Introduction to Vygotsky*, 1–27, London: Routledge.

Daniels, H. (1998) 'Researching issues of gender in special needs education', in P. Clough and L. Barton (eds) *Articulating with Difficulty*, London: Sage.

Daniels, H., Cole, T. and Visser, J. (2000) 'Values and behaviour in education: an activity theory approach to research', in K. Ruoho (ed.) *Emotional and Behavioural Difficulties*, Joensuun Yliopisto: University of Joensuu.

Daniels, H., Hey, V., Leonard, D. and Smith, M. (1998) 'Differences, difficulty and equity: gender, race and SEN', *Management in Education* 12, 1: 5–8.

Daniels, H., Hey, V., Leonard, D. and Smith, M. (1999) 'Issues of equity in special needs education as seen from the perspective of gender', *British Journal of Special Education* 26, 4: 189–95.

Daniels, H., Hey, V., Leonard, D. and Smith, M. (2000) 'Issues of equity in special needs education as seen from the perspective of gender', in H. Daniels (ed.) *Special Education: Beyond Rhetoric*, London: Falmer.

Daniels, H., Holst, J., Lunt, I. and Johansen, L. (1996) 'An intercultural comparative study of the relation between different models of pedagogic practice and constructs of deviance', in *Oxford Review of Education (Special Issue on Vygotsky in education)* 22, 1: 63–77.

Davies, B. (1994) 'On the neglect of pedagogy in educational studies and its consequences', *British Journal of In-Service Education* 20, 1: 17–34.

Davydov, V.V. (1988) 'Problems of developmental teaching: the experience of theoretical and experimental psychological research', *Soviet Education* xx, 8: 3–87, 9: 3–56, 10: 2–42.

Davydov, V.V. (1990) 'The content and unsolved problems of activity theory', paper presented 22 May 1990 at the 2nd International Congress on Activity Theory, Lahti, Finland.

Davydov, V. (1995) 'The influence of L.S.Vygotsky on education theory, research and practice', *Educational Researcher* 24: 12–21.

Davydov, V.V and Radzikhovskii, L.A. (1985) 'Vygotsky's theory and the activity oriented approach in psychology', in J.V. Wertsch (ed.) *Culture, Communication and Cognition: Vygotskian Perspectives*, Cambridge: Cambridge University Press.

Day, J.D. and Cordon, L.A. (1993) 'Static and dynamic measures of ability: an experimental comparison', in *Journal of Educational Psychology* 85: 75–82.

del Rio, P. and Alvarez, A. (1995) 'Directivity: the cultural and educational constructions of morality and agency', in *Anthropology and Education Quarterly* 26, 4: 384–409.

Dennett, D. (1991) *Consciousness Explained*, New York: Little, Brown and Co.

Department of Education and Science (1975) *A Language for Life* (The Bullock Report), London: HMSO.

Diamond, C.T. (1985) 'Becoming a teacher: an altering eye', in D. Bannister (ed.) *Issues and Approaches in Personal Construct Theory*, London: Academic Press.

Diaz, M. (1984) 'A model of pedagogic discourse with special application to the Colombian primary level of education', unpublished PhD thesis, University of London Institute of Education.

Dixon-Krauss, L.A. (1995) 'Partner reading and writing – peer social dialog and the zone of proximal development', *Journal of Reading Behavior* 27, 1: 45–63.

Donald, M. (1991) *Origins of the Modern Mind: Three Stages in the Evolution of Culture and Cognition*, Cambridge, MA: Harvard University Press.

Duffield, J. (1998) 'Learning experiences, effective schools and social context', *Support for Learning* 13, 1: 3–8.

Edwards, A., Daniels, H. and Ranson, S. (2000) Mimeograph. University of Birmingham.

Emihovich, C. and Souza Lima, E. (1995) 'The many facets of Vygotsky' *Anthropology and Education Quarterly* 25, 4: 375–85.

Engeström, Y. (1984) 'Students' conceptions and textbook presentations of the movement of the moon: a study in the manufacture of misconceptions', in H. Nielsen and P.V.Thompsen (eds) *Fysk I Skolen: Problemer og Perspecktiver* (pp. 40–62), Aarhus: Aarhus Universitet, Det Fysiske Institut.

Engeström Y. (1987) *Learning by Expanding*, Helsinki: Orienta-Konsultit Oy.

Engeström, Y. (1990) 'Activity theory and individual and social transformation', open address at the Second International Congress for Research on Activity Theory, Lahti, Finland, May 21–5, 1990.

Engeström, Y. (1993) 'Developmental studies on work as a test bench of activity theory', in S. Chaikin and J. Lave (eds) *Understanding Practice: Perspectives on Activity and Context*, Cambridge: Cambridge University Press.

Engeström, Y. (1996) *Perspectives on Activity Theory*, Cambridge: Cambridge University Press.

Engeström, Y. (1999a) 'Innovative learning in work teams: analysing cycles of knowledge creation in practice', in Y. Engeström, R. Miettinen and R.L. Punamaki (eds) *Perspectives on Activity Theory*, Cambridge: Cambridge University Press.

Engeström, Y. (1999b) 'Changing practice through research: Changing research through practice'. Keynote Address, 7th Annual International Conference on Post Compulsory Education and Training. Griffith University. Australia.

Engeström, Y. and Cole, M. (1997) 'Situated cognition in search of an agenda', in J.A. Whitson and D. Kirshner (eds) *Situated Cognition. Social, Semiotic, and Psychological Perspectives*, Hillsdale, NJ: Lawrence Erlbaum.

Engeström, Y. and Middleton, D. (eds) (1996) *Cognition and Communication at Work*, Cambridge: Cambridge University Press.

Engeström, Y. and Miettinen, R. (1999) Introduction in Y. Engeström, R. Miettinen and R.L. Punamaki (eds) *Perspectives on Activity Theory*, Cambridge: Cambridge University Press.

Engestrom, Y., Miettinen, R., Punamaki, R.J. (1999) *Perspectives on Activity Theory*, Cambridge: Cambridge University Press.

Engestrom, Y., Brown, K., Christopher, L.C. and Gregory, J. (1997) 'Co-ordination, co-operation and communication in the courts: expansive transitions in legal work', in M.C. Cole, Y. Engeström and O. Vasquez (eds) *Mind, Culture and Activity*, Cambridge: Cambridge University Press.

Epstein, D., Elwood, J. and Hey, V. (eds) (1998) *Failing Boys?: Issues in Gender and Achievement*, Milton Keynes: Open University Press.

Erickson, F. (1990) 'Qualitative methods', in *Research in Teaching and Learning*, Volume Two, by R.L. Linn and F. Erickson, New York: Macmillan.

Erickson, F. (1996) 'Going for the zone: the social and cognitive ecology of teacher–student interaction in classroom conversations', in D. Hicks (ed.) *Discourse Learning and Schools*, Cambridge: Cambridge University Press.

Fielding, S., Daniels, H., Creese, A., Hey, V. and Leonard, D. (1999) 'The (mis)use of SATs to examine gender and achievement at Key Stage 2', *The Curriculum Journal* 10, 2: 169–87.

Fodor, J. (1983) 'Modularity of mind', in M. Cole (ed.) *Cultural Psychology: A Once and Future Discipline*, Cambridge, MA: Harvard University Press.

Foley, J. (1991) 'Vygotsky, Bernstein and Halliday: towards a unified theory of 11 and 12 learning', in *Language, Culture and Curriculum* 4, 1: 17–42.

Forman, E.A. and McPhail, J. (1993) 'Vygotskian perspective on children's collaborative problem solving activities', in E.A. Forman, N. Minick, and C.A. Stone (eds) *Contexts for Learning: Sociocultural Dynamics in Children's Development*, Oxford: Oxford University Press.

Gagne, R. (1988) *The Conditions of Learning*, 4th edn. New York: Holt Rinehart & Winston.

Gearhart, M. and Newman, D. (1980) 'Learning to draw a picture: the social context of an individual activity', *Discourse Processes*, 3: 169–84.

Gergen, K.J. (1999) *An Invitation to Social Construction*, London: Sage.

Gibson, E.J and Walker, A.S. (1984) 'Development of knowledge of visual-tactual affordances of substance', *Child Development* 55: 453–60.

Gibson, J.J. (1979) *The Ecological Approach to Visual Perception*, Boston: Houghton Mifflin.

Giddens, A. (1979) *Central Problems in Social theory: Action Structure and Contradiction in Social Analysis*, Berkeley: University of California Press.

Glaser, R. (1999) 'Expert knowledge and processes of thinking', in R. McCormick and C. Paechter (eds) *Learning and Knowledge*, London: Paul Chapman.

Glassman, M. (1996) 'Understanding Vygotsky's motive and goal: an exploration of the work of A.N. Leontiev, *Human Development* 39: 309–27.

Greenfield, P.M. (1984). 'A theory of the teacher in the learning activities of everyday life', in B. Rogoff and J. Lave (eds) *Everyday Cognition: Its Development in Social Context*, 117–38, Cambridge, MA: Harvard University Press.

Greeno, J. (1991) 'Number sense a situated knowing in a conceptual domain', *Journal for Research in Mathematics Education* 22, 3: 117–218.

Greeno, J., Collins, A. and Resnick, L. (1996) 'Cognition and learning', in D. Berliner and R. Calfee (eds) *Handbook of Educational Psychology*, New York: Macmillan.

Gutierrez , K.D. and Stone, L.D. (2000) 'Synchronic and diachronic dimensions of social practice: an emerging methodology for cultural-historical perspectives on literacy learning', in C.D. Lee and P. Smagorinsky (eds) *Vygotskian Perspectives on Literacy Research: Constructing Meaning Through Collaborative Inquiry*, Cambridge: Cambridge University Press.

Haenen, J. (1996) *'PiotrGal'perin: Psychologist in Vygotsky's Footsteps'*, Commack, NY: Nova Science Publishers.

Hakkarainen, P. (1999) 'Play and motivation', in Y. Engeström, R. Miettinen, R-L Punamäki (eds) *Perspectives on Activity Theory*, Cambridge: Cambridge University Press.

Hall, S. (1996) 'Who needs "identity?"', in S. Hall and P. du Gay (eds) *Questions of Cultural Identity*, London: Sage.

Hatano, G. (1993) 'Time to merge Vygotskian and constructivist conceptions of knowledge acquisition', in E.A. Forman, N. Minick and C. Addison Stone (eds), *Contexts for Learning – Sociocultural Dynamics in Children's Development*, Oxford: Oxford University Press.

Hatano, G. and Inagaki, K. (1991) 'Sharing cognition through collective comprehension activity', in L.B. Resnick, J.M. Levine and S.D. Teasley (eds) *Perspectives on Socially Shared Cognition*, Washington, DC: American Psychological Association.

Hawkes, T. (1977) *Structuralism and Semiotics*, London: Methuen.

Hedegaard, M. (1990) 'How instruction influences children's concepts of evolution', *Mind, Culture and Activity* 3: 11–24.

Hedegaard, M. (1998) Situated learning and cognition: theoretical learning of cognition', *Mind, Culture and Activity* 5, 2: 114–26.

Hedegaard, M. and Chaiklin, S (1990) Review of Davydov, V.V. (1986), *Quarterly Newsletter of the Laboratory of Comparative Human Cognition*, October 1990, 12, 4: 153–4.

Hey, V. (1997) *The Company She Keeps: An Ethnography of Girls' Friendship*, Buckingham: Open University Press.

Hey, V., Creese, A., Daniels, H., Fielding, S., Leonard, D. and Smith, M. (2000) 'Sad, bad or sexy boys: girls talk in and out of the classroom', in W. Martino and B. Meyenn, *Teaching Boys: Issues of Masculinity*, Milton Keynes: Open University Press.

Hey, V., Leonard, D., Daniels, H. and Smith, M. (1998) 'Boys' underachievement, special needs practices and questions of equity', in D. Epstein, J. Elwood, V. Hey and J. Maw (eds) *Failing Boys? Issues in Gender and Achievement*, Buckingham: Open University Press.

Hildebrand, G. (1996) 'Redefining achievement', in P. Murphy and C. Gimps (eds) *Equity in the Classroom: Towards Effective Pedagogy for Girls and Boys*, 149–72, London/Paris: Falmer/UNESCO.

Hirst, P. (1996) 'The demands of professional practice and preparation for teaching', in J. Furlong and R. Smith (eds), *The Role of Higher Education in Initial Teacher Training*, London: Kogan Page.

Hirst, W. and Manier, D. (1995) 'Opening vistas for cognitive psychology', in L.M.W. Martin, K. Nelson and E. Tobach (eds) *Sociocultural Psychology: Theory and Practice of Doing and Knowing*, Cambridge: Cambridge University Press.

Hoetker, J. and Ahlbrand, W. (1969) 'The persistence of recitation', in *American Educational Research Journal* 21, 145–67.

Holland, D. and Cole, M. (1995) 'Between discourse and schema: reformulating a cultural-historical approach to culture and mind', *Anthropology and Education Quarterly* 26, 4: 475–90.

Holzman, L. (1995) 'Creating developmental learning environments – a Vygotskian practice', *School Psychology International* 16, 2: 199–212.

Holzman, L. (1997) *Schools for Growth: Radical Alternatives to Current Education Models*, London: Lawrence Erlbaum.

Hood-Holzman, L. (1985) 'Pragmatism and dialectical materialism in language development', in K.E. Nelson (ed.) *Children's Language Volumes*, Hillsdale, NJ: Lawrence Erlbaum.

Hundeide, K. (1985) 'The tacit background of children's judgments', in *Culture, Communication and Cognition*, Cambridge: Cambridge University Press.

Hutchins, E. (1986) 'Mediation and automatization', *Quarterly Newsletter of the Laboratory of Comparative Human Cognition*, April 1986, 8, 2: 47–58.

Hutchins, E. (1995) *Cognition in the Wild*, Cambridge, MA: MIT Press.

Il'enkov, E.V. (1977) *Dialectical Logic. Essays on its History and Theory*, Moscow: Progress.

Il'enkov, E.V. (1982) *The Dialectics of the Abstract and the Concrete in Marx's Capital*, Moscow: Progress.

Ivic, I. (1989) 'Profiles of Educators: Lev S. Vygotsky (1896–1934)', *Prospects*, XIX, 3: 427–36.

Jarning, H. (1997) 'The many meanings of social pedagogy: pedagogy and social theory in Scandinavia', *Scandinavian Journal of Educational Research* 41, 3–4: 413–31.

John-Steiner, V. and Mahn, H. (1996) 'Sociocultural approaches to learning and development: a Vygotskian framework', *Educational Psychologist* 31: 191–206.

Joravsky, D. (1987) 'L.S. Vygotski: the muffled deity of soviet psychology', in M.G. Ash and W.R. Woodward (eds) *Psychology in Twentieth Century Thought and Society*, Cambridge: Cambridge University Press.

Karpov, Y.V. and Haywood, H.C. (1998) 'Two ways to elaborate Vygotsky's concept of mediation', *American Psychologist* 53, 1: 27–36.

Kirshner, D. and Whitson, J.A. (eds) (1997) *Situated Cognition: Social, Semiotic and Psychological Perspectives*, Mahwah, NJ: Lawrence Erlbaum.

Knox, J.E. and Stevens, C. (1993) 'Vygotsky and Soviet Russian defectology, an introduction to Vygotsky', *The Collected Works of L S Vygotsky, 2, Problems of Abnormal Psychology and Learning Disabilities*, New York: Plenum Press.

Kozulin, A. (1986) 'The concept of activity in Soviet Psychology: Vygotsky, his disciples and critics', *American Psychologist* 264–74.

Kozulin, A. (1990) *Vygotsky's Psychology: A Biography of Ideas*, London: Harvester.

Kozulin, A. (1996) 'A literary model for psychology', in D. Hicks (ed.) *Discourse, Learning and Schooling*, Cambridge: Cambridge University Press.

Kozulin, A. (1998) *Psychological Tools. A Sociocultural Approach to Education*, London: Harvard University Press.

Kundera, M. (1988) *The Art of the Novel*, New York: Grove Press.

Langer, J.A. and Applebee, A.N. (1986) 'Reading and writing instruction: toward a theory of teaching and learning', in E.Z. Rothkopf (ed.) *Review of Research in Education* 13: 171–94, Washington, DC: American Educational Research Association.

Lave, J. (1988) *Cognition in Practice*, Cambridge: Cambridge University Press.

Lave, J. (1993) 'The practice of learning', in S. Chaiklin and J. Lave (eds) *Understanding Practice: Perspectives of Activity in Context*, Cambridge: Cambridge University Press.

Lave, J. (1996) 'The practice of learning', in S. Chaiklin and J. Lave (eds) *Understanding Practice: Perspectives on Activity and Practice*, Cambridge: Cambridge University Press.

Lave, J. and Wenger, E. (1991) *Situated Learning: Legitimate Peripheral Participation*, Cambridge: Cambridge University Press.

Lawrence, J.A. and Valsiner, J. (1993) 'Conceptual roots of internalization – from transmission to transformation', *Human Development* 36, 3: 150–67.

Lee, B. (1985) 'Intellectual origins of Vygotsky's semiotic analysis', in J.V. Wertsch (ed.) *Culture, Communication and Cognition*, Cambridge: Cambridge University Press.

Lee, C.D. (2000) 'Signifying in the Zone of Proximal Development', in C.D. Lee and P. Smagorinsky (eds) *Vygotskian Perspectives on Literacy Research: Constructing Meaning through Collaborative Inquiry*, Cambridge: Cambridge University Press.

Lektorsky, V.A. (1995) 'Activity approach and science about man', Plenary meeting 27 June 1995 at the 3rd International Congress on Activity Theory and Social Practice, Moscow.

Lektorsky, V.A. (1999) 'Activity theory in a new era', in Y. Engeström, R. Miettinen and R.-L. Punamäki (eds) *Perspectives on Activity Theory*, Cambridge: Cambridge University Press.

Lemke, J.L. (1990) *Talking Science: Language, Learning and Values*, Norwood, NJ: Ablex.

Lemke, J. (1997) 'Cognition, context, and learning: a social semiotic perspective', in D. Kirshner (ed.) *Situated Cognition Theory: Social, Neurological, and Semiotic Perspectives*, New York: Lawrence Erlbaum.

Leont'ev, A.N. (1978) *Activity, Consciousness, and Personality*, Englewood Cliffs: Prentice Hall.

Leont'ev, A.N. (1972/1981) 'The concept of activity in psychology', in J.V. Wertsch (ed.), *The Concept of Activity in Soviet Psychology*, Armonk, NY: M.E. Sharpe.

Lewis, R. (1997) 'An activity theory framework to explore distributed communities', *Journal of Computer Assisted Learning* 13: 210–18.

Lightfoot, C. and Valsiner, J. (1992) 'Parental belief systems under the influence: social guidance of the construction of personal cultures', in I. Sigel, A. McGillicuddy-DeLisi and J. Goodnow (eds) *Parental Belief Systems: The Psychological Consequences for Children*, 393–414, Hillsdale, NJ: Lawrence Erlbaum.

Lima, E.S. (1998) 'Education of experience with the Tikuna: a look into the complexity of concept construction', *Mind Culture and Activity* 5, 2: 95–104.

Matusov, E. (1998) 'When solo activity is not privileged: participation and internalization models of development', *Human Development* 41: 326–49.

Meadows, S. (1998) 'Children learning to think: learning from others? Vygotskian theory and educational psychology', in *Educational and Child Psychology*, 15, 2: 6–13.

Mehan, H. (1997) 'Students' interactional competence in the classroom', in M. Cole, Y. Engeström, and O. Vasquez (eds) *Mind, Culture and Activity: Seminal Papers from the Laboratory of Comparative Human Cognition*, Cambridge: Cambridge University Press.

Mercer, N. (2000) *Words and Minds: How We Use Language to Think Together*, London: Routledge.

Mercer, N., Wegerif, R. and Dawes, L. (1999) 'Children's talk and the development of reasoning in the classroom', *British Educational Research Journal* 25, 1: 95–111.

Michaels, S. (1990) 'The dismantling of narrative', in A. McCabe and C. Petersons (eds) *Developing Narrative Structure*, 303–51, Cambridge: Cambridge University Press.

Miettinen, R. (1999) 'Transcending traditional school learning: teachers' work and networks of learning', in Y. Engeström, R. Miettinen, and R-L. Punamäki (eds) *Perspectives on Activity Theory*, Cambridge: Cambridge University Press.

Minick, N.J. (1985) 'L.S. Vygotsky and soviet activity theory: new perspectives on the relationship between mind and society', unpublished PhD thesis, Northwestern University, USA.

Minick, N. (1987) 'The development of Vygotsky's thought: an introduction', in R.W. Rieber and A.S. Carton (eds) *The Collected Works of L.S. Vygotsky*, 1, New York: Plenum Press.

Minick, N. (1990) 'Mind and activity in Vygotsky's work: an expanded frame of reference', *Cultural Dynamics* 2: 162–87.

Minick, N., Stone, C.A., and Forman, E.A. (1993) 'Introduction: integration of individual, social and institutional processes in accounts of children's learning and development', in E.A. Forman, N. Minick, and C.A. Stone (eds) *Contexts for Learning: Sociocultural Dynamics in Children's Development*, Oxford: Oxford University Press.

Moll, I. (1994) 'Reclaiming the natural line in Vygotsky's theory of cognitive-development', *Human Development*, 37, 6: 333–42.

Moll, L.C. (1990) 'Introduction' L.C. Moll (ed.) *Vygotsky and Education. Instructional Implications and Applications of Sociohistorical Psychology*, 1–27. Cambridge: Cambridge University Press.

Moll, L.C. (2000) 'Inspired by Vygotsky: ethnographic experiments in education', in C.D. Lee and P. Smagorinsky (eds) *Vygotskian Perspectives on Literacy Research: Constructing Meaning Through Collaborative Inquiry*, Cambridge: Cambridge University Press.

Moll, L.C. and Greenberg, J.B. (1990) 'Creating zones of possibilities: combining social contexts for instruction', in L.C. Moll (ed.) *Vygotsky and Education, Instructional Implications and Applications of Sociohistorical Psychology*, 319–48, Cambridge: Cambridge University Press.

Moll, L.C. and Whitmore, K.F. (1993) 'Vygotsky in classroom practice: moving from individual transmission to social transaction', in E.A. Forman, N. Minick and C. Addison Stone (eds) *Contexts for Learning – Sociocultural Dynamics in Children's Development*, Oxford: Oxford University Press.

Moll, L.C., Tapia, J. and Whitmore, K.F. (1993) 'Living knowledge: the social distribution of cultural resources for thinking', in G. Salomon (ed.) *Distributed Cognitions: Psychological and Educational Considerations*, Cambridge: Cambridge University Press.

Moore, R. (1984) 'Education and production: a generative model', unpublished PhD thesis, University of London.

Moscovici, S. (1996) 'Who is the most Marxist of the two?' *Swiss Journal of Psychology* 55, 2–3: 70–3.

Murphy, P. and Elwood, J. (1998) 'Gendered experiences, choices and achievement – exploring the links', in *International Journal of Inclusive Education* 1, 2: 95–118.

Nardi, B.A. (1996) 'Studying context: a comparison of activity theory, situated action models, and distributed cognition', in B.A. Nardi (ed.) *Context and Consciousness. Activity Theory and Human-computer Interaction*, 69–102, Cambridge, MA: MIT Press.

Nelson, K., (1981) 'Cognition in a script framework', in J.H. Flavell and L. Ross (eds) *Social Cognitive Development*, 97–118, Cambridge: Cambridge University Press.

Nelson, K. (1995) 'From spontaneous to scientific concepts: continuities and discontinuities from childhood to adulthood', in L.M.W. Martin, K. Nelson and E.

Tobach (eds) *Sociocultural Psychology: Theory and Practice of Doing and Knowing*, Cambridge: Cambridge University Press.

Newman, D., Griffin, P. and Cole, M. (1989) *The Construction Zone: Working for Cognitive Change in School*, Cambridge: Cambridge University Press.

Newman, F. and Holzman, L. (1993) *Lev Vygotsky: Revolutionary Scientist*, London: Routledge.

Nicolopoulou, A. and Cole, M. (1993) 'Generation and transmission of shared knowledge in the culture of collaborative learning: the fifth dimension, its play-world, and its institutional contexts', in E.A. Forman, N. Minick and C. Addison Stone (eds) *Contexts for Learning, Sociocultural Dynamics in Children's Development*, New York: Oxford University Press.

O'Connor, C. and Michaels, S. (1993) 'Aligning academic task and participation status through revoicing: analysis of a classroom discourse strategy', in *Anthropology and Education Quarterly* 24, 4: 318–35, American Anthropological Association.

Osin, L. and Lesgold, A. (1996) 'A proposal for the reengineering of the educational system', *Review of Educational Research* 66, 4: 621–56.

Palincsar, A. and Brown, A.L. (1984) 'Reciprocal teaching of comprehension-fostering and comprehension-monitoring activities', *Cognition and Instruction* 1, 2: 117–75.

Palincsar, A.S. and Brown, A.L. (1988) 'Teaching and practising thinking skills to promote comprehension in the context of group problem solving', *Remedial and Special Education* 9, 1: 53–9.

Parrilla, A. and Daniels, H. (2000) 'Diversidad y educacion: El asesoramiento pedagogico como estrategia de cambio,' in A. Estebaranz (ed.) *Construyendo el cambio: Perspectivas y propuestas de innovacion educativa*, Sevilla: Universidad de Sevilla.

Pea, R.D. (1993) 'Practices of distributed intelligence and designs for education', in G. Salomon (ed.) *Distributed Cognitions: Psychological and Educational Considerations*, Cambridge: Cambridge University Press.

Piaget, J. (1978) *Recherches sur la generalisation*, Paris: Presses Universitaires de France.

Piaget, J. (1995) *Sociological Studies*, L. Smith (ed.) London: Routledge.

Popkewitz, T.S. (1998) 'Dewey, Vygotsky, and the social administration of the individual: constructivist pedagogy as systems of ideas in historical spaces', *American Educational Research Journal* 35, 4: 535–70.

Popper, K.R. (1972) *Objective Knowledge: An Evolutionary Approach*, Oxford: Springer-Verlag.

Prawat R.S. (1999) 'Cognitive theory at the crossroads: head fitting, head splitting, or somewhere in between?', *Human Development* 42, 2: 59–77.

Premack, D. (1984) 'Pedagogy and aesthetics as sources of culture', in M. Gazzaniga (ed.) *Handbook of Cognitive Neuroscience*, 15–35 New York: Plenum.

Prior, P. (1997) 'Literate activity and disciplinarity: the heterogeneous (re)production of American studies around a graduate seminar', *Mind, Culture and Activity* 4, 4: 275–95.

QCA (1998) *Can Do Better: Raising Boys' Achievement in English*, London: QCA.

Ratner, C. (1997) *Cultural Psychology and Qualitative Methodology. Theoretical and Empirical Considerations*, London: Plenum Press.

Ratner, C. (1998) Prologue in R. Rieber (ed.) M.J. Hall (trans.) *The Collected Works of L.S. Vygotsky: Volume 5 Child Psychology*, London: Plenum Press.

Ratner C., (1999) 'Three approaches to cultural psychology: a critique', *Cultural Dynamics* 11: 7–31.

Reeve, R.A., Palinscar, A.S., Brown, A.L. (1987) 'Everyday and academic thinking: implications for learning and problem solving', *Curriculum Studies* 19, 2: 123–33.

Reid, D.K. (1998) 'Scaffolding: a broader view', *Journal of Learning Disabilities*, 31, 4: 386–96.

Reid, D.K. and Stone, C.A. (1991) 'Why is cognitive instruction effective? Underlying learning mechanisms', *Remedial and Special Education*, 12, 3: (May/June 1991).

Resnick, L.B. and Nelson LeGall, S. (1996) 'Socializing intelligence', paper presented at the 1996 Annual Conference of The British Psychological Society: The Piaget–Vygotsky Centenary Conference, 11–14 April at the Brighton Centre.

Riegel, K.F. (1976) 'The dialectics of human development', *American Psychologist*, October, 689–700.

Rogoff, B. (1990) *Apprenticeship in Thinking: Cognitive Development in Social Context*, New York: Oxford University Press.

Rogoff, B. (1992) 'Three ways to relate person and culture: thoughts sparked by Valsiner's review of Apprenticeship in Thinking', in *Human Development* 35, 3: 16–320.

Rogoff. B. (1994) 'Developing understanding of the idea of communities of learners', *Mind, Culture and Activity*, 1: 209–29.

Rogoff, B. (1995) 'Observing sociocultural activity on three planes: participatory appropriation, guided participation and apprenticeship', in J.V. Wertsch, P. del Rio and A. Alvarez (eds) *Sociocultural Studies of Mind*, NY: Cambridge University Press.

Rogoff, B., and Lave, J. (eds) (1984) *Everyday Cognition: Its Development in Social Context*, 95–116, Cambridge MA: Harvard University Press.

Rogoff, B., Gauvain, M. and Gardner, W. (1987) 'The development of children's skills in adjusting plans to circumstances', in S.L. Friedman, E.K. Scholnick and R.R. Cocking (eds) *Blueprints for Thinking: The Role of Planning in Cognitive Development*, Cambridge: Cambridge University Press.

Rogoff, B., Mistry, J., Göncü, A. and Mosier, C. (1993) 'Guided participation in cultural activity by toddlers and caregivers', *Monographs of the Society for Research in Child Development*, Serial No. 236, 58 (8).

Rosenholtz, S. (1989) *Teachers' Workplace: The Social Organization of Schools*, White Plains, NY: Longman.

Rueda, R. and Mehan, H. (1986) 'Metacognition and passing: strategic interactions in the lives of students with learning disabilities', *Anthropology and Education Quarterly* 17: 145–65.

Rumelhart, D. (1978) 'Schemata: the building of cognition', in R. Spiro, B. Bruce and W. Brewer (eds) *Theoretical Issues in Reading Comprehension*, 33–58. Hillsdale, NJ: Lawrence Erlbaum.

Rumelhart, D.E., Smolensky, P., McClelland, J.L. and Hinton, G.E. (1986) 'Schemata and sequential thought processes in PDP models', in J.L. McClelland, D.E. Rumelhart and the PDP Research Groups (eds) *Parallel Distributed Processing: Explorations in the Micro Structure of Cognition*, 2: 7–57 Psychological and biological models, Cambridge, MA: MIT Press.

Russell, D.R. (1997a) *Rethinking Genre in School and Society: An Activity Theory Analysis*, Iowa State University.

Russell, D.R. (1997b) 'Writing and genre in higher education and workplaces: a review of studies that use cultural-historical activity theory', *Mind, Culture, and Activity* 4, 4: 224–37.

Salomon, G. (1993a) Editor's introduction, in G. Salomon (ed.) *Distributed Cognitions: Psychological and Educational Considerations*, Cambridge: Cambridge University Press.

Salomon, G (1993b) 'No distribution without individuals' cognition: a dynamic interactional view', in G. Salomon (ed.) *Distributed Cognitions: Psychological and Educational Considerations* 4: 111–38, Cambridge: Cambridge University Press.

Sameroff, A.J. (1980) 'Development and the dialectic: the need for a systems approach', in W.A. Collins (ed.) *The Concept of Development – Minnesota Symposia on Child Psychology* 15: 83–103.

Sampson, E.E. (1981) 'Cognitive psychology as ideology', *American Psychologist* 36, 7: 730–43.

Scardamalia, M. and Bereiter, C. (1991) 'Higher levels of agency for children in knowledge building: a challenge for the design of new knowledge media', *The Journal of the Learning Sciences* 1, 1: 37–68.

Scardamalia, M. and Bereiter, C. (1996) 'Student communities for the advancement of knowledge', *Communications of the ACM* 39, 4: 36–7.

Scardamalia, M., Bereiter, C. and Lamon, M. (1994) 'The CSILE project: trying to bring the classroom into world 3', in K. McGilly (ed.), *Classroom Lessons: Integrating Cognitive Theory and Classroom Practice*, 201–28, MA: MIT Press.

Schank, R. and Abelson, R. (1977) *Scripts, Plans, Goals and Understandings: An Inquiry into Human Knowledge Structures*, Hillsdale, NJ: Lawrence Erlbaum.

Schneuwly, B. (1994) 'Contradiction and development – Vygotsky and paedology', *European Journal of Psychology of Education* 9, 4: 281–91.

Schoenfeld (1985) *Mathematical Problem Solving*, New York: Academic Press.

Scribner, S. (1990) 'Reflections on a model', *The Quarterly Newsletter of the Laboratory*.

Serpell, R. (1999) *Sociocultural-historical Genesis of Vygotsky's Theory*, email posted on XMCA.

Shibutani, T. (1962) 'Reference groups and social control', in A. Rose (ed.) *Human Behaviour and Social Processes*, London: Routledge & Kegan Paul.

Shore, B. (1996) *Culture in Mind*, New York: Oxford University Press.

Shotter, J. (1993a) 'Vygotsky – the social negotiation of semiotic mediation', *New Ideas In Psychology* 11, 1: 61–75.

Shotter, J. (1993b) 'Bakhtin and Vygotsky – internalization as a boundary phenomenon', *New Ideas In Psychology* 11, 3: 379–90.

Simon, B. (1985) 'Why no pedagogy in England', in B. Simon (ed.) *Does Education Matter?* London: Lawrence and Wishart.

Slee, R., Weiner, G. and Tomlinson, S. (1998) *School Effectiveness for Whom? Challenges to the School Effectiveness and School Improvement Movements*, London: Falmer Press.

Smith, L. (1996) 'The social construction of understanding', in A. Tryphon and J. Voneche (eds) *Piaget Vygotsky. The Social Genesis of Thought*, Hove: Psychology Press.

Star, S.L. (1998) 'Working together', in Y. Engeström and D. Middleton (eds) *Cognition and Communication at Work*, Cambridge: Cambridge University Press.

Steffe, L.P. (1996) 'Sociocultural processes: a discussion', in H. Mansfield, N.A. Pateman and N. Bednarz (eds) *Mathematics for Tomorrow's Young Children*, 79–99, Dordrecht: Kluwer.

Stone, C.A. (1998) 'The metaphor of scaffolding: its utility for the field of learning disabilities', *Journal of Learning Disabilities* 31, 4: 344–64.

Stringer, P. (1998) 'One night Vygotsky had a dream: "children learning to think . . ."

and implications for educational psychologists', *Educational and Child Psychology* 15, 2: 14–20.

Subbotsky E.V. (1996) 'L.S. Vygotsky's distinction between lower and higher mental functions and recent studies on infant cognitive development', *Voprosy Psikhologii* 6: 88–108.

Sutton, A. (1980) 'Backward children in the USSR: an unfamiliar approach to a familiar problem', in J. Brine, M. Perrie and A. Sutton (eds) *Home, School and Leisure in the Soviet Union*, London: George Allen & Unwin.

Tharp (1993) 'Institutional and social context of educational practice and reform', in E.A. Forman, N. Minick and C.A. Stone (eds) in *Contexts for Learning: Sociocultural Dynamics in Children's Development*, Oxford: Oxford University Press.

Tharp, R.G. and Gallimore, R. (1988a) *Rousing Minds to Life: Teaching, Learning, and Schooling in Social Context*, Cambridge: Cambridge University Press.

Tharp, R.G. and Gallimore, R. (1988b) 'Rousing schools to life', *American Educator* 13, 2: 20–5, 46–52.

Tomasello, M. (1999) *The Cultural Origins of Human Cognition*, Cambridge, MA: Harvard University Press.

Tomasello, M., Kruger, A.C. and Ratner, H.H. (1993) 'Cultural learning', *Behavioural and Brain Sciences* 16, 3: 495–552.

Toulmin, S. (1999) 'Knowledge as shared procedures', in Y. Engeström, R. Miettinen and R.-L. Punamäki (eds), *Perspectives on Activity Theory*, Cambridge: Cambridge University Press.

Tudge, J.R.H. (1992) 'Processes and consequences of peer collaboration: a Vygotskian analysis', *Child Development* 63: 1364–79.

Tudge, J. (1997) 'Internalisation, externalisation and joint carving: commenting from an ecological perspective', in B.D. Cox and C. Lightfoot (eds) *Sociogenetic Perspectives on Internalisation*, Hillsdale, NJ: Lawrence Erlbaum.

Tudge, J.R.H. and Rogoff, B. (1989) 'Peer influences on cognitive development: Piagetian and Vygotskian perspectives', in M.H. Bornstein and J.S. Bruner *Interaction in Human Development*, Hillsdale, NJ: Lawrence Erlbaum.

Tudge, J.R.H. and Winterhoff (1993) 'Vygotsky, Piaget, and Bandura: Perspectives on the relations between the social world and cognitive development', *Human Development* 36: 61–81.

Tudge, J.R.H., Winterhoff, P.A., and Hogan, D.M. (1996) 'The cognitive consequences of collaborative problem solving with and without feedback', *Child Development* 67, 6: 2892–909.

Tul'viste, P. (1988) 'Some causes of the unsatisfactory state of Soviet Psychology', *Vop. Psikhol* 2: 5–18.

Tyler, W. (1983) 'Organisations, factors and codes: a methodological enquiry into Bernstein's theory of educational transmissions', unpublished doctoral thesis, University of Kent.

Valsiner, J. (1988) *Developmental Psychology in the Soviet Union*, Sussex: Harvester Press.

Valsiner, J. (1997) *Culture and the Development of Children's Action: A Theory of Human Development* (2nd edn), New York: John Wiley.

Valsiner, J. (1998) *The Guided Mind: A Sociogenetic Approach to Personality*, Cambridge, MA: Harvard University Press.

Van der Veer, R. (1994) 'The concept of development and the development of concepts in education and development', in Vygotsky's *Thinking, European Journal of Psychology of Education* 9, 4: 293–300.

Van der Veer, R. (1996) 'The concept of culture in Vygotsky's *Thinking*', *Culture and Philosophy* 2, 3: 247–63.

Van der Veer, R. (1998) 'From concept attainment to knowledge formation', *Mind Culture and Activity* 5, 2: 89–94.

Van der Veer, R. and Valsiner, J. (1991) *Understanding Vygotsky: A quest for synthesis*, Oxford: Blackwell.

Van der Veer, R. and Van Ijzendoorn, M. (1985) 'Vygotsky theory of the higher psychological processes – some criticisms', *Human Development* 28, 1: 1–9.

Veresov, N. (1999) *Undiscovered Vygotsky*, Berlin: Peter Lang.

Voloshinov, V.N. (1973) *Marxism and the Philosophy of Language*, trans. L. Matejka and I. R. Titunik, New York: Seminar Press.

Vygotsky, L.S. (1934/1987), *Thinking and Speech. Collected Works*, 1: 39–285, New York: Plenum.

Vygotsky, L.S. (1956) *Izbrannie psibhologicheskie issledovania* [Selected psychological research]. Moscow: Izdateel'stro Akademli Pedagogicheskikh Nak.

Vygotsky, L.S. (1960/1981) 'The instrumental method in psychology', in J.V. Wertsch (ed. and trans.) *The Concept of Activity in Soviet Psychology*, 134–43. Armonk, NY: M.E. Sharpe.

Vygotsky, L.S. (1962) *Thought and Language*, E. Hanfmann and G.Vakar (eds and trans.), Cambridge, M.A.: MIT Press.

Vygotsky, L.S. (1978) *Mind in Society: the Development of Higher Psychological Processes*, M. Cole, V. John-Steiner, S. Scribner and E. Souberman (eds and trans.), Cambridge, MA: Harvard University Press.

Vygotsky, L. (1981) 'The development of higher forms of attention', in J. Wertsch (ed.) *The Concept of Activity in Soviet Psychology*, 189–240, Armonk, NY: M.E. Sharpe.

Vygotsky, L.S. (1983) 'From the notebooks of L.S. Vygotsky', *Soviet Psychology* XXI, 3: 3–17.

Vygotsky, L.S. (1986) *Thought and Language*, A. Kozulin (ed. and trans.) Cambridge, MA.: MIT Press.

Vygotsky, L.S. (1987) *The Collected Works of L.S. Vygotsky. Vol. 1: Problems of General Psychology*, including the volume *Thinking and Speech*, R.W. Rieber and A.S. Carton (eds), N. Minick (trans.), NY: Plenum Press.

Vygotsky, L.S. (1997a) *The Collected Works of L.S. Vygotsky. Vol. 4: The History of the Development of Higher Mental Functions*, R.W. Rieber (ed.), M.J. Hall (trans.) NY: Plenum Press.

Vygotsky, L.S. (1997b) *Educational ·Psychology*, Boca Raton, FL: St Lucie Press. (Originally written 1921–1923).

Vygotsky L.S. (1998) *The Collected Works of L.S. Vygotsky: Vol. 5: Child Psychology*, in R. Rieber (ed.), M.J. Hall (trans.) London: Plenum Press.

Waddington, C.H. (1951) *The Strategy of Genes*, London: George Allen & Unwin.

Wardekker, W.L. (1998) 'Scientific concepts and reflection', *Mind Culture and Activity* 5, 2: 143–54.

Warren, S. (1997) 'Who do these boys think they are? An investigation into the construction of masculinities in a primary classroom', *International Journal of Inclusive Education*, 1, 2: 207–22.

Wartofsky, M. (1973) *Models*, Dordrecht: D. Reide.

Watkins, C. and Mortimore, P. (1999) 'Pedagogy: What do we Know?' in J. Mortimore (ed.) *Understanding Pedagogy and its Impact on Learning* 1–19, London: Paul Chapman.

Wells, G. (1993) 'Re-evaluating the IRF sequence: a proposal for the articulation of theories of activity and discourse for the analysis of teaching and learning in the classroom', *Linguistics and Education* 5: 1–37.

Wells, G. (1994a) 'Learning and teaching "Scientific Concepts": Vygotsky's ideas revisited', paper presented at the Vygotsky and the Human Sciences Conference, Moscow, September 1994.

Wells, G. (1994b) 'The complementary contributions of Halliday and Vygotsky to a "language-based theory of learning"', *Linguistics and Education* 6: 41–90.

Wells, G. (1999) *Dialogic Inquiry: Toward a Sociocultural Practice and Theory of Education*, Cambridge: Cambridge University Press.

Wertsch, J. V. (1980) 'The significance of dialogue in Vygotsky's account of social, egocentric, and inner speech', *Contemporary Educational Psychology* 5: 150–62.

Wertsch, J.V. (1985a) *Vygotsky and the Social Formation of Mind*, Cambridge, MA: Harvard University Press.

Wertsch, J.V. (1985b) *Culture, Communication and Cognition: Vygotskian Perspectives*, Cambridge: Cambridge University Press.

Wertsch, J.V. (1991) *Voices of the Mind: A Sociocultural Approach to Mediated Action*, Cambridge, MA: Harvard University Press.

Wertsch, J.V. (1998) *Mind as Action*, Oxford: Oxford University Press.

Wertsch, J.V. (2000) 'Vygotsky's two minds on the nature of meaning', in C.D. Lee and P. Smagorinsky (eds) *Vygotskian Perspectives on Literacy Research*, 19–30, Cambridge: Cambridge University Press.

Wertsch, J.V. and Lee, B. (1984) 'The multiple levels of analysis in a theory of action', *Human Development* 27: 193–6.

Wertsch, J.V. and Stone, C.A. (1985) 'The concept of internalization in Vygotsky's account of the genesis of higher mental functions', in J.V.Wertsch (ed.) *Culture, Communication and Cognition: Vygotskian Perspectives*, 162–79, New York, Cambridge University Press.

Wertsch, J.V. and del Rio, P. and Alvarez, A. (1995) 'Sociocultural studies: history, action and mediation', in J.V. Wertsch, P. del Rio and A. Alvarez (eds), *Sociocultural Studies of Mind*, 1–34, New York: Cambridge University Press.

Wertsch, J.V. and Tulviste, P. (1992) 'L.S. Vygotsky and contemporary developmental psychology', *Developmental Psychology* 28, 4: 548–57.

Wertsch, J.V. and Tulviste, P. (1996) 'L.S. Vygotsky and contemporary developmental psychology' in H. Daniels (ed.) *An Introduction to Vygotsky*, 53–74, London: Routledge.

Wertsch, J.V., Tulviste, P. and Hagstrom, F. (1993) 'A sociocultural approach to agency', in E.A. Forman, N. Minick, and C.A. Stone (eds) *Contexts for Learning: Sociocultural Dynamics in Children's Development*, Oxford: Oxford University Press.

Wilson, B.G., Teslow, J.L. and Taylor, L. (1993) 'Instructional design perspectives on mathematics education with reference to Vygotsky's theory of social cognition', in *Focus on Learning Problems in Mathematics* 15, 2 and 3: 65–85, Center for Teaching/ Learning of Mathematics.

Winegar, L.T. (1997) 'Can internalisation be more than a magical phrase? Notes toward the constructive negotiation of this process', in B.D. Cox and C. Lightfoot (eds) *Sociogenetic Perspectives on Internalization*, Hillsdale, NJ: Lawrence Erlbaum.

Wood, D.J. (1998) *How Children Think and Learn: The Social Contexts of Cognitive Development*, Oxford: Blackwell.

Wood, D., Bruner, J.C. and Ross, G. (1976) 'The role of tutoring in problem solving', *Journal of Child Psychology and Psychiatry* 17: 89–100.

Wood, D. and Wood, H. (1996a) 'Commentary: contingency in tutoring and learning', *Learning and Instruction* 6, 4: 391–7.

Wood, D. and Wood, H. (1996b) 'Vygotsky, tutoring and learning', *Oxford Review of Education* 22, 1: 5–16.

Wood, D., Wood, H. and Middleton, D. (1978) 'An experimental evaluation of four face-to-face teaching strategies', *International Journal of Behavioural Development* 1: 131–47.

Woods, P. (1983) *Sociology and the School*, London: RKP.

Wozniak, R.H. (1975) 'A dialectic paradigm for psychological research: implications drawn from the history of psychology in the Soviet Union', *Human Development* 18: 18–34.

Yaroshevsky, M. (1989) *Lev Vygotsky*, Moscow: Progress Publishers.

Yates, L. (1997) 'Gender, equity and the boys' debate. What sort of challenge is it?', *British Journal of Sociology of Education* 18: 337–47.

Zinchenko, V.P. (1985) 'Vygotsky's ideas about units of analysis for the analysis of mind', in J.V. Wertsch (ed.) *Culture, Communication, and Cognition: Vygotskian Perspectives*, New York: Cambridge University Press.

Index